Perilous Journey

The authorised
Gordon Giltrap Biography

Perilous Journey

The authorised
Gordon Giltrap Biography

Steve Pilkington

WYMER
PUBLISHING
Bedford, England

First published in Great Britain in 2018
by Wymer Publishing
Bedford, England
www.wymerpublishing.co.uk
Tel: 01234 326691
Wymer Publishing is a trading name of Wymer (UK) Ltd

First edition. Copyright © 2018 Steve Pilkington / Wymer Publishing.

ISBN 978-1-908724-78-6

Edited by Jerry Bloom.

The Author hereby asserts his rights to be identified
as the author of this work in accordance with sections
77 to 78 of the Copyright, Designs & Patents Act 1988.

All rights reserved. No part of this publication may be
reproduced or transmitted in any form or by any means,
electronic or mechanical, including photocopying, or any
information storage and retrieval system, without written
permission from the publisher.

This publication is sold subject to the condition that it shall not,
by way of trade or otherwise, be lent, re-sold, hired out or
otherwise circulated without the publishers prior consent in any
form of binding or cover other than that in which it is published
and without a similar condition including this condition
being imposed on the subsequent purchaser.

Every effort has been made to trace the copyright holders of the
photographs in this book but some were unreachable. We would
be grateful if the photographers concerned would contact us.

Typeset by The Andys.
Printed and bound in Great Britain by
Clays Ltd, Bungay, Suffolk

A catalogue record for this book is available from the British Library.

Cover design by The Andys.
Cover photos © Rob Jewell.

CONTENTS

	Foreword	*1*
	Preface	*3*
1	Roots	5
2	London	11
3	Adolescent Years	19
4	Fast Approaching	29
5	The Entertainer	37
6	When I See My Son	43
7	Starting All Over	51
8	The Visionary	57
9	Revelation Highway	65
10	Perilous Journey	71
11	To The High Throne	81
12	Fear Of The Dark	89
13	Indomitable	97
14	Gypsy Lane	103
15	Wherever There Was Beauty	109
16	Airwaves	115
17	The Long Road Home	114
18	Shining Morn	119

19	Elegy	123
20	One To One	129
21	The Price Of Experience	136
22	In Unison	141
23	A Hint Of Blue	147
24	Heathcliff	155
25	Troubadour	160
26	Janschology	165
27	Under This Blue Sky	170
28	Drifter	175
29	Circle Of Friends	181
30	Ravens And Lullabies	187
31	Ravens Will Fly Away	193
32	A Tapestry Of Tears	198
33	A Promise Fulfilled	205
	Afterword	211
	Discography	213
	Acknowledgements	231

Foreword

Gordon and I have known each other for half a century and it gave me great pleasure and a big surprise when he suggested that I write a foreword for his biography.

We first met in 1970 when he was making a record for MCA. Later in 1973 I was asked to work with him again. The last time we worked together was in 1997 when we made the *Troubadour* album, which I consider to be amongst his best work.

I found it interesting that in the earlier days Gordon wrote songs and the nature of the lyrics were often Biblical. Years later he told me he had stopped writing lyrics completely and concentrated on the melodic content of his work. He reminded me of the lute performers of the middle ages, who abounded in the royal courts of Europe and Britain. He is unique in his creations and always a pleasure to listen to.

Gordon always expressed his enthusiasm for the orchestral backgrounds behind his work. There are two categories of arranger: Arranger/Arranger and Composer/Arrangers. The first only deals with the material they are given and the second brings to the material completely new melodies and colours that were not there before.

Concerning the material of Gordon's book I'm certain that the readers will be pleasantly surprised to learn about a superb musician and a generously giving person that I have been proud to know as a friend and colleague.

Best Wishes

Del Newman

Preface

It is a common thread in the lives of many successful people that there will be one single event which serves as a catalyst, a moment in time which cements their career path for the rest of their lives. This is particularly so in the case of those with an artistic muse, and for Gordon Giltrap it came at the age of sixteen, when he faced what can only be described as an ultimatum.

Leaving school at the age of fifteen, and after a brief dalliance with signwriting, owing to a talent for lettering he had shown at school, the young Gordon managed to secure employment at a local building firm, eventually progressing to a position as a plumber's mate just before his sixteenth birthday. Knowing the boy's love of music, though sceptical of its ability to put food on the table as a profession, his father agreed to sign the hire purchase documents for a Hofner Verithin guitar from Len Styles' music shop in Lewisham. A beautiful instrument, complete with a Bigsby tremolo arm as used by Bert Weedon, it came with a hefty price tag of sixty guineas, which Gordon promised faithfully to pay off from his meagre £3-a-week earnings. The guitar quickly became his prized possession and he was rarely seen without it.

The plumbing apprenticeship however, was fast wearing thin in comparison with the joy of creating music and after a little under a year, Gordon decided it wasn't for him, despite the practical skills it had provided. Handing in his notice with the vague intention of finding something more suitable, it was clearly not likely to meet with approval. Nonetheless he dutifully informed his parents of his decision that night at the meal table. Unsurprisingly his father was less than impressed by this news. An old-school working man who had come through the war and rationing he was no stranger to the challenges of providing for a family. His rigid belief was that his son was to learn a trade and find himself a secure way to earn a living and leave such idle fancies as music for the evenings and weekends. After the meal he pulled the boy to one side. "Son", he began, "I am going to tell you what I am going to do. Next Monday you will leave this house to find a job — there are plenty in the newspaper and there is no reason you can't secure one. If you come home without a job on that day, I am going to take that guitar of yours, take a hammer to it and you will find the pieces in the dustbin. Do I make myself clear?"

Though accustomed to his father's stubborn streak and occasional temper, this particular threat hit home in a way that left Gordon cold. Surely he wouldn't do that, he reasoned with himself — while being equally certain that the threat was very real. On that Monday morning he left the house with the image of his beloved guitar in pieces haunting him and went from place to place with increasing desperation, as the doomed instrument weighed heavier and heavier on his mind. In the end, almost by dint of sheer force of will he secured a position and was able to return home and rescue the guitar from its ignoble fate. However, the emotions of that day never left him.

From that day forward, Gordon Giltrap was certain of one thing. Plumbing be damned, the tools of his trade throughout his career would not include any spanners, wrenches or other such mundane items; they would have six strings and a fretboard, and would allow him to give voice to the music he heard in his head and his heart throughout the rest of his life.

This book is the story of that journey...

1
Roots

According to his birth certificate, Gordon Giltrap came into this world on 6th April 1948 in a building called Moatlands in the very select area of the Royal Borough Of Tunbridge Wells — though such a location belies the circumstances. His family were living in south-east London, yet his parents travelled to leafy Kent for his mother to give birth, at The British Hospital For Mothers And Babies, housed in Moatlands, just outside a small town called Paddock Wood. Quite a journey in those days, yet the reason behind it was somewhat prosaic. Their local maternity hospital in Woolwich had been bombed during the war. The former private residence of Moatlands was set up as an 'evacuation hospital' for expectant mothers who came under the Woolwich jurisdiction.

This salubrious start in life was to only last ten days as the young Gordon and his parents returned to his grandmother's house in West Greenwich, home of the Cutty Sark and the great maritime tradition of the area. Here they stayed for a few months until they moved to a rented house in nearby Deptford.

Gordon's father Leonard Giltrap was born on the Isle Of Sheppey in Kent in 1918. The young Gordon would later go there for his holidays. Leonard was the son of an Irishman and his mother was of Burmese extraction. He was brought up in Bexleyheath in the wonderfully-named Fanny-On-The-Hill (where, incidentally, Kate Bush also grew up). Leonard was one of nine children — a fairly large family, even for the time, though nothing compared to Gordon's maternal grandmother, who came from an astonishing brood of seventeen! Growing up with eight siblings — Charlie, Ted, George, Olive, Rhoda, Louise, Eva and Kath — just after the First World War, things were tough to say the least. Leonard was hospitalised with pleurisy when he was young and it was a common occurrence for the children to faint during school assembly from sheer lack of food. Such an upbringing may not have been easy but it did instil a sense of frugality and work ethic which would never leave him.

Not that lack of food was the only problem to overcome in Leonard Giltrap's home. Indeed, his father lived up to the reputation of his Irish lineage by being a hard drinking man and this could often spill over into domestic violence between Leonard's parents. In later years Gordon recalls his father relating tales of sitting on the floor, eating bread and jam and begging his parents to stop fighting, as another argument would come to physical blows. Such a mixture of deprivation and violence would be seen as unthinkable to today's sensibilities, but in those days would have been regarded as a quite unremarkable environment in which to be raised and a common theme of working class family life. The old maxim of 'what doesn't kill you makes you stronger' holds true, children did emerge, if not unscathed, then at least as survivors.

On leaving school at fourteen Leonard took on various jobs, including a spell as a butcher's delivery boy, before eventually taking up a trade as a rough carpenter. At this stage he obtained work on a nearby estate laying floorboards with his brother Charlie, a rough and ready character in Gordon's recollection, to say the least. The work was hard but the amount the pair would get through was astonishing by today's standards, especially considering they were doing the job by hand, with only the most rudimentary of tools. They would regularly manage to finish the floorboards for four houses in one day. Leonard would often tell of the way they would finish off the last board in a room — fitting it into place so that it bowed up, and then jumping on it until they saw the walls physically move as it snapped into place. Hanging around the Woolwich area, they managed to secure some work at the Royal Arsenal, just as their father had before them. By dint of sheer hard graft the boys were managing to earn a living, although Gordon still has his suspicions that his uncle Charlie may have occasionally supplemented his income by slightly shadier means!

By this time the Second World War had broken out and Leonard first attempted to volunteer for the Parachute Regiment, unfortunately failing the medical for reasons that he never managed to find out. With this ambition closed to him, he joined the Royal Artillery, as had his father before him, managing to come through the war unscathed. He was on the Howitzers — the short-barrelled big guns seen so often on grainy black-and-white footage — and he often said later that the whole of his wartime experience was one of the best periods of his life. He had never been abroad before and he managed to travel all over the world, making the kind of fast friendships that only shared adversity or danger can forge.

His love of the army life may have had something to do with the fact that, as a very good looking man by all accounts, he was able to attract his share of the ladies and there would certainly have been ample scope for that sort of activity on his travels. He later confided to Gordon that when he left Germany for the final time to be demobbed, his then-girlfriend over there was actually pregnant, which would undoubtedly have been a wrench to leave. He never, ever went back however, so thereby hangs a loose branch on the Giltrap family tree. Shortly after his return, he met a young factory worker named Olive Manchester in a pub in Woolwich and they were married in 1947...

******

Alice Olive Emily Mary Manchester — always known simply as Olive — was born and raised in a small two up, two down cottage in Roan Street, Greenwich — the location of local factory The Roan Works, which made armaments during the war. A relatively small family for the time, she was the only girl among four brothers; Albert, Bill, Tom and George — the latter of whom sadly died aged 12, from meningitis brought on by a fall. Having lost her father to Tuberculosis at the age of fourteen, when he was 48 years old, she was brought up by her mother and she went on to meet the man who was effectively the love of her life, Johnny Hills. They were inseparable and looked set to be together for life when tragically Johnny was killed with his parents in an air raid shelter. Olive was shattered beyond belief and never really got over the incident, continuing to grieve in silence until the day she died. To this day Gordon believes that she was very much 'on the rebound' from this grief and trying to bury it when she met his father, and that she was never really able to give him the whole of her heart, with a piece of it forever with the memory of Johnny.

Nevertheless, Leonard and Olive married in a church named St Alfege.[†] Having married in these beautiful and historic surroundings the Giltraps moved in with Olive's mother in her house very near to the church. They remained there until soon after Gordon was born when

---

[†] Named after an archbishop who was abducted by Danish pirates and murdered in Greenwich in 1012. Knowing full well that his ransom would plunge his would-be saviours into penury, Alfege refused to let them pay and was bludgeoned to death. Soon after, a miracle was reported whereby a Danish oar which had been dipped in his blood sprouted leaves and he was ultimately canonised in 1078. With his last words in response to the Danish demands for gold being, "The gold I give you is the word of God", St Anselm later said of him, "He who dies for justice dies for God"; these words are engraved in stone outside the Greenwich church which bears his name. The church was later further immortalised when the legendary composer Thomas Tallis was organist there in the sixteenth century.

they moved, as we have already seen, to a rented house in nearby Deptford.

******

43 Elverson Road, Deptford, was to be Gordon's home throughout his formative years. The street was situated by the river Ravensbourne, a tributary of the Thames — and presumably the home to eels, giving rise to the 'Elver' part of the name. It was affectionately known to the locals by the rather underwhelming nickname of 'The Quaggie'. Although the house itself was in Deptford, the other side of the road was actually in the Lewisham district; by one of those quirks of geography, despite being officially in Deptford, number 43 was actually closer to Lewisham.

The house was a straightforward bay-windowed two up, two down but was shared by two families. There was a communal front door and upstairs lived another family, the Towners. They had a front room and a back bedroom, and then down some steps was the kitchen and the scullery. Through a side door was a communal passage that the families shared with access to the kitchen and leading out to the back yard with its outside toilet, so typical of the times. Hanging off the fence outside were two tin baths, a large one and a smaller one. As Gordon remembers, "the small one would be brought inside and would go onto the New World gas cooker, and then be put inside the large one in front of the fire. A scene typical of working class families up and down the country at that time, not just London. I lived in that house until the age of eleven, as an only child and I can say quite categorically, hand on heart, that it was a very happy childhood spent there".

At the back of the houses was a large disused railway embankment, which had been bombed during the war — the local children used to call it 'the bank'. As Gordon got a little older his parents allowed him to play up the bank, which he remembers as a wonderful place seen through the imagination of a young boy: "It was magical, a child's playground. You'd go through the back garden, up the slope, and it was this wonderful green hill which backed onto a wooded area. It was like magic, it really was".

How different to the children of today, or even of thirty or forty years ago, when a railway embankment could seem like a gateway to a kingdom of delights — but such, of course, is the power of imagination when given free rein, shorn of the distractions and, indeed, comforts, of life in the present day.

At the age of five Gordon began developing severe stomach pains and the family doctor was summoned. An Irish doctor, a bluff character named Dr Brosnan, who was known to live up to stereotyping by being fond of a drink, he dismissed Gordon's pains as a case of the gastric flu. Things worsened however to the point where Leonard actually feared Gordon had died, so unresponsive had he become. A particularly violent bout of vomiting persuaded them to seek a second opinion and Olive carried him to Great Ormond Street hospital. She was informed that this action had undoubtedly saved the boy's life as he had appendicitis, which was on the cusp of rupturing and turning to peritonitis, which was almost certain death at that time. To this day, Gordon feels a debt of gratitude to the hospital, and the staff who worked so quickly to save his life.

It was around this time that he started his education at St Stephen's, a very small church school in Gerrard Street, Lewisham, with no more than a hundred pupils. One of his recollections was that it actually backed onto the Coca Cola factory and during the summer months many of the braver kids would manage to beg the odd bottle from the men who worked there. Although Gordon does not remember ever being successful in this aim, he does recall those who did manage to secure the odd exotic prize being regarded as very lucky. Coca Cola would have been far from the everyday beverage it has become today for the St Stephens pupils of the time!

The headmaster was a Welshman named Mr Hughes, a larger-than-life character who projected quite a fearsome demeanour to the boys; a chain-smoker, he had a persistent and hacking cough which seemed to go hand in hand. However, it was only later that it became known he had served in the trenches in the First World War and had been gassed — a somewhat poignant fact on reflection.

On regular occasions the children would go from the school to a local swimming baths, Ladywell Baths. A fair distance away in the Catford end of Lewisham, they nevertheless had to walk there and it is not a place which Gordon remembers fondly. Already with a fear of water, the oppressive chlorine smell and the freezing temperature in the pool did nothing to endear it to his young mind. As a result he was thirteen before he had learnt to swim properly and even then it was self-taught.

Although Gordon was never a natural sportsman and had no great love of football or the like (his father had taken him to a game at The Valley, home of Charlton Athletic in an unsuccessful endeavour to instil in him a passion for the game) but when he was eight years old he developed an unlikely love for judo. The Green Man pub had a judo club in the cellar called the AJM Club (named after the owner Anthony John 'Tony' Moore). A mutual friend of his and Gordon's father had a child who had recovered from polio and had taken up the sport to help strengthen his limbs. It was recommended to Gordon and despite some initial trepidation he took to it like the proverbial duck to water. Indeed, he still treasures a 'Most Improved Member' trophy he received. Despite only attending the club for a couple of years he became quite proficient and filed away the skill for possible use against the attentions of school bullies. Ironically however, it was this very scenario which helped turn him away from the art as he only once used it in anger, throwing a larger boy to the ground in such a way that, provoked or not, terrified him at how easily he could have administered real physical harm. In addition Tony Moore was apparently was something of a drinker and had started taking advantage of Gordon's aptitude by having him teach other members. Consequently he simply stopped developing so his love affair with the martial arts came to a somewhat premature and unfulfilled conclusion.

At home, his family life was settled and he had a fairly loving upbringing, at least in his early years. He remembers his mother obviously doting on him and he was also close to his father at first, although as time went on their relationship grew more strained and became a defining feature of the boy's early life. Across the street from number 43 was Leithwell Road. There were always stories of a guy named Spike Milligan. The young Gordon was unaware of him at that time but it turned out later that Milligan had indeed actually lived in Leithwell Road. His parents lived there and after he came out of the army he came back to live there again. Obviously he was a local 'character' even then, with the tales circulating about him, but it was only later, when the Goons became a household name that many people realised that they had had their own 'Leithwell Road celebrity'.

Going up Elverson Road the other way it was crossed by Thurston Road, before continuing as Little Elverson Road and coming to an end at a railway viaduct — the main Lewisham-St John line, straight through from Charing Cross out to Kent. This was the scene in 1957 of one of the most traumatic incidents in Gordon's childhood when a massive train wreck caused ninety people to lose their lives in one of the worst disasters that area of London has ever seen...

2
London

One evening in December 1957 Gordon was sitting in the kitchen drawing something at the table as he often did when the house was shaken by an enormous 'bang'. He and his parents all looked up startled at the same moment and asked each other what on earth they thought it could have been. The next thing they knew there was a knock at the door and one of the neighbours brought the news that there had been a train crash on the viaduct. Straight away Gordon's mother and father got blankets and pots of tea together and rushed out to do whatever they could to help, along with most of the surrounding streets — Gordon, being only nine, was ordered to stay in the house; probably sensibly, as it would surely have been an extremely traumatic event to witness at that age. In another example of what a small world it can appear to be at times, another one of the helpers on that fateful night was a young local man named Val Doonican in the days before he achieved fame as the cardigan-clad easy-listening entertainer he later became. In fact, years later, Gordon was to appear as a guest on Val's show, and they swapped stories about the event.

The accident was apparently the result of thick fog. These were the days when London was still notorious for the 'pea-souper' fogs and even worse, smog, created through excessive burning of coal. The bridge was actually a dual level track — one rail with another track above it. In the terrible visibility, two trains had crashed into one another head-on. What made it even worse was that this happened on the lower track, so that when the trains smashed into each other, they went straight up and crashed through the track above, causing carnage that one can only imagine. Although Gordon didn't go out that night to see it he still recalls vividly the scene the following morning: "I can still remember going to school the next day and seeing this burnt-out engine — completely blackened and burnt — and they were *still* rescuing people from it or sadly in some cases retrieving bodies I suppose. There were still people dying up there and it's a scene I'll never forget. Thankfully I didn't go out to see it when it happened — not only did my parents not let me go, they weren't letting any children up there anyway for obvious reasons. I'd have been told to stay in and watch the telly or listen to the radio. I do remember them coming back from helping with the rescue though and being in a state of shock. My mum more so than my dad, because he'd seen it all before during the war, but it was clear what a dreadful thing it had been to witness".

It was reported after the rescue operations had taken place that the death toll was only the beginning of the tragedy, as reportedly many of the survivors were horrifically injured. In one of those rare strokes of fortune that happen whenever such a disaster occurs, Gordon's uncle Albert was actually supposed to catch that very train from Charing Cross out to Blackheath, but at the last minute he decided to wait for the next train because it was already so overcrowded. The phrase 'there but for the grace of God' often gets bandied around in such situations, but one can only imagine the melting pot of emotions for Leonard Giltrap in particular, in terms of witnessing such a horrendous accident, but then finding out that his brother could so easily have been one of the bodies he helped to pull from the wreckage. In a grimly ironic postscript to the disaster, when the nearby hospital mortuaries filled up and could take no more of the deceased, a temporary mortuary was set up at Ladywell Baths, the very place that the young Gordon had such unpleasant memories of from his school visits...

******

Oddly enough Gordon didn't come from a particularly musical family. His parents both loved music, and were both quite good singers (his father loved Bing Crosby while his mother was a big Gracie Fields fan), but neither played an instrument. If there was a genetic link it would be through his paternal grandfather who was a very skilled, classically trained musician, but it wasn't a direct link. It was an unexpected revelation therefore when one day in the house at Elverson Road he was to have his first ever encounter with a guitar. It was through a boy named Roy Satie (though the spelling of the surname is uncertain), who lived up the road and one day came to the Giltraps' house with an acoustic guitar on which he knew one chord. From this seemingly unremarkable experience was born Gordon's lifelong love of the instrument. Hearing it was a revelation as he explains: "The guitar must have been vaguely in tune because he was able to strum this one chord which he'd learned. As he played that chord, I swear to God, it was the most beautiful sound I had heard in my entire life! I asked him 'Play it again! Play that chord again!' — it must have been a simple G chord or something like that — but as he kept playing it to me it seemed that the sound that came out of this guitar was the most glorious sound I'd ever heard. It's a turning point in your life when something like that happens, a life-changing moment. I remember that I brought him into the kitchen and said to my mum and dad, 'Listen to this! Play it again Roy, play it again!' so excited. At that moment I think they must have realised that I wanted a guitar. I didn't demand one or anything, but it must have been clear."

In actual fact, what Gordon got first may have been a musical instrument but it wasn't a guitar as they bought him a four-string ukulele from the Freeman's catalogue! The instrument was noteworthy in itself as it was made by Selmer — a company that had been set up by an Italian named Mario Maccaferri.[†]

The four-string instrument Gordon had complete with small round picture of Elvis Presley in the headstock may have been far from sophisticated, but it did teach him the basic mechanics of the guitar. Indeed, coming as it did with a push-button gadget, which you strapped onto the neck for it to form chords for you, it took Gordon down a crucial, if accidental, path: "What happened was, I could never get the hang of this chord gadget, so what I did was to just tune it to an open chord — I hadn't learned to form chords, and that was what pleased my ear. That of course is what's known as open tuning and I still use it quite often to this day. Necessity as they say is the mother of invention and without the use of the 'gadget', or the knowledge of chord shapes, I learnt open tuning by ear as the best way I could get the sound I wanted out of it! Of course, from there I experimented and I found that by moving my fingers up and down the frets I could change the notes, which was a revelation to my nine-year-old mind!"

Shortly after this time the first major upheaval in Gordon's life took place. Having failed the Eleven Plus examination ("I think I even put my name in the wrong bloody place on the form!" he says now, "and I've had an aversion to forms ever since"), he was sent to a new school near to where the family moved to a brand new house. New however, did not equate to 'better' in Gordon's eyes. Quite the contrary, in fact...

******

[†] A noted guitar maker responsible for the Selmer Maccaferri model guitar used by the great Django Reinhardt. He had become a pioneer of the use of plastic in musical instruments; even eventually working on a plastic violin so sophisticated that it was used in performance at Carnegie Hall before his death in 1993. He set up the plastics company Selmer and began making instruments such as this in the 1940s, though they would only be refined to real commercial success much later.

The new location for the Giltraps to call home was situated in the far from salubrious surroundings of East Greenwich near the Blackwall Tunnel in the less than exotically named Blackwall Lane. Gordon recalls that he discovered later that noted guitarist Albert Lee lived in the next street, Tunnel Avenue (which does beg the question as to what these titans of imagination would have done with the third road!) and he was of the same opinion as to the surroundings. Gordon says now "I met him some time later and we discovered we lived around the corner from each other. The first thing he asked me was 'Were you afraid to go out at night in case you got beaten up?' — which speaks volumes. Albert came from gypsy stock — he was actually related to Gypsy Rose Lee and that gypsy blood might explain the fire in his playing, I think".

The Giltraps' house was situated in a block of three on the end of Blackwall Lane with constant traffic going to and from the tunnel, which was completely alien to them at the time, coming from a quiet road where you could play in the street. Across the road was a factory and next to that the much more pleasant Rothbury Hall, which doubled as the local church hall and youth club and whose turreted and exotic design marked it as utterly incongruous to its mundane surroundings. The other way across the roundabout was a bombsite where, like many such locations in those days of London still rebuilding after the war, the children made their playground. One of Gordon's mother's favourite sayings was "we don't get dust here, we get soot". This was especially true in the summer months when the smell of a nearby grain factory pervaded everything and the traffic was at its height. Running one's finger along the window frames outside the house revealed a layer of black grime, indicating the levels of air pollution in the area.

The house itself was structurally a big step up. Unlike Elverson Road it actually boasted an indoor toilet and a real bath and for the first time Gordon had a bedroom to himself. This luxury had a spin-off however as the removal from his friends and familiar surroundings, coupled with a new ability to lock himself away in his own room by himself, led him to become increasingly introverted, retiring for hours at a time to read or draw in self-imposed isolation. Some of the people and the children his own age who lived there were, in Gordon's own words, very, very rough and often unsavoury. There was one boy, who shall remain nameless, who was widely known and had been witnessed as such, to be sleeping with his own sister. Such was the environment that this was merely remarked upon rather than being the scandal and shock that one might expect. Making friends was accordingly not easy.

All was not lost however as it was not too long after the move that Gordon persuaded his parents to buy him his first actual six-string guitar, an archtop Martin Coletti acoustic. He went with his mother to a shop in Deptford High Street called Furlongs to choose it. She then paid for it on hire purchase with her factory earnings. "I can still remember to this day, looking out of the front kitchen window at Blackwall Lane watching the bus stop across the road and seeing her get off the bus after picking the guitar up. It came in a brown canvas case and I can see it like it was yesterday and still feel the excitement of her carrying it across the road and bringing it in. It had a little buckled clip to open the case and I can still recall the feeling as I opened it up and pulled out this thing of beauty, sunburst finish with a cutaway. The thrill of it has never really left me and I still love the feeling of opening a guitar case and taking the guitar out. Of course it was a horrendous thing to play, with a high action and heavy strings — no truss rod to adjust it of course — but you didn't know about those things at the time; it was a guitar and it had six strings! It came with a book called First Step written by a guy called Geoffrey Sisley and it showed you how to tune it with a set of pitch pipes. So I sat there figuring how to relate the strings to the sound of the pipes and I taught myself to tune it, which I was really proud of. It had the chord boxes as well, showing you where to put your fingers and when I played my first chord the sky opened up, it was like a revelation! I knew this was what I wanted to do."

******

Away from the world of new guitars however, things were still not going too well for Gordon in the new environment. One thing which certainly didn't help matters was that when he was due to start secondary school he was a week late, owing to a family caravan holiday in Kent (this incident in itself speaks volumes about how low a priority was placed on education at that time, as the thought of a holiday being arranged to clash with a week of school nowadays is unthinkable). As misfortune would have it that missed week was when the streaming exams were held, whereby the pupils were put into their designated 'stream', or grade of class; missing this meant that Gordon was put into the B Stream with, as he recalls it, "some of the biggest psychopaths you could imagine sharing a class with". The school, Blackheath And Bluecoats, was in a quite well-to-do area of Blackheath but that was only half the story as it backed onto an area known as the Cherry Orchard Estate. This had a reputation belying its name, as one of the roughest estates you could imagine, with seemingly the lion's share of its more unruly inhabitants ending up in class 1B with the young Giltrap.

Starting at the school he recalls being petrified to enter this twilight world wherein smaller children were routinely menaced by the larger predatory hooligans and when he was deposited into 1B this only intensified. To this day he recalls some of the most insalubrious of his classmates — one particular boy who is presumed to have gone on to serve prison time for violence, demonstrated his handiness with his fists at every opportunity. His behaviour was matched by another who repeatedly marked class visits to church by exposing himself within the church itself.

So traumatic was this breeding ground of villainy and moral turpitude that Gordon realised very quickly that the only way to escape it was to apply himself, work hard and get the grades to climb up into the coveted, and relatively civilised, A Stream. This he duly did by dint of sheer effort and he managed to finish top of the class in no less than six subjects — though he now suggests that this feat may have had as much to do with the lack of competition from his peers, most of whom were, even if not entirely without intelligence, then certainly uninterested in making any sort of effort to learn. One boy in particular he remembers well as he used to bring knives in to school and throughout lessons would often sit at the back of the class with a pack of playing cards, pointedly ignoring the efforts of the teachers to get through to him.

On one particular day with a female teacher taking the class, this boy became so obstructive that he eventually suggested that she 'piss off' — not a sentiment appreciated by schoolteachers in those days, to say the least. She duly went off to fetch the headmaster George Galloway, who Gordon recalls as being a lovely man who used to travel up from Brighton every day on the train. On this occasion however, he was so incensed by the behaviour of this boy that he burst into the class, bellowed his name and dragged him across the class from his desk by the scruff of the neck, thrashing him with his cane every step of the way, leaving him as a "snivelling, sobbing wreck", as Gordon describes it. The rest of the class watched in shock but still aware that in truth he had deserved it, because of his persistent and intolerable behaviour. The punishment would be out of the question in today's educational environment, but that pack of playing cards were never seen again and the rest of the boys knew very well what might happen if they dared to push the boundaries in such a fashion.

The move into the A Stream managed to make the school atmosphere more bearable, but Gordon was still very introverted, spending long hours in his own company on pastimes like coin collecting, painting, drawing and of course, his music — indeed, such was his perceived isolation that his father, in a typically well-meaning but misguided way, made him go for a two-hour walk every Sunday, by way of getting him out of the house for a change. All this resulted in was two more hours of solitude but it was at least in a different location!

He was beginning to develop an interest in spiritual matters, which would exert an influence on his songwriting for some time to come. He even had a brief dalliance with the Jehovah Witnesses through his grandmother, who had become involved with the organisation. He didn't make much in the way of real friends, until he was introduced to another boy, Ray Maddox, the son of a work colleague of his mother's — a lad with a very similar temperament, they became firm friends. They would take trips to places like the Natural History Museum. Ray also introduced him to the pursuit of angling. Another solitary pursuit perhaps, but they could at least sit and share the experience, which pleased his parents.

Gordon's main subjects at this time were Art and English and he regularly excelled at both. Indeed, he regularly topped the class and his art teacher — a lady by the unlikely name of Mrs Spong — thought him extremely gifted and blessed with a fertile and free-roaming imagination. She was very keen for him to stay in school to continue his studies. When Gordon was 15 and his parents came into school to discuss his future, Mrs Spong made strong representations to allow him to stay on. Unfortunately, this was not to be, as his father was doggedly insistent that he leave as soon as possible and 'learn a trade'. Gordon's thoughts on the matter even today are illuminating: "It was very disappointing, because she practically begged them to let me stay on, but my father had his mind made up. In some ways, even now, I blame him for denying me an education — though I know that's kind of a cop-out really, because if you really want an education, as an adult you'll pursue it. So I can't shift that responsibility entirely, but I still believe that I would have liked to stay on, get some O Levels, Art, English and something else and then go on to Art College. That would have been a natural progression and I'm certain that Art College would have suited my temperament. It would have been an easier life path, but it was denied to me".

So at 15, leave school he did, to enter the world of work. More crucially than that however, another chapter was about to open in Gordon's life. He had already started to spend time in the youth club over at Rothbury Hall and along with three other young men, Colin Cabell, Malcolm Aylott and John Snow, formed what was to be his first band. The world of music was finally beckoning him in...

3
Adolescent Years

By some margin, Gordon Giltrap was the youngest among the crowd of would-be musicians who hung around in the Rothbury Hall youth club, yet he found himself being accepted into their circle due to his ability on the guitar. One of the first young men he got to know there was an 18-year old aspiring guitarist Colin Cabell who had suffered a serious motorcycle accident and as a result had a steel pin in his leg. Owing to this and the leather gear he still wore, despite being unable to ride since the injury, he fancied himself as something of a Gene Vincent character and had an air of danger about him. Like the similarly attired John Lennon with the younger George Harrison, however, musical ability and potential was to override the usual youthful 'peer system' and Gordon found himself in Cabell's circle.

The drummer was Malcolm Aylott — an intimidating character who, according to Gordon, "you would still walk the other way from if you saw him today". He wore a smart Italian suit with the fashionable short 'bum-freezer' jacket, but set it off with a pair of hobnail boots ("the weapon of choice in Greenwich", as Gordon puts it). He hailed from a nearby council estate at the top of Blackwall Lane, which had been created when a lot of Gypsy families had been re-housed from their caravans and there was some heavy company in that environment. Gordon recalls one family of brothers named Bleach, led by the oldest boy Billy. It was well known that Billy Bleach was someone who you would not cross if you knew what was good for you. He and his brothers used to come to the youth club to play table tennis and listen to the jukebox and this all contributed to the volatile atmosphere. Malcolm had a caste in one eye which meant his eyes would not look correctly in the same direction — clearly a result of the fact that his parents couldn't, or wouldn't, get him the corrective glasses he needed when he was younger — and he would openly talk about bolstering his meagre income with some petty crime; all adding to his general air of menace.

Completing this fledgling line-up was bass player John Snow. A bass player in name only, he was unable to play a note when he was drafted in to the band. He was left-handed but managed to procure a bass and the line-up, to all intents and purposes, was complete. Cabell had a Hofner Galaxy guitar, with Gordon still armed with the Coletti (by this time complete with pick-ups which he had attached in a sort of Frankenstein attempt to convert it to an electric), while Aylott's kit consisted of just a single snare drum and a cymbal! "He was a good drummer though", Gordon says now. "Such a shame that his upbringing stifled all that, while he wasted his talents on a life of drifting in and out of trouble. Years later, I went back to the area, and I actually saw Malcolm sitting there on a bench, as if no time had passed, looking as if he was waiting for the betting shop or the pub to open. I didn't speak to him, but I wish I had really. Quite sad, in a way".

Christening themselves 'The Young Ones', reflecting Gordon's obsession with Cliff Richard and the Shadows, the young hopefuls began rehearsing in the nearby Glenister Road school, an all-boys establishment attended by Gordon's friend Ray Maddox. The name still makes him cringe to this day but at the time, as he freely admits, he wanted to look and sing like Cliff and play guitar like Hank Marvin. Better than the other way round, I suppose! They played their very first public performance at the youth club where they first formed — an event which left the untrained Snow stricken with stage fright and standing rigidly on the stage without playing a note. Gordon's mother, in attendance at the show, laughingly remembered him as standing there "like a frightened rabbit" and his contribution was non-existent. Manfully, however, the other three powered on without bass accompaniment, making what was by all accounts an impressively loud racket between them, effectively covering up their stricken comrade. Some time after this, they entered a talent contest at Eltham Little Theatre where, to Gordon's astonishment even now, they managed to secure second place. Sadly, soon after this high point, The Young Ones fizzled out and Gordon's initial brush with performance was over.

******

Away from the world of music, Gordon was having to make his way into the world of gainful employment. The first job he took was at a signwriting company called Hall Signs in the New Cross Area on the border with Bermondsey — a notoriously rough area in those days. By his own admission he was basically the 'dogsbody', making the tea in the morning, collecting the lunchtime sandwich orders and doing things like sweeping up in between, although he did sometimes get the task of delivering signs to customers, which involved travelling round by tube to their locations. For these endeavours he was paid the princely sum of three guineas a week (three pounds three shillings), though after six months he did get a raise of another ten shillings a week, which felt like a king's ransom! Being still a bit of a dreamer by his own admission, he did fall victim to the practical jokes played by some of the rough-and-ready characters who worked there — filling his donkey jacket pockets with water was one favourite, as was the old trick of pinning a note to his back which he would only find later (these notes often referred to him by the bizarre nickname 'Speedy Knobs Giltrap'). Another activity they enjoyed was trying to shut him into one of the large ovens which were used to dry the signs, although his remaining judo instincts helped him to resist this and eventually they gave up without success.

Although his job responsibilities were mundane, his artistic instincts did occasionally surface, as on one memorable occasion involving graffiti on the toilet wall. One of his great loves was the drawings of Leonardo Da Vinci and one day at work Gordon found himself in the toilet, bored and with a pencil, so he drew a facsimile of a Da Vinci drawing of a Roman Centurion on the wall. He thought nothing more of it until lunchtime the next day, when some of the staff were talking about it, saying how good this drawing was. Gordon piped up immediately that it was his, but was met with scorn as they would not believe that a 15-year-old shop boy could have done that. They proffered a piece of paper for him to reproduce it to prove his claim, which he duly did, earning praise in particular from one old hand Jim, who commented that Gordon's talent was clear and that he would bring some of his own drawings in to show him. "He brought in this portfolio the next day of drawings he'd done and they were incredible! He used to draw animals; cats and things like that and portraits — he was such a gifted artist! I told him how marvellous they were but he shrugged it off, saying they were okay. I was really touched that he'd chosen to share his work with me like that and take an interest in a 15-year-old kid in that rough factory environment — and it showed me how much artistic talent there is buried within people who don't have the chance to express it, or to escape their environment."

To briefly escape the factory confines, and to vicariously scratch his artistic itch, Gordon used to walk up to a nearby cafe at lunchtime, which was frequented by the students from the nearby Goldsmith's College — Exactly the type of establishment he would have wished to attend had he not been forced to abandon his education when he did. He would sit with a cup of coffee and a sandwich and feel, just for that time, as if he was a part of that college-scarf, bohemian environment, far away from the drudgery of the factory. In a nice twist of fate Gordon would later end up playing some gigs at that very college shortly after the release of his first album and therefore became the 'artist' that the arty students he so envied were wanting to see.

He stayed at Hall Signs for about nine months but by that time he wanted to earn a little more money. So, just before his sixteenth birthday he took up employment at a small building firm called Manners in Greenwich, run by Sam Manners. It consisted of a plumber, a carpenter and a painter. Working there as the plumber's mate, under the auspices of Fred Button (who Gordon remembers as 'a master builder and plumber with extraordinary skills, but an anti-Semitic travesty of a man on a personal level'), he spent a year learning all facets of the building trade.

Given his artistic leanings, it may seem surprising that he voluntarily left the signwriting business for a seemingly more mundane position, but as he now explains, there was a reason behind it: "The thing was, I was never going to get any real chance to do the creative signwriting work — the nearest I got was making the signs in the moulding shop. There was only one guy there who did the artistic writing, the gold-leaf stuff, that sort of thing and that was old Fred who was about 85. He was never going to teach me anything, because he didn't have the time, so as an apprenticeship it was a non-starter. So, when the opportunity came to earn more money as a plumber's mate, I had no hesitation. I suppose subconsciously I wanted to do the kind of work that would please my dad as well, manual work and a proper trade. This was well before health and safety regulations though. The stuff they had me doing as a sixteen year old was unbelievable; going up scaffolding, up triple ladders sixty feet in the air, doing lead work on roofs — it was so Dickensian it's a wonder they didn't send me up bloody chimneys! However, I learnt practical skills there which have stayed with me my whole life, so I'll never say it was time wasted."

It was during this spell that Gordon acquired his next guitar, the Hofner Verithin model described at the beginning of this book and so memorably threatened with demolition by his irate father some time afterward! A cheaper copy of a Gibson 335, the guitar replaced the partly-electrified Coletti as more suitable for the kind of music he was playing (although, ironically, he soon became more drawn to acoustic guitar playing and once again found himself with an unsuitable instrument). For now however, this was his dream guitar. Soon after this, the yearning for a more creative job began to reassert itself and after a year or so he quit the plumber's mate position, leading to the incident described earlier, wherein his father demanded he go out and get another job on the following Monday, or that beloved instrument would be in pieces in the dustbin.

As it happened, the job he did secure to rescue the guitar from its ignoble fate went some way to satisfying his creative desires. It was a part-time job at a photographer's called John's Studio. Run by a man who was completely deaf, it gave Gordon an interesting grounding in printing and developing and soon led to a full-time position. They also provided him with a Lambretta scooter to carry out deliveries. As something of a mod at the time it was a dream come true. Or at least would have been had he not spent so much time falling off it! From here the jobs became quite frequent and often short-lived. His next position was working for a shop in Blackheath which sold TVs, fridges, electric irons, toasters and all manner of electrical goods. Given a little bit of instruction in fixing irons and toasters and a set of tools, Gordon assumed the rather imperious official title of 'The Iron Manager', which in reality meant repairing these goods. He became quite skilled in the art of mending toasters and enjoyed the work, not least because he was able to listen to Pirate Radio all day. He recalls the very first time he heard Bob Dylan singing *Mr Tambourine Man* while he was mending a toaster and being struck by the intensity of the delivery, although Dylan was never a major favourite of the teenage Giltrap. Indeed his first true life-changing musical discovery came when he heard the debut album by future Pentangle guitarist Bert Jansch, the second album he ever purchased (the first being *With The Beatles*). Jansch's acoustic playing influenced him more deeply than his other favourites such as The Who, Donovan or Peter Paul And Mary ever did.

Quite soon, the lure of something else job-wise — this time for more money — reared its head again. Quitting the shop he took a job delivering laundry under the mistaken impression that it would pay well. When it became clear that the dull work was matched by the paucity of the wages it was time for another change; this time to yet another photographer, Harry Harvey, at his studio in Nelson Street, Greenwich, just up the road from the Cutty Sark as it happens.

Initially the work at Harry's photo studio was largely the same as he had done before, although he was able to put those hard-learned plumbing skills to use when he installed all of the piping for a new darkroom being built for colour photography — a use of his talents which was guaranteed to go down well! What might not have gone so well, had it been discovered, was the fact that he spent some time writing songs on the back of the expensive photographic paper. A significant musical opportunity came Gordon's way when Marty Wilde, who he had met while working in the Blackheath electrical shop, offered him a position in his band. Despite the drawback of being required to don a costume more suitable to a Robin Hood Pantomime, this was obviously an exciting offer and significant as he was to replace none other than future Moody Blue Justin Hayward. He spent some time rehearsing round at Wilde's house, where two toddlers were running around at the time; one of these of course was none other than Wilde's daughter, Kim. Sadly, it turned out that Wilde was ultimately unable to use him owing to financial constraints and delivered the news via a letter of apology which Gordon still possesses, framed, in his music room. He was devastated and in an awkward situation having given in his notice at the photographic studio, but Harry agreed to take him back.

After a while he started working as a wedding photographer at the weekends, a role which he still insists taught him the mechanics of crowd control. "When you're at a wedding, and you have a camera and a tripod, you can make people do anything", he says now. "It gives you an amazing sense of power!" The money again wasn't great however and three months later, now aged 18, something a little better rewarded was definitely needed. That position duly arrived when his father managed to get Gordon a reliable job as a 'brickie's labourer', working for the local Borough Council. Not without consequences though, since, having already taken him back once, Harry took a dim view of Gordon jumping ship again. When he returned for a social call some time later, he was shown the door quite unceremoniously.

There was a sense of responsibility in taking this role, because his father was full of pride at having secured the position for him. There was an amount of 'Now, you mustn't let me down after I've found this job for you' advice delivered. In truth, it was a good opportunity, as Leonard Giltrap, for all his faults, was an extraordinarily good labourer — a strong, wiry man renowned for being able to serve three bricklayers with materials while also digging a trench. As such he had an enviable reputation with the council and it was directly through his skills and influence that the job was offered. But this brought greater expectations along the lines of 'Well, we hope you're half the workman your father is! You'd better live up to it!' Gordon accepted the responsibility and began working for a man named Harry Driver, who Gordon recalls today as being "possibly the most remarkable man I've ever met".

Around ten to fifteen years earlier, Harry Driver had been pointing a chimneystack on a scaffolding platform sixty feet from the ground. With no guardrail present, as was often the case in those days, he reached backward to get another load of mortar and fell backward off the platform. He told Gordon that he still remembered the sensation of spinning through the air and having the presence of mind to land on his feet. Doing so allowed him to survive, but at a considerable price; he broke practically every bone in his feet and legs and doctors told him he would never walk again. He spent fifteen months in hospital but he was determined. Not only did he manage to walk, he returned to full-time work. He also had terrible dermatitis from years of working without gloves — being forever encrusted with sand, cement and lime, he was in pain every day of his life, though he never missed a day of work as his pride would not let him cry off sick.

"He was a miserable bugger to work with, but he was also a lovely, lovely man. I didn't know that at the time, though — I didn't realise that the pain he was in made him so grumpy and of course he took it out on me. He came to the house once, while I was still living with my parents as he had some firewood to drop off for dad. I was really pleased that he'd called round and I still remember him saying to dad, 'Let me tell you, your boy is the finest labourer I've ever worked with'. I have to say that was one of the best compliments I could have possibly received. As a boy having just turned 18, to be told by this man, who had been a very skilled bricklayer all his life, that I was up there with the best people he'd worked with was truly special. I still carry it with me to this day."

Around this time came a notable experience whereby Gordon found himself on the receiving end of some peer-group violence when he and an old school friend Hugh Little had a run-in with some pretty aggressive local youths. The pair had been for a drink one Sunday and were walking home when they encountered three "pretty rough-looking individuals led by a tall, blond skinny chap", as Gordon remembers it. He had, perhaps unwisely, shouted something less than complimentary to this blond-haired lad when he didn't like the way he and his friends were talking to a girl on the bus the week before. Approaching Gordon enquiring as to whether he was the same person who had dared to give him this back-chat he initially denied it, but then another one of the three, whom Gordon recalls quite vividly as being "dark haired with tattoos and rings on both hands" started on Hugh, twisting up his jacket and asking if he wanted trouble. When Hugh replied with the rather nice comment that he would prefer not to have trouble as he didn't want to mess up his suit, Gordon decided in a rush of bravado that he wasn't going to take this intimidation and stepped up to his own aggressor asserting that he did remember him from the bus after all.

"I think he was a bit unnerved by the fact that I had made this about turn to stand up to him, but his mate with the tattoos then turned his attention to me asking if I wanted some bother. Seeing trouble coming I was just about to put my knuckles up to defend myself when before I knew it he'd smashed me two or three times hard in the face, almost laying me out and leaving me with a black eye and a very bloody nose". On returning home in this dishevelled state with torn clothing to add to the injuries, both of his parents were shocked at what they saw, and demanded to know the identity of his attackers. All he could tell them was the pub they frequented, the Royal Albert in Greenwich, prompting some protective action from his father. "I remember I'd get to that pub and my father would be outside on his motorbike and sidecar with a large spanner in his pocket, asking if they were there! I never saw them there when he was and to be honest I'm glad, because I swear to God if he'd caught them he'd have used that spanner and he might have ended up in prison. It did show one thing though and that was how much my father actually did care about me, despite the fact that we had difficulty connecting and being close and that was his way of showing it really, by his actions and trying to protect me".

******

By this time Gordon's musical endeavours were progressing. Realising that the Hofner was unsuitable for the acoustic style he was embracing he had traded it for a Hoyer 12-string acoustic, from the same Len Styles shop and begun to take his first strides as a folk singer. He had realised that the Hofner was unsuitable when he had formed a short-lived duo with a somewhat bohemian friend, Jim Hughes, an acoustic guitarist with an abiding love of Bob Dylan. The pair actually played their first show in the same Green Man pub where Gordon had attended those boyhood judo classes in the basement. The pub was used to hosting jazz on some nights (fielding some top-class musicians, including renowned saxophonist Sonny Stitt), but on other nights became a folk club. It was on one of these nights when he came across acoustic finger-style guitar for the first time in the hands of Tony Shaw and it was a revelation to him.

Armed with the new guitar he would get home from working at the site, then play at a local pub or club whenever he had the opportunity — with the Royal Albert in Blackheath Road, that very scene of his father's motorcycle protection, being one such venue. He hadn't yet started writing in earnest so was playing a mixture of Dylan covers and folksongs but the experience was invaluable. He met some people there who became great friends, including Bill McGillivray, whose then-girlfriend would later go on to become Gordon's first wife. Bill went on to study trumpet at the Guildhall and became a respected session musician — playing alongside such greats as Big Jim Sullivan, the legendary session guitarist who gave the young Jimmy Page his first session and also gave lessons to Ritchie Blackmore.

Armed with this newfound experience, Gordon even took his guitar into work one day and played for his workmates: "I think they quite enjoyed it. One of them actually said to my dad 'You know what? Your boy shouldn't be doing this work, because of his hands'. Which dad should have realised himself I guess, but he just didn't have that awareness, bless him. Dad wasn't entirely unsupportive by this time, he just had difficulty embracing my world and bringing it into his own. There were moments, such as one day I arrived home to find him playing a Bert Jansch album which I'd talked about and saying, 'Son, this guy is incredible!' — his personality was such that it stopped him fully buying into things he wasn't familiar with, even though sometimes it prevented him from being happy himself."

One of the most important people in terms of the fledgling Giltrap writing career was his uncle, Albert Manchester, his mother's brother. An enormously important figure to him growing up, he had taught the young Gordon to tell the time, to swim and perhaps most significantly, to love and appreciate classical music. A working class man like all of the Giltrap / Manchester clan, he was nonetheless very cultured in his own way and took great joy in introducing the receptive ears of Gordon to the music of Elgar in particular. He had also been awarded the British Empire Medal 'for services to his fellow workers', no small achievement in itself. A man possessed of the patience and attentiveness that he often wished his own father had, whenever Uncle Albert would visit the house Gordon would always make sure he would play him any of the pieces he was working on, as a sort of sounding-board. His reaction and advice in these instances was more often than not both accurate and worth heeding.

Around this time he acquired a manager of sorts named Moreton Coles — who later went on to become a Conservative MP. Moreton ran the folk club in the basement of the Royal Albert pub and had given Gordon his first opportunity to play there after his parents went in for a drink one night and mentioned that their boy 'played the guitar a bit'. Following a favourable reaction at the venue he offered to represent Gordon's interests as his first manager. One night Moreton took him to the legendary Les Cousins club to play a couple of songs. With Pentangle personnel John Renbourn and Jacquie McShee on the bill that same evening, he felt somewhat out of his depth as he now admits, and can't even remember what songs he played.

Under Moreton's guidance he managed to record a demo of his material, get it pressed onto vinyl and send it out to various people in the business. It featured one of his own early songs — an instrumental called *Spider's Run* — together with two other songs, one being a Paul Simon cover. Transatlantic Records, who were influential in the folk scene at the time liked what they heard, having been nagged by Gordon's persistent calling of them. He was contacted by record producer Bill Leader with the offer of a contract, subject to developing his own material and getting himself known. The stage was set for Gordon Giltrap to take his first tentative steps into the spotlight.

4
Fast Approaching

The promise of an actual record deal, subject to raising his profile, was something which obviously focused Gordon's attention to be even more single-minded about his ambitions. He set about contacting every folk club and pub that he could find to get floor spots and if at all possible, a paying gig. Sure enough, he began to get his name known, to the point where he was getting regulars turning up at his shows and developing something of a following.

However, while Transatlantic demanded a higher profile before putting an album out, they were happy to be recording it — with the proviso that he write his own repertoire of original music. So, matched up with producer Bill Leader, he began to do just that. He would write a couple of songs, then get the bus up to Bill's flat in Camden Town and play them to him. When they had a few together, Bill would book some time in Livingstone Studios to record the material. Oddly enough, while Bill's flat was kitted out with adequate recording technology — complete with egg-boxes soundproofing the walls — he didn't want to record Gordon there, despite having done recording sessions there with such names as Bert Jansch. Gordon recalls him saying later that he had seen straight away that he needed a slightly better production in order to do the songs the justice that he felt they needed.

The very first studio session was not without note as it was delayed by the appearance of violinist Dave Swarbrick and vocalist Sandy Denny (both then of Fairport Convention) — a couple at the time, looking for something which Dave had recorded but had been lost. He was taking up considerable time talking with Bill Leader and engineer Nick Kinsey about this elusive recording, while Gordon became ever more frustrated in the background as he was fired up to start the session. He remembers Sandy as being very pretty and very quiet, but although his recollection of Swarbrick was much more vivid, when they met years the violinist had no recollection of the meeting.

When the sessions began they were always done live with the vocals and guitar recorded at the same time. It wasn't always the first take, but everything was recorded in a single go — Gordon remembers no editing at all taking place. In between sessions, he would write further material and then return to record it. Sometimes Bill would come over to Lewisham where Gordon was living in a flat with his parents at the time, very close to a pub called the Rose Of Lee in Lee High Road, where Kate Bush would later play her first live shows with her first band. Legendary blues musician and bandleader John Mayall also lived in a flat nearby, which he shared for some time with Eric Clapton and so too did Tom McGuinness of Manfred Mann and McGuinness Flint — once again Gordon had happened upon something of a musical hotbed as he seemed to have a habit of doing! Bill would drive over in the old converted ambulance that he owned, to enable him to do mobile recording and transport the gear. He would take Gordon — who didn't own transport at that time — back to his place in Camden to work through more recordings. One thing Gordon does remember Bill advising him was to 'listen to plenty of music, but not guitar'. He gave him a list of works he believed would prove inspirational to Gordon's compositional abilities, for him to borrow from the local record library and they worked extremely well. One such record that he remembers was of harpsichord sonatas by the composer Scarlatti. He still credits this with awakening his interest in the baroque style, which has influenced significant amounts of his writing. In this way he was able to draw musical inspiration without becoming derivative of other guitarists in the process, which was extremely shrewd advice.

At this time in 1968 Gordon was still working on the building site so he used to stay at Bill's flat at the weekend to work on the songs. He recalls one particular time when Bill announced that two guys named 'Bill and Tam' were coming down from Scotland to do some recording. He assured Gordon they were great characters he'd like. When they arrived Gordon was actually in the kitchen running through one of his pieces. He still recalls a booming, broad Scottish voice saying "That's great! Who's that? That's some great playing!" — and it was none other than Billy Connolly, along with Tam Harvey, the first incarnation of his duo The Humblebums, later featuring Gerry Rafferty. He recalls Connolly as being a larger than life, intimidating character and a big drinker, yet enormously entertaining company — indeed even then he had a great reputation in the clubs for his humour and personality while performing.

The recording sessions were going well but there was still the pressing matter of getting more gigs to attain the profile Transatlantic wanted before releasing an album. Bill having the contacts and the knowledge of the folk scene (the nearest fit for Gordon at that time) helped. The first thing he did was to get an advertisement placed in a publication named *Folk Directory* and he enlisted photographer John Harrison (who had previously been a musician in influential folk band the Watersons) to take the very first Gordon Giltrap publicity photograph. Gordon describes it as looking like "a very young Al Pacino type figure, very moody with a neckerchief which I thought was cool at the time". Business cards were also printed up and Bill managed to arrange a residency at the Les Cousins club. Gordon felt that he was incredibly fortunate to get breaks like this but only came to realise through time that having the backing of a label like Transatlantic and a producer like Bill Leader was able to open those doors for him. Even to this day he is fulsome in his praise for Bill who he credits with discovering him. Asked about this today, Bill himself refutes this idea. "I didn't discover Gordon Giltrap", he insists. "Gordon Giltrap discovered himself. All I did was to allow his natural talent to flourish. There was no need to discover it". Gordon however insists that Bill Leader's standing and importance at that time within the folk music scene could not be overstated: "Bill was quite simply a god within that scene at the time", he says now. "He knew everybody and the people he'd worked with was astonishing — he was the first person to record Bert Jansch, John Renbourn, Martin Carthy, all of these incredible musicians, yet the average man wouldn't even know who he was; even most music fans today wouldn't know him, because he never sought recognition or fame for himself. He was actually the person who arranged for Bob Dylan to be hosted and shown round London the first time he came over, after recording his first album. He came over to play harmonica in a play — just for that and to get to know a few people. His character in the play was reportedly Blind Boy Grunt and the record label wanted someone to show Dylan London's sights. They called Bill and he got in touch with Jansch and Carthy, arranged for them to meet Dylan, take him round London, get drunk in some pubs, all of that. What a meeting that must have been! While he was over on that visit, Dylan made his first UK appearance, a floor spot at the Troubadour. I can't stress enough how much I owe Bill Leader for having the faith in me that he did, and taking me under his wing".[†]

When the album finally appeared, simply titled *Gordon Giltrap* in late

---

[†] Madhouse On Castle Street was a play broadcast by BBC Television on 13th January 1963. Dylan featured in it performing four songs:- *Blowin' in the Wind; Hang Me, O Hang Me; Cuckoo Bird* and *Ballad of the Gliding Swan*. He was simply billed as Bobby.

Blind Boy Grunt was a pseudonym that Dylan apparently used at the Troubadour for his first UK performance the previous month. He also used it for some recordings for the Broadside label in America.

1968 it was a somewhat uneasy, yet oddly effective mix of vocal tracks and instrumental pieces, sequenced to alternate between the two in a way that accentuates the dichotomy of styles still further. Gordon was to later state in the sleeve notes to a CD reissue that his lyrics were 'very naive' at the time although the songs are, in the main, quite accomplished pieces. It is true that the lyrics are clearly the work of a young artist with the attendant poetic fancies accompanying such an age. The songs exude a sophistication and maturity that takes them beyond the simple folk songs that many of his contemporaries were producing and is very much indicative of a guitarist accompanying himself on vocals, rather than the reverse.

The album opens with *Gospel Song*, a straightforward and clear addressing of Gordon's religious and spiritual beliefs of the time and influenced by Pete Townshend as regards the aggressive strumming underpinning the song. This continues with *Fast Approaching*, a piece which he revisited and rewrote later on *Fear Of The Dark* in 1978 in much expanded form. One of the pieces closest to his heart was *Ives Horizon*, inspired by a childhood trip to St Ives, which he remembers as life-changing such was the contrast between the palm tree-lined roads leading to the beach and his own urban upbringing. The memory stayed with him so clearly that he was determined to write a piece which evoked and celebrated those feelings of freedom and elation. Elsewhere he winces slightly at what he calls the 'tortured young man' in the songs *Don't You Feel Good* and *Don't You Hear Your Mother's Voice*, though as he points out, "there again, I probably was tortured; I had a father who bullied me and I worked on a building site! It was shit! But seriously, I must have been insufferable at the time, thinking I was a tortured poet and writing songs looking back on a life that I hadn't even lived yet — though I suppose all lyric writers go through that phase at first. Paul Simon, genius that he was had a huge chip on his shoulder about being short but that grudge against the world worked for him brilliantly".

The final song on the album and the only one to go over the three minute mark is *Willow Pattern* — at four minutes and seventeen seconds almost an epic by comparison! A lyrically oblique song, Gordon remembers it being inspired by his love of art, particularly Picasso and Da Vinci, though he doesn't recall where the title came from ("perhaps it was inspired by my mother's dinner set!"). One of the things he is most proud of is that the great Ralph McTell once commented on how much he liked the song and the imagery it portrayed, an incredible compliment for a song at such a formative time in his career.

The cover of the album was photographed by the noted '60s lensman Brian Shuel. It featured a moody-looking Gordon looking back over his shoulder at the camera, accompanied by a blonde girl who was actually his then-fiancée Susan Creswell. In the wake of Bob Dylan's iconic cover of his *The Freewheelin' Bob Dylan* album, which had him walking down a New York street with his girlfriend of the time Suze Rotolo, it had become quite common for an artist to feature their 'other half' on an album cover. Bert Jansch and John Renbourn had done so and even Paul Simon on his *Paul Simon Songbook* album.

On the album's release one of the first things Gordon did was to dash round to Susan's house with a copy as she was also referenced in the song *Won't You Stay Awhile Suzanne*. As the most important thing that had happened to him at this point he was understandably anxious to show it to her. He went into the house almost breathless with excitement and handed her the album cover, with her picture emblazoned on it. "Look! The album, it's finally here!" — expecting her to be as thrilled as he was. However, to his dismay and disbelief she simply didn't grasp the importance and just said "Oh, great" and tossed it onto the sofa. Today he can see that in perspective it was Gordon the man rather than Gordon Giltrap the musician which was important to her, but at the time it was a kick in the guts that he never really got over. Though he tried to put it to one side it was as if something had been lost between them, a huge part of his world that she could never share and they broke up soon afterward. Ironically it seemed that the very gesture of sharing the moment by putting her on the cover served to drive them apart. For the first time, Gordon's professional life had taken a toll on his personal life and it is something that he regrets even to this day.

******

During the making of the album the thorny problem of the increasingly untenable role on the building site came to a head. He would come home from work, hands raw, then grabbing his guitar and rushing out to do a floor spot somewhere. It was a situation that couldn't continue for much longer. Even some of his workmates were commenting on the fact that it couldn't be good for his chosen vocation. To that end he obtained what he calls 'a soft job', working as a salesman in Cheeseman's, a large department store in Lewisham selling electrical goods. Not a dream job, but immeasurably better for his hands!

Shortly after the first album was released, the stream of new material led to recording sessions starting for the second album *Portrait*. Gordon also managed to secure a slot on a prestigious radio programme *Country Meets Folk*, broadcast on BBC Radio 2. This was the point when even his father came to the conclusion that this was more than a passing fancy and that he had to be given free rein to pursue it. By then Gordon could point to the fact that he had an album in the shops, he was earning money from playing gigs (enough to secure him the Hagstrom guitar he had used to record the album) and he was about to appear on national radio — so there weren't too many arguments when he decided he wanted to quit the sales job.

"I knew by this time that I wanted to get out and be done with it, so I said to a pal of mine 'okay, if I'm going down, I'm going to go down in a blaze of glory — let's go out to the pub at lunchtime and get pissed!" Sure enough I left work at lunchtime and we arrived back three hours later. The manager took one look at me and called me into his office. I thought 'this is it, finally'. Anyway, he said, 'Look Gordon, this isn't good enough. We've had a chat about it and we're going to give you one more chance; you're on a warning'. I was thinking, what on earth do I have to do to get the bloody sack around here? He came back an hour later and said they'd talked it over again and that they'd decided to sack me. I thought 'Thank God' as I had no idea what to do next to make them get rid of me!"

Now there was no obstacle remaining in the way of an increasingly busy schedule of live appearances and he soon had the material ready for what would become the *Portrait* album. Released in 1969, stylistically the record followed the same template as the debut, but with growing levels of sophistication and experimentation woven into the songs. Bill Leader, again at the production helm, was also starting to use a few more effects such as delay and reverb to give the songs more depth. As Bill recalls now, "There wasn't a massive amount of studio experimentation from what I recall. This was at a time when multi-track recording was about to take off very rapidly, when you would be saying, almost daily it seemed, 'Four-track? Eight-track?? What — Sixteen?' but we were still working more or less in stereo, just a two-track system. I do remember a bit of panning of the guitar from one side of the speakers to the next; that was quite interesting".

In the same way as the first album had included a song (*Fast Approaching*) which would later be re-recorded and would remain in Gordon's repertoire for many years, so too did the second — this time in the shape of *Lucifer's Cage*, later re-recorded on the landmark *Visionary* album and performed on *The Old Grey Whistle Test* with Gordon's full band. The version included on *Portrait*, while a little more rudimentary still stands up and displays the potential that it had to become the show-stopping piece it would morph into.

Lyrically the album explored slightly greater depths than its predecessor with the songs becoming less direct and more veiled by layers of opaque meaning. *William Taplin* is a great example, being inspired by the old man who lived upstairs when the Giltraps first moved into Elverson Road, which was later recorded by Gordon's future musical collaborator Don Partridge (more on which later).

"William Taplin was an elderly guy who lived upstairs when we arrived, though he later got moved to an Old People's Home and the Towners then moved in. He was an old soldier, he wore a bowler hat and I know my mother used to look after him a bit. I remember thinking that when I start writing songs, I'd like to write one about this man who has served his country and then grown old and come towards the end of his life, always living alone. It's a song about him but also about the themes of growing old, loneliness and bereavement in general. I was quite pleased with it at the time, I think."

Other highlights from a lyrical perspective include the drama of *Hands Of Fate* and the existential angst of *Never Ending Solitude*, but musically the album should be rightly lauded as a step up from the debut. Gordon today recalls some of the material being inspired by the D chord (D in the second position), which he says today that he still loves. "I find it very uplifting — I was inspired by Pete Townshend at the time certainly, because he used that chord shape a lot. The beginning of *Substitute*, for example, is centred around that, and it's irresistible."

At this time Gordon was using another new guitar that he had obtained and it was to be one of his prized possessions for many years: It was made by acclaimed guitar maker John Bailey. Such was his desire to own one, Gordon actually went to see Bailey armed with £70, which was all he was able to scrape together. It was to prove a fortuitous trip as there just happened to be a spare instrument. Apparently someone who was a huge Roy Harper fan had asked Bailey to replicate one of Harper's guitars, a beautiful instrument with a distinctive winged shape headstock. Such was the quality and aesthetic appeal of the guitar in question that he took on the commission. For whatever reason the man never came back to claim it. Gordon absolutely fell in love with it at first sight. Bailey, who admitted later that he 'saw something in him', allowed Gordon to purchase it for his £70, when it should have been £90. It is this guitar that he is proudly pictured with on the front cover of the *Portrait* album.

For the cover design — again photographed by Brian Shuel — he obviously wanted an image which reflected the title, a photograph of himself, smartly dressed in suit and neck scarf, standing with the John Bailey guitar in front of the palatial backdrop of the Queen's house in Greenwich Park. Framed with a green and black border the cover is much more striking than the straightforward photograph of the debut,

but it is certainly a somewhat awkward pose! Standing proudly, one arm across the chest and the other on the neck of the guitar, it resembles the sort of picture a 19th Century mill owner might have had, standing before his stately residence. Indeed, such was the appearance of the picture that after the album's release one Estate Agency actually contacted Gordon enquiring if he wished to sell his house, believing him to be the owner of what was actually the royal residence! Nevertheless, the cover did its job and Gordon's concept of himself in a dapper, dandified image was eye-catching enough to help the album sell quite respectably.

Already however, Gordon was looking to his next move. While making the album he had come into contact with renowned singer-songwriter Don Partridge, best-remembered for his 1968 hit *Rosie*, performed in his trademark 'one-man band' style. Partridge penned the distinctive sleeve notes for *Portrait* and after the recording they were to team up in an acoustic-based group named Accolade and the next phase of Gordon's career would begin...

5
The Entertainer

Don Partridge had been, in Gordon's words, "famous before he became famous" as he started out as a busker, entertaining the queues at theatres and suchlike across London. So well known a figure did he become that he acquired the unofficial title 'King of the Buskers'. His reputation landed him a record contract, going on to record his big hit single *Rosie*, still in that same manner. When Gordon came across him he remarked on Don's tremendous collection of guitars, including Gibsons, Martins, Guilds — worth, as Gordon says, thousands of pounds in today's money — and was told that he actually was able to buy them, not from his record sales, but from the busking days, which speaks volumes for how talented he was as having that sort of earning power performing on the street was almost unprecedented.

Both men shared a vision for a group in which they would both play guitar, with Gordon handling the lead duties, albeit on acoustic. When the five-piece band came together (completed by Brian Cresswell on flute, Malcolm Pool on bass and drummer Ian Hoyle), their debut album, released in 1970, proved a fascinating mix of psychedelic folk and a sort of early jazz-fusion. The most notable track on the album is probably the superb 10-minute version of the old Nat King Cole classic *Nature Boy* featuring a remarkable extended, quite mesmerising instrumental workout reminiscent of early Jethro Tull. Another extended track, the 13-minute and bizarrely misspelled *Ulyssees*, continued this approach, with the remainder of the album being made up of shorter and more conventional, songs. One surprise was a version of Gordon's own *Gospel Song* from his debut album, though this is less than totally successful, with a very promising opening descending into something of a 'pub sing-along' in the chorus and is something of a missed opportunity. Gordon's other contribution, *Starting All Over*, would be revisited on his next solo album *A Testament Of Time*.

Overall the album was an extremely interesting debut and is now quite sought-after among collectors. The band went on to do some live work to promote it, with Gordon squeezing some solo shows in as well. The involvement with the Accolade project certainly did his growing reputation no harm as Partridge's name gave the band a certain level of attention right from the word go and the name of Gordon Giltrap was starting to become known. However, just when it seemed the band might go on to be more successful, Gordon elected to jump ship and disappointed his bandmates — Partridge in particular. Looking back on it now, he ascribes his decision to leave to one thing: "Impatience. That was what it came down to. I was enjoying being in the band and doing the odd gig, but things were moving too slowly for me. I'd had the two albums out under my own name and I was keen to get into the studio and do more, to build on that. Looking back, I could have stayed with the band and had my solo career in tandem with it, but in those days that wasn't anything like as common as it is now. Like when Godley And Creme left 10cc — they could have done their own stuff alongside the band, but back then 90% of the time you would do one thing or the other and for me it had to be my solo career."

Accolade continued with respected Croydon-born folk guitarist Wizz Jones (still active today) in Gordon's place, but the end was nigh and the magic was gone. After one more album, *Accolade 2*, in 1971 (on which Gordon's *William Taplin* was featured) the band split up.

At this point, in 1970, Gordon had just got married to his first wife Maureen and he felt the acute need to be bringing in some money to support her. Although, as he admits now, she could have worked herself and helped support them financially, he was very proud, as were many men at the time, and wanted to be the main 'breadwinner' — still expected in those times. Feeling the need to bring some money in for this responsibility — and ironically, considering the factors behind his resignation from Accolade — he responded to an advertisement in *Melody Maker* which read 'lead guitarist wanted for new band'. It seemed as if he was jumping out of the frying pan and heading purposefully for the fire...

******

He arrived at a big house in the well-to-do St John's Wood area of London to meet with the band, who were named, in extremely 1970s fashion, Stonefeather. He entered with his acoustic guitar in one hand and his albums in the other. He admits now he wasn't a good fit for the band that really wanted an electric player, while he was still almost exclusively acoustic. As it happened, it didn't even get as far as an audition as he was met by an American man who took one look at him and said 'There's no point you auditioning for this band, you're too good'. Asking how he knew this, Gordon received the answer 'Well, you've made albums. You've got to be too good, you've already made it'. Seemingly a blow, this actually turned out to be a remarkably serendipitous moment — the man turned out to be none other than Miles Copeland (older brother of drummer Stewart Copeland), who went on to manage The Police to massive global success and by this time was already managing the fledgling Wishbone Ash, who were yet to record their first album.

The house was the home of Miles' and Stewart's father, Miles Snr, who had been an extremely important figure within the CIA, hence the impressive property he owned. Having brushed aside the idea of Gordon joining Stonefeather, Miles wanted to know about what he'd done so far, so Gordon ended up playing him some of his material. Sufficiently impressed with what he heard, Copeland announced right there and then that he was interested in managing him and would like to introduce him to a few people. A meeting was arranged for an evening when they were joined at the house by Copeland's management partner John Sherry and also Derek Lawrence, who was lined up to produce the first Wishbone Ash album and in fact went on to work as their producer for several years. Indeed, Wishbone Ash used to rehearse in the basement of that very house in St John's Wood at that time.

Miles already had considerable ties to MCA Records through label signings Wishbone Ash and also through Derek Lawrence, so brokering a contract for Gordon with MCA was an obvious next step. Everything was set up, from the management to the label, to the producer, to the recording studio. Gordon began working with Derek, playing him some of the new material he had been writing. While impressed by the material, Derek's first suggestion was that he could very much hear the songs with string arrangements to enhance them. He recommended string arranger Del Newman who had already worked with Cat Stevens and Peter Sarstedt. Newman would later become incredibly respected and well known, working with an enormous range of artists, from Elton John to George Harrison. A meeting was arranged and Gordon, Derek and Miles all travelled to Del's house. When they arrived, they knocked on the door and Del shouted down from the window. Interestingly, with none of the three having met Newman —all three were surprised to find that he was black. At that time, few apart from Jimi Hendrix and perhaps Arthur Lee from Love, had broken down the 'glass wall' between the worlds of white rock and folk music and the Motown and soul arena and it was still noteworthy to find someone crossing that divide. The glass wall was still in place, but each time someone like

Hendrix or Lee or Phil Lynott kicked it down, it would be rebuilt weaker than before.

Having met and discussed things, the other two left Gordon to it. He and Newman spent the afternoon at the piano with Del transcribing and transposing the songs to the keyboard. This led to the next album *A Testament Of Time* on which Newman played keyboards and did all of the arrangements. The resulting album was a great leap forward in terms of sophistication and depth of songwriting and one which Gordon was extremely proud: "I thought it was wonderful at the time. I was so pleased with everything about it and Del was absolutely superb". A string section and Chris Lawrence's bass guitar rounded out the accompaniment — not yet a full band, but a much fuller sound than the first two albums, to say the least.

The album was recorded in the prestigious De Lane Lea studios in London[†], a world apart from Gordon's previous studio experience.

Opening the album was *Starting All Over*, which had appeared on the Accolade album. A very effective opener, it finds Gordon waxing nostalgic about his life and is a model of concise songwriting. Perhaps an interesting listen after reading this book, in many ways! The track that garnered the most attention and proved to have the most traction going forward was ironically one of the shorter pieces, the instrumental *Catwalk Blues*. Only two minutes long, it is nevertheless both a very skilled piece of playing and also a memorable one for the listener. Indeed, so durable did this song prove, that it appeared in reworked form on two later Giltrap releases, as a bonus track on the *Fear Of The Dark* album and also on the 2004 release *The River Sessions*, expanded and, in Gordon's words, improved each time. In fact, the very first time Gordon appeared on television was on the programme *Disco 2*, the forerunner to *The Old Grey Whistle Test*, playing *Catwalk Blues* and *Starting All Over*.

Elsewhere on the album highlights abound — the beautifully arranged guitar work in *Gypsy*; the deep, almost impenetrable imagery of the excellent *Cycle*; the charming almost-instrumental *Candlelight Lady*; the catchy *Lady Jae* and the story-telling of *The Entertainer*. Looking back over the album, Gordon recalls some of the influences today: "Some of the lyrical meanings are so far removed I can't remember them

---

[†] Originally founded in 1947 by a Frenchman named Major Jacques De Lane Lea — a French intelligence attaché for the British government — the studio's original role was for the somewhat mundane purpose of dubbing French films into English. By the 1960s it had been adapted to keep up with technology and by the time Gordon recorded there it had already been used for recordings by artists including the Beatles, The Who, The Rolling Stones, Pink Floyd, Fleetwood Mac and Deep Purple. Big footprints in which to walk for a 22 year old London lad with an acoustic guitar!

all myself, such as *Cycles*, for example, which I think was written about having got married, but also couched the message in a lot of quasi-religious or philosophical imagery. *Gethsemane* was a straightforward Christian song, but that part of me was still very strong at that time. It's the only overtly religious song on there, although there are many nods to my faith at the time. *Lady Jae* I remember was about a cat, while *The Entertainer* was inspired by an old black-and-white film of the same name, which told the story of a washed-up old seaside entertainer for whom the show must go on. I do remember a dissonant chord, which I put in the chorus of that one deliberately — trying to be a bit too clever in a way I think, because it disrupts the flow a bit. The instrumental *Harlequin* was another of my many nods to the great John Renbourn, very influenced in that way. I was still carrying a lot of Jansch and Renbourn influences at the time, unashamedly so".

The cover of the album, while an undeniable step forward in terms of artistic concept from the first two, was to prove a significant bone of contention to Gordon. It is certainly eye-catching and even an attempt to be sophisticated in an early '70s kind of way, but the execution is poor. A gloomy-looking image of (presumably!) Gordon stares unrecognisably out of a large oval, looking for all the world as if asking 'mirror, mirror on the wall, who designed this cover at all?' while another circular, vague painted shape is presumably intended to be a man with a guitar, but matches none of the rest of the artwork. This wouldn't be the only or indeed the last album of the decade to appear with artwork which disappointed the artist, but in this case the issue ran somewhat deeper, as the original designs were done by no less a team than the legendary Hipgnosis — Storm Thorgerson and Aubrey Powell, the men behind so many iconic designs for Pink Floyd, Led Zeppelin, UFO and a lot more. Gordon is still unsure how on earth the decision to turn away from Hipgnosis came about: "I remember the original design that the Hipgnosis guys came up with, because it was absolutely wonderful. It was a picture of a stream with me in it and all of these memories floating past, like the stream of time. There was a rosary for example, I think some flowers, some other old things from my childhood and earlier life. It was such a strong concept and it would have made a fabulous cover, absolutely fabulous. To this day I have no idea why the record company decided to change it. I was just happily assuming that the Hipgnosis design was going to be the cover but then out of the blue they got this guy from the States to do this alternative illustration. You see that picture of me in the mirror, as it were? That was painted from a photograph taken by Aubrey Powell in Kew Gardens. The original photograph is great, but the painting is awful! And what's that all about in the circle? It just mystifies me why they made that U-Turn, whether it was a question of money or something. At the time I probably just thought 'well, it's all right I suppose, but it's not as good as the original', but it's frustrated me ever since that such a cool album cover was scrapped".

The back cover is much better, featuring a half-shadowed black-and-white photo of a moody-looking Gordon in rapt concentration hunched over his guitar — by this time emerging from the fresh-faced young man from the earlier albums into something a little more shaggy, unshaven and generally freer-spirited in appearance. The classic troubadour / drifter image if you will. "That's right", agrees Gordon "I like that picture, always have. That was actually taken by a pal of mine who I'm still in contact with now. I really like the mysterious half-shadow of the picture, it lends it an air of mystery almost, which the front cover was completely lacking".

Any perceived shortcomings in the cover imagery though, however irksome they might be, should not overshadow the fact that this album was a major step forward in Gordon's career, and many would say the best album he recorded up until 1975's breakthrough *Visionary*. As it stood in 1971, things were moving in the right direction. With the benefit of greater distribution and the status of a label like MCA, *A Testament Of Time* sold significantly more copies than the first two Giltrap albums, and bigger and better gigs were coming in on the back of it. Things were looking good...

6
When I See My Son

With Gordon having got married to Maureen on 6th June 1970 the couple decided straight away that they would like to start a family. Confident that his work would now afford them enough income to support a child and with his touring schedule generally allowing him to have a semi-regular home life at least, Gordon says now that he felt the pull of fatherhood very strongly. Maureen soon fell pregnant and the planning for the next stage in Gordon's development began in earnest.

The pregnancy was relatively straightforward. Far from the present day regime of avoiding anything from peanuts to caffeine and seemingly all points in between, many children in those days were raised *in utero* on a diet of cigarettes and beer! While not perhaps being quite so cavalier, the Giltraps were able to enjoy a relatively normal and trouble-free period of expectancy. They were living in Grove Park, South East London in a flat in Coopers Lane, which, oddly enough, Gordon's mother had found for them, having seen it advertised in a tobacconist's window. Gordon remembers it as an optimistic time, with "that feeling of hope which all young married couples go through and the magic of feeling the bump getting bigger and all that sort of thing".

Eventually, when the time came, Maureen was whisked off to Bromley Hospital to give birth. Gordon remembers the labour as not being too arduous in comparison with some and without significant complications, though as he admits "it's never 'straightforward' in reality is it though. Like all births, unless you are going to go for epidurals and that sort of thing, it was hard for her". In those days natural childbirth was more the norm and as he puts it "the woman basically had to scream her head off and push"!

So it was that on 27th May 1971 Jamie Giltrap came into the world. At that time it was quite uncommon for fathers to be present at the birth — the usual scenario was of expectant fathers pacing up and down the waiting room before handing out cigars — but Gordon insisted that he be in attendance and witnessed his son being born. An event which he remembers even now as having a significant effect on him: "The thoughts that went through my head were that I knew there was a child in there, logically of course, but then when this baby appeared I just thought 'Oh my God, it's a person! It's a real human being'. It really is a feeling that you'll never be the same again. The elation is hard to put into words. When I held him, it was a mixture of this overwhelming feeling of joy, together with a sense that you've really accomplished something major. I was 22 and I had just become a father; it's hard to explain, but you feel as if you've done what you were meant to do, carrying on your line and it was really quite a profound thing. Even now, whenever there is a significant birthday in Jamie's life and I write a card, I always put in it something to the effect of 'The night you were born was one of the most extraordinary nights of my life'. It was, as I'm sure it is for most parents".

When he left the hospital, he remembers just walking all the way home without even thinking about it: "It must have been about five miles or so, quite a distance, but I just walked, and probably half ran, I think. Your mind doesn't seem your own at the time, with the adrenalin and all of that; it's a state of bliss. It might have been cold, or raining, I honestly can't remember, as it just wasn't registering".

After this came the difficult part when the sleepless nights began. "You really start to forget what it's like to have a good night's sleep! All parents go through it of course, but it still comes as a shock the first time". Nevertheless he still remembers Jamie as being "a really good boy and an absolute delight to be with". He was still having to do gigs to support them financially, but these were arranged whenever possible to be one-night affairs, without too much travelling, so that he could always get back to a stable home life in which to raise the child.

Interestingly, Jamie has since gone on to follow his father into the music business, if in a very different way, as he has established himself as a very successful Drum And Bass DJ and producer. So the apple, while not falling too far from the tree, has gone far enough not to be in the shade of it, as one might say...

******

One notable concert that Gordon played at this time was actually supporting David Bowie, just before the release of his iconic *Ziggy Stardust* album. It was Friday 25th February 1972 at Avery Hill College in Eltham, just before Bowie's popularity sky-rocketed in July of that year when the *Ziggy* album took the charts by storm. Also on the bill were cult theatrical progressive rock outfit Principal Edward's Magic Theatre. Bowie's band at the time were of course the Spiders From Mars with Mick Ronson on guitar along with Trevor Bolder and Woody Woodmansey making up the rhythm section. Gordon had seen Bowie playing several times in his slightly earlier days when he used to play the clubs in and around London. While not a fan of his music or image as such he was obviously delighted to secure the gig supporting the man whose career was even then clearly on a fast upward trajectory. At the time Gordon was playing as a duo with bass player Alan Hall who would go on to appear on the following year's *Giltrap* album. The pair travelled round in an old black cab which Gordon had bought, despite not yet holding a driving licence. They had removed the back seats so that they could fit all of their gear in it, and it turned out to be an extremely reliable workhorse. He vividly remembers Bowie making a point of coming to seek him out before the gig, chatting about it and wishing him luck for the show. He looks back fondly on what a polite and friendly character Bowie actually was, behind the make-up and the glam.

As time went on Gordon's relationship with Miles Copeland was growing ever more distant, with the palpable feeling that Copeland was losing interest in his other clients as he became more and more focused on Wishbone Ash — his 'star pupils', if you will. Matters were certainly not helped by the fact that an American tour he was arranging for Gordon fell through at the last minute. A band had been put together with the exciting prospect of the *Testament Of Time* material being arranged for full band treatment and Gordon's collaborator Del Newman had been installed as musical director. Everything was lined up, including an appearance at the famed Troubadour club in Los Angeles when at the eleventh hour a call came through from Miles simply stating 'The tour isn't happening — sorry'.   It was a severe blow as this was to have been a huge opportunity although Maureen wasn't too happy, but had accepted the fact that this sort of thing had to come with the territory if the opportunity arose. Gordon states that to this day Del Newman bitterly resents Copeland for his treatment of them: "Del will say even now how let down he felt. He'd been promised this was going to happen, a period of rehearsals had been arranged; he'd cancelled a lot of work for it and without even being properly told about it, everything was suddenly cancelled. But that's often the way things were back then, unfortunately. It could have been a big thing, who knows, but it wasn't to be".

[†] His real first name is Michael and the nickname reportedly comes from the name of a teddy bear.

Despite the fact that Wishbone Ash were claiming more and more of his manager's attentions, Gordon asserts that he has never had anything but good things to say about the band, with whom he became good friends, and also toured alongside, as we will read later.

"I was actually at a party a while ago in Malvern and I bumped into Ted Turner [Wishbone guitarist]. He lives in the States now, but he'd come home to visit family. I was having a good chat with him about the old days and when I first saw Wishbone who were an incredible live band. The first time I saw them they went into the song *Blind Eye* from their first album with no count in or anything. They were so tight it seemed almost telepathic, absolutely fantastic. Anyway, I was talking to Ted, and he suddenly said to me 'Gordon, the one thing I can see about you is that you haven't changed a bit! You're still the same romantic person, with the same outlook on life, and I love that!' — and that got me thinking that he's right in a way. I still remember now the way I felt about things back then, and my feelings now are much the same. I remember my attitude to music, love and relationships was always sincere and from the heart and I still feel the same way. I'm still the same bloke — it's just that I'm old now..."

Things had to change, that much was obvious — and change they did when Gordon encountered Martin Clark who expressed an interest in working with him. Martin worked for a music publishing company, April Music, but also did freelance work. He told Gordon that he would be very interested in producing his next album and he could get him a prestigious record contract. Sure enough he made good on that promise and arranged for Gordon to sign with Philips Records for the album, which ended up simply being called *Giltrap*.

The idea this time was to further increase the instrumentation and personnel on the album and to that end a team of musicians were assembled. Probably the most noteworthy of these was a very early recorded appearance by Nicko McBrain[†] who plays drums throughout the album. He was later to become a member of Iron Maiden where he remains over thirty years on. Most of the bass guitar on the album is courtesy of Brian Belshaw, who had been a member of cult '60s band Blossom Toes along with future Rod Stewart collaborator Jim Cregan. Alongside this rhythm section there were appearances by a number of guest musicians, including pedal steel virtuoso BJ Cole, bass player Alan Hall and guitarist Gordon Smith, while backing vocals were provided by future Pink Floyd backing singers Vicki Brown and Liza Strike.

Despite this impressive line-up Gordon feels that the album was a little bit of a disappointment after *A Testament Of Time*, regarding it as patchy in places and unsure of exactly what direction it wanted to go in.

There is some truth to this but there is also some very strong material on the record. One of the best songs is *Touch And Sound* concerning a blind man who 'moves around inside a world of touch and sound', inspired very strongly as Gordon admits, by Jose Feliciano. It is one of the best examples of music and lyrical ideas blending together in his whole repertoire.

A further highpoint and a favourite of Gordon's is *Passing Of A Queen*, another song he later reworked, this time on the 2010 album *Shining Morn*. That re-recording is in purely instrumental form but this original vocal piece deserves to be heard, with its evocative lyric about a condemned queen going to her fate being perfectly matched by the accompaniment, which carries echoes of a Tudor madrigal — a very under-appreciated song in Gordon's catalogue and another of his very best vocal pieces. After this record the vocals were to disappear as he became an almost exclusively instrumental performer. At this point however he was producing strong songs with vocals; as with the previous albums there is one overtly Christian song in the shape of *Miracle*, which takes a Good Samaritan type story as its starting point to create a song which not only does Gordon still remember fondly, but which also caught the ear of his friend of the time Cliff Richard. Again though this would be the last of his directly Christian songs for reasons that will become evident.

Opening the album and a very clear indicator of how fatherhood had impacted his life was his ode to Jamie, *When I See My Son*. Lyrically a little trite in places, the sentiment and sincerity of the song ultimately carries it. It can be viewed as the signature song on the album, especially with the use of young Jamie in the cover photographs. Speaking about the song now, Gordon says: "I think if you forget about some of the lyrics, the sentiment of the song still shows through. If I tried to rewrite it now I could probably do a better job I suppose, but it still holds a very pleasant memory of a genuinely happy time in my life. Even more so now in a way because Jamie is a father himself and when he recently commented on social media about the birth of his son, I felt as though I could have written the same words four decades previously. So it still holds a lot of magic for me".

The cover of the album is a collage of photos of Gordon with Jamie, while on the back he is holding his guitar; all of these photographs show a bearded Gordon wearing a tank-top and sporting a very 'Cat Stevens' look.

"Looking back on that cover, I probably shouldn't have done it, I suppose. It was very 'of the moment' and doesn't really date all that well. However, in another way I'm glad I did, because it created a lovely memory for my son. He's never been embarrassed by it — which I suppose he could have been and he even has one of those photos on his fridge. I suppose the main photo of us blowing bubbles might have been a bit much though, now you come to mention it! The thing is you could get away with that sort of thing more back then. People were more comfortable with picturing themselves with their kids on an album cover. John Renbourn did it [on the album *The John Renbourn Sampler*], and John Martyn as well; it was never cool, but it was accepted. I'd never do it now, though — expose images of your family for the whole world to see? People would shy away from that today, which is a shame in a way. The Cat Stevens thing is really obvious, though — it's clear to see what a huge fan I was and that I was modelling myself on him entirely! The thing is it didn't really work because even with the hair and the beard I clearly looked nothing like him! The beard itself let me down, because it would never join up to the moustache; it took me decades to manage to finally get a joined-up beard!"

The album was released with something of a media fanfare from Philips, certainly compared to the relatively low-key releases of his previous records. "I remember opening up the *Melody Maker* and seeing this full page advert with the album cover and the words 'Giltrap's Back!' in big letters. I thought that was great, he thing of 'He's been away, you must have missed him, well now you'll be stunned by his new direction', which of course, people weren't! It didn't really sell all that well, and it proved to be my only album for the label".

In truth the album falls between two stools. There was potential for a new step, with the band accompaniment and also the fact that Gordon himself was enjoying playing a lot more electric guitar as he absorbed more and more rock influences. Unfortunately, it never really took off in that way as there is also a feeling of an artist unwilling to step away from the comfortable style he was used to. As a result the album is somewhat hamstrung by the past while trying to take a step towards something new. There was good material across these styles, but less of a defining identity than on his previous work.

There was some live work around this time — in particular a support slot on a UK tour by a Gloucestershire progressive rock band named Decameron. Formed back in 1968, the band — who had once been managed by comedian Jasper Carrott of all people — released their debut album *Say Hello To The Band* in 1973, and had high hopes for success. The tour got off to a slightly sour start owing to one episode when a disbelieving Gordon was asked by a (nameless) member of the band for money to cover using their PA system! This request was understandably given short shrift, but it did instigate something of a bad taste, as it were.

A much more humorous episode came during a foray into Wales when Gordon, having taken details of the night's gig over the phone, arrived in Carmarthen, near Swansea, after a long arduous drive. Looking for the venue Trinity College, he stopped at a police station to ask directions. In desperation, he trudged in; a disconsolate looking figure in a blue duffle coat, having alighted from a matching blue mini! When he asked the desk sergeant for directions he was greeted by the reply 'Ah yes, we get that a lot. Let me show you on this map...' At which point he pointed to Carmarthen, said 'Now you're here...' and then pointed to a location on the Anglesey coast some 127 miles north, adding with a flourish 'And you want to be here!' The gig was actually at Trinity College, Caernarfon, the other end of Wales. There is clearly a very funny side to this story, but it was entirely lost on this dejected travelling musician with only an enormous double guitar case to keep him company! Having given up any hope of getting within 100 miles of the gig, he bemoaned his troubles over the phone to Maureen, found a local Bed And Breakfast, procured a bottle of wine from a nearby off-licence and proceeded to spend a gloomy evening attempting to drown his sorrows.

Needless to say, Decameron and the rest of the tour party immediately saw the light side of this and at the following gig Gordon was immediately greeted with enquiries as to whether he had enjoyed his tour of Wales. Overall, it is not a tour which lingers long in his memory — or at least not for the right reasons and 1973 rather petered out in something of a blaze of indifference.

The next album, 1975's *Visionary* was set to be a whole different story, as Gordon's career was to be propelled to another level. Before this however, there were to be some hurdles in the way, both in his personal life and his professional career. For Gordon the road travelled was rarely the simple one...

7
Starting All Over

Around this time, and partly as a result of the regular Christian lyrics appearing on his albums, the spiritual and religious side of Gordon's life and career began to grow. Already possessed of a strong religious faith, his work had come to the attention of the 'Christian Rock' scene and he became quite involved with the magazine *Buzz*, published by the Musical Gospel Outreach (MGO).

MGO had founded a decade or so earlier, as a loose-knit organisation dedicated to helping and advancing the cause of Christian musicians and groups playing contemporary pop and rock music, and *Buzz*, evolving from an earlier title *Crusade*, was their flagship publication. In fact, over the years, *Buzz* grew in popularity as the Christian rock scene grew, around such artists as Larry Norman, Graham Kendrick, Nutshell and Resurrection Band, and of course Cliff Richard and the Greenbelt Festival, becoming a glossy, professional publication by the late 1970s, before going through a series of name changes prior to its eventual demise. At this time, around 1973, however, the magazine and MGO in general were still quite small, and Gordon became one of their figureheads as a popular artist spreading the Christian message.

As he admits today, there was certainly an element of self-interest in this liaison, as MGO were a good source of fairly regular gigs on the Christian circuit, which he could play in tandem with his regular shows. By the same token he was a man of some faith, who took his beliefs seriously, and so this seemed to be the perfect arrangement for both parties. Doing these shows, however, began introducing him to people who had much more rigid and strictly defined manifestations of their faith, and he began getting asked at gigs, 'What church do you attend', and even 'Do you tithe?' ('tithing' referred to the giving of ten per cent of a person's income to their church or religious organisation). As someone whose faith was very much a personal thing, these were unfamiliar waters. He began mixing increasingly with those of the Pentecostal faith, or 'charismatics' as they were often known as at that time, whose elements of faith healing and 'speaking in tongues' among other demonstrative expressions, intrigued him.

One weekend in 1973, seeking to get to know more about the Pentecostal beliefs, Gordon went on a seminar based around the movement, and in particular the 'laying on of hands', or faith healing, side of things. As he says now, he was "quite full of this stuff", and excited by what he'd been encountering and witnessing. At the same time, he was a little conflicted as he had met quite a number of avowedly Christian people since moving in these circles whose day to day behaviour seemed to him to be at odds with their beliefs — in many ways quite hypocritical, but he remained fascinated, and personally quite inspired, by what he had been learning.

On returning from that pivotal weekend he visited his parents at their maisonette in Lee High Road, Lewisham. His father, by this point, had been stricken quite badly with arthritis, which had progressed quite quickly over the past couple of years and left him unable to work any more. His knees were giving him a lot of trouble walking, his hands were in significant pain, and the problems with his neck rendered him unable to turn his head beyond the most basic movement. Seeing this, and talking animatedly to them about the weekend experience he had just had, Gordon suggested that he try the route of prayer to see if it would help.

"I remember I was talking about all of the laying on of hands which I had witnessed and it just came to me to suggest trying the power of prayer. I didn't say I'd try to heal him, or anything directly like that, but what I did say was that, if we joined in prayer and asked God to help, then maybe something might come from it, because I'd seen it happen. I was really stepping out on thin ice, especially because I'd never talked about anything like this with my parents, but I believed in this stuff quite strongly. So there were just the three of us sitting at the kitchen table. I asked them to join hands with me and close their eyes while I said a short prayer. Even as I said it, I remember thinking to myself 'If this doesn't work, I'm going to feel pretty stupid', as if it's a trick that's gone wrong or something, but at the same time I thought that, even if nothing happened — and deep down I don't think I expected it to — I thought 'Well, this is nice, if nothing else, that we're doing this'. So, I said a little prayer while we held hands, and then when we opened our eyes, my dad got up and walked out of the room without a word. I could tell my mum was upset, so I just told her he was probably a bit overwhelmed and not to worry. I followed him out of the room to see what was happening, and I caught up with him at the bottom of the stairs. I asked him what the matter was, and he turned to me — I'll never forget this — and he had tears streaming down his cheeks. 'Son', he said, 'you've healed me!'"

Understandably shocked and taken aback by this announcement, Gordon could only reply "what??", while his father reiterated, "You've cured me, son. Look — the pain is gone!" and flung his arms above his head in a way that he had been physically unable to do for the previous twelve months. Not only that, he started running up and down the stairs, with no trace of the pain or impairment which had been his constant companion for so long. He had, with no shadow of a doubt, undergone a transformation which seemed nothing short of miraculous. Apart from elation, relief or any sense of triumph, however, Gordon's first thought was: "I was scared to death to be honest! I hadn't really expected it to work and I thought I hadn't done anything, so what was going on? I remember dad going on and on, repeating 'You've cured me'. I said to him right there that I hadn't done anything, that God had cured him. 'I'll never doubt God again', my dad was saying, through his tears of joy, and I have never seen someone so overcome with relief, happiness and newfound faith. I left that house like a man reborn."

Tragically, however, there was a twist in this tale: "You know what, though? Despite all of that, within a week — in fact within two days — the pain came back. As bad as ever, just like that. He started going to church, praying for God to take the pain away — it really screwed him up, and me as well in a way. My mum would say he's gone to church, so I'd go there and see this old man, struggling to kneel, just asking God to give back what had been taken away, and I was so angry. It wasn't right, and I was furious. Of course, he went rapidly worse as well, it was awful to watch. Now, looking back on it, it was a mind-over-matter thing, with his pain being lifted by something in his brain, like a huge surge of adrenaline because the mind is such a powerful thing, but at the time I was young, full of faith, and so resentful of a God who would take away someone's pain only to give it back to him. I just thought I didn't want any part of a God so cruel or malicious. Now, at a time like that, I really needed the support of my fellow Christians, but again I was let down enormously, as all they would say was the stock answer of 'Oh, it's all God's plan', and brush it aside. This to me represented the worst kind of whitewash, and I just thought it was completely unacceptable to treat such a massively important event so flippantly. From that moment on, my relationship with Christianity, the church and spiritual faith in general was never the same again. If that was my faith, I was done with it."

This wasn't the first time Gordon had felt at odds with this way of worship, however. Some time before this, he had gone to a big Pentecostal church event in Stroud, where he was to be baptised — largely because he had been urged strongly to do so by people within the movement. They duly carried out the baptism and he still recalls now that when he emerged he knew he was expected to start speaking in tongues.[†] As he puts it, he "started talking gibberish. Total nonsense, but they loved it! I knew in my heart that was a load of old rubbish!" It was about this time that he first met Cliff Richard but as he remembers it, "Cliff was never into that sort of scene. He had his beliefs, and he did the Christian festivals, but he was much more of a traditional, Church Of England man. He had very little time for what I might call the fringe nutters, which is one of the reasons we got on".

This period had not been without its highlights however. Not only had the Christian-based shows in churches and the like provided an extra stream of income but there had also been big shows. One memorable occasion was when Gordon played at Wembley Stadium, sharing the bill with none other than evangelical preacher Billy Graham (playing *Lucifer's Cage*, as it happens). Nevertheless, his creeping disillusionment with the whole situation meant that something was going to have to give sooner or later. The catalyst was when he first encountered the work of poet, artist and visionary William Blake. The impact Blake had on Gordon was profound and Blake's work went on to form the basis for the landmark *Visionary* album. Part of his appeal was that he had always been something of a rebel and free-thinker, reacting against the dogmatic conventions of the church, in much the same way as Gordon was attempting to do himself, some 150 years later. This anti-establishment ethos, coupled with the extraordinary nature of his poetry and artwork, and the romantic and esoteric appeal of the fact that he claimed to have seen visions which informed his work, was enough to leave the conflicted and transitionary Gordon Giltrap entranced. His schism from the world of organised religion and the Christian faith was complete.

His mind freed, Gordon's creative energies channelled themselves into what would coalesce into *Visionary*, but for now there were more earthbound concerns coming to the surface. Whether as a result of the Christian circuit ceasing to provide work, or the comparatively cool reception the *Giltrap* album had received from the public, or a mixture of several factors, the reality was that the live work was beginning to dry up, and with none of his work thus far having been commercially successful enough to provide enough in the way of royalties, Gordon was suddenly faced with a career crossroads.

******

[†] The act of speaking in an alien language as the Holy Spirit supposedly speaks through you.

To supplement his gig money Gordon opted to give guitar tuition, a route taken by many professional musicians over the years. He placed an advertisement in the *Melody Maker* stating 'Gordon Giltrap — Advanced Guitar Tuition', with the telephone number. There was a reasonable response and he enjoyed giving tuition to the people at his home. Most of them knew of him as he had a sufficient name that serious acoustic guitar players would generally have come across his work. Gordon remembers a phone call with his old friend Davy Graham: "I used to speak with Davy often", remembers Gordon. "He'd had a lot of troubles with heroin addiction and he had done guitar tuition himself when times were a little tough. I mentioned the ad to him, and I still remember him saying 'Yes, I thought that was a bit much, saying Advanced Tuition' — kind of ticking me off, as if I was getting above my station. I suppose I was in a way if you compared me to someone like Davy who was truly advanced, but I explained to him that the reason I put that was not through any egotistical reason, it was simply that I didn't want to teach beginners, as I just wasn't equipped to do so, so I needed to have people who already knew the basics, that was all."

Despite this extra source of income, it was still insufficient to pay the bills, so the next move was to find some extra employment. He was determined to find a job, even if it was a part-time one and he went to the local Labour Exchange in search.

He was interviewed and asked what his profession was, to which he replied "I'm a guitarist — a musician", whereupon, with the classic bureaucratic literal-mindedness of the times, he received the reply "well, we don't have any vacancies for musicians at the moment". The ludicrousness of this response was not lost on Gordon, since he was "fully aware that you didn't go to the Labour Exchange to get a job as a musician, for God's sake! How ridiculous is that!" He was told that if he wanted to look for a job, he would have to sign on, and was handed the stack of forms it was necessary to complete — and that was that; at the age of 26, Gordon Giltrap signed on for benefit and registered as unemployed. It was a low point in his life and career, but one which would get lower before too long had elapsed.

Gordon began claiming his 'dole money' [unemployment benefit], and stopped playing gigs for the time being. What surprised him was that once all of the extra benefits such as help with things like milk, the mortgage payments and other 'essentials' had been factored in, he was actually better off claiming benefits than gigging. Gordon had to all intents and purposes retired as a professional musician. This went on for about six weeks, until one particular incident made him do an about-face.

He was signing on as usual at the Labour Exchange, however he arrived to find directly in front of him in the queue, one of his own guitar students. He was mortified at the thought of being seen. In his mind, the whole reason these students were coming to him was that he was this well-known and respected musician. To be seen lining up in the queue to collect his dole money was more than he could bear. Accordingly he left, waited some time until his student had left and then went back in to claim his money. But the realisation of how that made him feel was such a low point that he resolved that whatever happened, he would not continue to claim benefits. If his future was a job outside of the music business, then so would be his lot.

There was a lot of pressure on him, with not only his wife, but also her family constantly asking about when he would get a job, and how he needed to be bringing some proper money in. At this point, he felt as if he finally understood the pragmatic attitude of his father all those years ago when he insisted that he get a proper trade and keep the music as a sideline; this was the first time Gordon had been in the position his father had grown up in — of really, truly needing the money and he realised that there was only so far an artistic dream could get you if it was not putting food on the table or shoes on the children's feet. Accordingly he went to see his parents, ready to announce that he was giving up the music business and to see if they could help him get a 'proper' job.

However a role-reversal of incredible irony yet also deep poignancy took place. When he stated his decision to step back from the professional musician's life, his father instantly answered him with 'Son, you can't do that. You are the best acoustic guitarist in England, and there is no way you can give up on that dream now!' Astonishingly, the roles had been reversed, as he had become the pragmatic money-driven decision-maker while his father, long entrenched in that very position himself, had in his later life assumed the role of the dreamer, the romantic — determined that his son should not waste the God-given talent he had. It was an immensely powerful and symbolic moment — and indeed, one which has only magnified itself in Gordon's mind down the years. The end result was that, though it was essential that he start earning more of a living wage, he was going to do it, by hook or by crook, through music.

This had been the first time Gordon had attempted to turn his back on his life's dream and career as a professional musician — and in terms of such drastic action, it would be the last. Through highs and lows, good times and bad, he would remain a musician for the rest of his professional life. He was, to all intents and purposes, starting all over...

8
The Visionary

Once back on the road, and focused again on his true calling, new material was vital for Gordon to move forward. The *Giltrap* album had not lived up to his expectations or hopes, artistically or commercially. A work of real quality was paramount if he was to escape the position in which he found himself figuratively spinning his wheels. Fortunately, that inspiration had already come to him, without his knowing it.

The life and work of poet and artist William Blake had begun to fascinate Gordon more and more. He was not only inspired by the esoteric imagery which so fired his imagination, but also he saw much of his own spirit in that of the troubled genius which was Blake. As he looked more and more into Blake's writings and paintings he began to formulate the idea of composing music which was directly inspired by the material. Although the iconic nature of Blake's paintings especially had been plundered to an extent by the rock musicians of the day[†], his poetry had been less widely drawn upon and certainly no-one had thought of writing a conceptual work based entirely upon those writings. This was a little in the future yet, however, as the first fruits of this inspirational union were only just being sown.

After Gordon had begun writing some of his formative Blake-inspired material, with early incarnations of tracks like *Tyger* and *The Dance Of Albion*, he began thinking about getting a small band of musicians together to play it. By now he was being managed by Greg Thain and together they reached out to some musicians Gordon knew. The first was Andrew Van Der Beek, a man who was hugely experienced within the 'early music' scene, and a keyboard player named Dave Cook, who had played in a duo called McKenzie Cook with Julia McKenzie, and later went on to write a lot of music for television, and

---

[†] UK band Atomic Rooster had used his arresting and eye-catching — and slightly disturbing — 'Nebuchadnezzar' for their second album *Death Walks Behind You* in 1970.

children's programmes in particular. Through these, Gordon then came across bass player, David Etheridge, who was known to everyone as 'Brillo' on account of his head of bushy hair. An exceptional bass player, he played for a long time with a superb guitarist Isaac Guillory, but also did gigs with the likes of Stephane Grappelli. With this line-up assembled, they concentrated at first on an 'early music' direction, with Dave Cook often playing harpsichord, and Van Der Beek playing recorders and various wind instruments. They started playing some gigs at clubs and colleges, showcasing the new material which Gordon was beginning to produce. The gigs tended to be a mix and match sort of evening, with Gordon doing some solo songs, Dave Cook performing with McKenzie Cook, and the whole ensemble performing the embryonic *Visionary* music.

After a while they managed to get enough money together to record a demo of the material, which has latterly seen the light of day as a bonus track on CD releases of the *Visionary* album. Taking the form of one long piece, simply titled *Visionary*, it is still in the form originally envisaged by Gordon, as a baroque suite. Gordon is insistent that the individual sections had names, even at this early stage, but they are not credited as such on the CD releases. In truth, for the casual listener, it is somewhat hard going at times, especially compared to the more familiar shape of the material, but for the fan intent on looking into the development of the music as it transitioned into the familiar, it is a fascinating and illuminating artefact.

Meanwhile there was an addition to the Giltrap family, with daughter Sadie arriving on March 5, 1975. She was born in Lewisham hospital, but sadly Gordon was unable to attend the birth as he was stuck in the studio when the moment came. Nevertheless, he was utterly delighted to have a daughter alongside Jamie in completing the family, and says to this day that he could not have wished for two better children, or to have been more proud of them.

Back in the studio, however, there was some degree of frustration contrasting with the happy home situation as, for a while, nothing seemed to take off. The demo at first garnered little interest until a guy named Keith Lyons, who Gordon had actually given guitar lessons to, offered to put up some money to help finance things. Even then, however, it was to come to naught, as he ended up forming a partnership with Greg Thain, and sank his money into Thain's magazine project, called *College Event*.

What eventually got it moving was Gordon thinking back to a session he had done for Larry Norman, at George Martin's Air Studios. John Wetton had been on the same session, for an album called *Only*

Visiting This Planet, originally to have been produced by Martin, who had passed on it owing to pressure of work and passed it on to a production trio named Triumvirate. Gordon ended up playing on a track from the album called *The Outlaw*, and while he was struggling to get things moving with *Visionary* in a satisfactory way, thought back to the guys he'd worked with on that session, and got in touch again. Two of the musicians, guitarist Roger Hand and keyboard man Rod Edwards, came over to listen to the demos, and liked what they heard. It was at this point that the material began to take a sharp left turn, as Gordon remembers now: "I started recording with these guys, in their excellent studio, and we entered a whole new world to me: the world of click tracks. I asked why we needed a click track, only to be told that was for the bass and drums. I said 'Wait a minute, bass and drums? I wasn't expecting bass and drums; this is a baroque piece'. It was at this point that they began to guide me a little. It wasn't as if they sat me down and said 'Now, see sense, Gordon! This has got much greater potential', but they did have different ideas, and they were very persuasive as they dragged me kicking and screaming into my first real steps as a rock musician. In fact, though these were meant to be more demos, they ended up so good that most of them became the basis for the eventual *Visionary* masters. I have to say that I owe those guys a huge debt of gratitude — I had no concept of the direction my music could go in, and they showed me that I could be the rock musician I really should already have been."

Once the demos were finished and presented, a three album deal was offered by The Electric Record Company, and Gordon moved into Sound Associates Studio in October 1975, to begin work, while also writing more material to go with the original *Visionary Suite* (which had now been split into separate tracks) to complete the album. At this point, bassist John G Perry, a gifted musician and also a classically-trained violinist who had been a member of Caravan and Curved Air came into the band, along with drummer Simon Phillips[†]. Perry was already a friend of Gordon's, who he had known from playing gigs with Caravan around 1973, and he lived in Blackheath, so they were able to drive to the studio together. Simon Phillips was actually recommended for the job when Gordon's first choice, Bill Bruford, proved to be unavailable. Phillips was actually only eighteen years old at the time, but as soon as he came into the studio and played, it was obvious that he had something special. In fact, to this day, Gordon maintains that he has never played with a better rhythm section than the pairing of Perry and

---

[†] Phillips went on to become one of the most prolific and respected session musicians in rock history but was making his major recording debut here.

Phillips: "Simon was incredible, especially given his age. What I always say is that, despite the fact that he came in and played on basic tracks which had already been recorded, he somehow managed to play as if he'd written the stuff! His father was the well-known bandleader Sid Philips, so he had been raised in that environment, and was born to be a musician really. I do remember making a bit of an embarrassing blunder when I first met Simon though; I'd heard of Sid Phillips, as he was extremely well known and respected in those circles, so when I first met Simon I asked him how his father was, only for him to reply 'He passed away some years ago'! I hadn't realised, but it certainly isn't the best way to break the ice with someone!"

The album was produced (alongside Edwards and Hand) by Jon Miller, who also bankrolled much of the studio time and associated costs — Gordon remembers him as "a very driven, focused business character", while recalling that this attitude led to them having some disagreements but a very positive working relationship. Miller, Edwards and Hand were collectively known as Triumvirate Productions, and Gordon recalls one pivotal moment when his musical horizons were changed drastically: "I remember this one time when we were discussing the instrumentation on one particular track, and one of the guys said to me 'We need an electric guitar solo on that'. Now, I was so set in my musical ways that I immediately asked, in all innocence, 'Okay, who should we get to play that?' They just looked at me and said 'well, you, of course'! I'd never thought of myself as an electric guitarist, and it just didn't occur to me. In fact, I didn't even own an electric at that time, and they had to loan me a Telecaster for the session! Anyway, I did it, and they were all saying things like 'you said you couldn't play electric, that's great'. I did do all right when I got down to it, and I found I did have the chops to play some of that fancy stuff. The only thing I didn't have, which is very important, was vibrato. I didn't have the knack. The thing is, you often find that great electric guitarists start off playing electric — Peter Green for example, or Eric Clapton. They develop certain muscles, a certain ear and a certain way of approaching the instrument, and vibrato is a key part of that; especially when you're looking at a fantastic tone like the incredible 'woman tone', as it was known, that Clapton invented. There was a guy around that time who did lots of sessions for Triumvirate called James Litherland, who'd formed a band called Mogul Thrash. He used to come down and start giving me lessons on the electric guitar — I'd ask how he got that great vibrato, and he'd explain how you just squeeze the string, bend it a little and bring it back, but I just couldn't get it. I learnt to get away with it over the years, but it was never natural to me. But James was an electric guitarist, and he couldn't get the hang of some of the acoustic stuff I was doing either, so that really highlighted the difference".

The album was finally finished in June 1976. Being released shortly afterward it immediately struck a chord with the public in a way that none of his previous releases had. A very visible advertising campaign certainly aided in this success, but the truth was that the music on the album was at a level of sophistication and quality that his previous work had only hinted at sporadically. It was a completely unified album, and a musical statement of considerable weight.

Opening the album was the two-part *Awakening / Robes And Crowns*, a full-band grandiose statement of intent which works brilliantly as an opener. It manages to straddle the two sides of the album, the new electric band work and the acoustic guitar which was still Gordon's trademark — nowhere is this more evident than in the memorable descending guitar figure which underpins the piece, played on a nylon string guitar as it happens. The tone of the album had been set perfectly.

Following this is *From The Four Winds*, a largely solo piece using twelve-string guitar, which Gordon describes as being "in my Julian Bream mode". There are, he insists, some mistakes on the track, where he missed the odd note, but he recalls that the Triumvirate team, even though they were largely sticklers for perfection, urged him to leave it as it was, because the overall spirit of the piece outweighed any small blemishes. The string accompaniment plays a significant part on the track, as indeed do the string arrangements throughout the album. Interestingly, these arrangements were intended to be done by Del Newman, but as Gordon recalls "when I played him the demos, he said 'I can't do this album, because it would bring out a side of my music that I really want to reserve for my own album', though in actual fact that intended solo album never materialised. It therefore fell to Rod Edwards to arrange the strings, with the assistance of Roger Hand — a task which filled Edwards with trepidation as he had never done a string arrangement of this magnitude or complexity before. As it happened, his fears were groundless, as the work he did on the record was much-praised and of the highest quality.

Up third on the album is *Lucifer's Cage*, massively overhauled from the formative version which first appeared on the *Portrait* album. It had been rearranged already, when it had been played live with the "medieval line-up" as Gordon terms the Cook / Etheridge touring band, but the version here features a full band arrangement for the first time. It would go on to become even more forceful in subsequent live incarnations, but this is a fine statement nonetheless. Indeed, it seems surprising that it wasn't chosen to end at least the first side of the album, with its dramatic quality, but as Gordon admits, he "had nothing to do with the actual sequencing of the album. But yes, that would have seemed a likely thing to do, I agree". In actual fact, the side closes with the following piece, *Revelation*, which begins as mainly guitar-led with keyboard accompaniment, before the band come in midway. Full of dramatic, plangent guitar runs, the track is notable for a stunning wordless vocal by Shirlie Roden, soaring over the climactic band crescendos toward the end, before the whole thing tails off to a single reverberating note, effectively removing all doubts about the sequencing order of the side. It's a marvellous ending, career-defining in its scope, and finishing perfectly a side of music which was all inspired by the illustration and poem 'The Day Of Judgement' and 'The Last Judgement'.

It is difficult for the second side to compete with this, and wisely it doesn't really attempt to directly do so, being overall of a more reflective tone, and also consisting of six unrelated pieces inspired separately by the illustrations and poems whose titles they bear. It does, however, open with one more big-sounding piece in *The Price Of Experience*, which fills its two and a half minute duration with not only the band and the orchestration, but also a big brass sound which conveys the poem on which it is based. Underpinning the whole track is an insistent pizzicato rhythm, played by Gordon but actually put on a loop at the advice of engineer Gareth Edwards (younger brother of Rod), to ensure the precise, metronomic quality. This rhythmic figure was actually based on a part of Tchaikovsky's Third Symphony, and took a whole day to record on its own. Indeed, Gordon recalls one amusing point when, in the glorious spirit of the technology of the day, Gareth phoned Rod and sang the rhythmic guitar figure onto his answering machine so as not to forget it! Pro Tools and the like seem a long way off when faced with those improvised arrangements!

Up next is the reflective guitar piece *The Dance Of Albion*, before the following track *Tyger*, inspired by the famous poem that every schoolboy used to learn ('Tyger, Tyger, burning bright, In the forests of the night' etc); a band piece led very much by a strident and upfront acoustic guitar lead, conveying the dramatic imagery of the poem. This is followed by two more virtually solo guitar pieces *The Ecchoing Green* and *London*, which combine to give a sense of the album winding down to a calm after the earlier storm, before the stirring closing track *Night* features the band coming in with a dramatic conclusion similar to *Revelation*, which closes the album superbly.

Surprising, however, is the omission of another composition recorded at the sessions, *On Wings Of Hope*, included as a bonus track on some subsequent CD releases, which is a soaring, triumphal string-laden piece which finishes proceedings off in an even better fashion when following on the heels of *Night*. It was felt at the time not to fit the mood of the overall work, but this seems a strange decision, especially when the album as it appeared was only around 34 minutes long. Having said this, however, as Gordon states now, "the rule of thumb recording-wise with instrumental music was always 'less is more'. The mind finds it naturally easier to focus on music with vocals, and we were advised not to overload the concentration of the listener with too much purely instrumental material, for fear of diminishing returns".

Musically, the album was certainly both an artistic and commercial triumph, easily outstripping any of Gordon's previous work on either count. There was, however, one large fly still in the ointment, in the shape of his old bugbear of cover design — but in this case, far more seriously so. Given the fact that the album was conceptually a celebration and evocation of the works of William Blake, Gordon had naturally wanted the artwork to depict this. Indeed, he had thoughts of using the same 'Nebuchadnezzar' illustration that Atomic Rooster had used some years earlier, and he wanted the inspirational poems and illustrations to be fully credited alongside the songs. The record label however had other ideas and wanted to market the album in more of a Pink Floyd direction. They enlisted Chris Sharville of Dobney Johnson Studios to produce the image which ended up on the front cover — the familiar airbrushed illustration of the 'film noir'-looking man in the hat looking over a mysterious fence. Although it is a striking illustration in its own right, and worked well as a recognisable marketing tool, the connection to Blake was lost entirely. To the casual observer, the man on the cover would appear to be the Visionary of the title himself, which was totally at odds with the intended concept. When Gordon saw this cover, he was both immensely upset and desperately angry. To him, it had removed the heart and soul of the work and ripped out the guts of the whole concept. Seeing the back cover with the song titles within a triangle, which he swears to this day was a direct nod to *Dark Side Of The Moon*, only made things worse. The album cover had no gatefold sleeve, which again he would have liked, and even the inner sleeve, despite containing an excellent monochrome photograph of him playing the guitar under stark lighting, again made no reference to the Blake connection.

Today, Gordon is more circumspect about the cover design. He says he has come to look upon it with some affection, for the music and the success that it represents, and that he can also appreciate that as a stand-alone piece of art it is full of merit. He still steadfastly maintains, though, that despite the excellent sales of the album, it would have done better still had it come packaged as a complete Blake concept — and indeed, who can take exception with that view? Sadly, it is something we will never know for sure. Still, Gordon at last had a successful album on his hands, and a whole new audience — all that remained now was to get out there and play for them...

9
Revelation Highway

With the *Visionary* album selling healthily and pleasing the critics, the obvious next step was live work to promote it. In a way this would come as something of a relief from his home based 'chores', as the arrival of Sadie to the home had resulted in the old plumber and builder coming out in him again! The Giltraps were now living in Heather Road, Grove Park, which had been an easy move from the previous rented accommodation in Cooper Street, just two streets away. With the addition to the family he wanted to improve the house and he brought his plumbing skills to bear by installing extra gas pipes and general plumbing to create a decent bathroom and also heating in the downstairs lounge. This work was compounded however with Maureen, who had developed what Gordon describes as something of an obsession with creating space, which was achieved by him donning his builder's guise and, as he remembers it, "knocking every available non load bearing wall wherever possible". Nonetheless, and as testament to his evident artisanship, the house remained standing! It was a home which he loved — or, at least those parts he hadn't had to demolish — and he says now that he still regrets moving out from there a couple of years later when he sought to get away from London.

Returning to touring matters, once again, in his relative naiveté in terms of playing with a full band, Gordon had assumed he would most likely be rearranging the material for solo acoustic guitar and going out on his own to play it. Triumvirate, understandably, were having none of this. He had to have a band, they reasoned — after all, this album had completely reinvented his approach to recorded music, so to step back at this point would make little sense, commercially or artistically. The logic of this could not be argued with, but there was only one thing missing from the picture: a band!

The studio collective of Phillips, Perry and Edwards were unable, or unwilling, to commit to a full schedule of live work, so it became imperative to put together a touring band before any further planning could be undertaken. Before this could be achieved however there arose a necessity for a publicity shot for a press release about plans for touring the album. This led to the slightly absurd situation in which Gordon was summoned one day to a photo session, posing along with his 'band', who were in reality Leo Sayer's backing band — none of whom he had ever met before, nor had any arrangement to work with. It is safe to say that it was difficult to say which side appeared the more bemused by the surreal goings on, guitarist or band! Sure enough, they never worked together, and that odd, orphan publicity photo remains the only evidence of that particular non-liaison. An answer to the problem arrived in the unlikely shape of little-known Yorkshire-based progressive rock band Strange Days, whose sole album *9 Parts To The Wind* had appeared in 1975 on EMI. The way the band came into the Giltrap orbit was through Shirlie Roden, partner at that time of Jon Miller, who had, of course, contributed vocals to *Visionary*. Her sister was the girlfriend (now wife) of Eddy Spence, keyboard player with Strange Days, and from there came the suggestion that they should, en bloc, become Gordon's live backing band.

In truth, Strange Days were an excellent group of musicians, whose album remains something of an overlooked gem in the world of Genesis-influenced mid-'70s progressive rock — containing just six tracks, ranging from the commercial overtones of *Be Nice To Joe Soap* and *Monday Morning* to ambitious epics such as *A Unanimous Decision*, *The Journey* and *18 Tons*. The material was all written by guitarist / vocalist Graham Ward, with the band being completed by Spence, bass player Phil Walman and drummer Eddie McNeill, though the latter was replaced by the younger Ward brother Dave in Gordon's band. Ward's lyrics were intelligent, dealing with some serious matters of the day with deft social commentary, all with an undercurrent of humour which prevented it from taking itself too seriously and self-importantly. It was something of a surprise when they were asked to move over to Gordon, but this was balanced somewhat by the fact that, on the first tour of the UK, Strange Days effectively acted as their own support band, opening the shows with a short set of their own material before returning with Gordon for the main event, thus simultaneously giving their own material some promotion and also scratching their own collective creative 'itch' while still playing the Giltrap material. The 'Ward connection' was completed by Graham's other sibling, older brother Pete, who had been Strange Days' sound engineer and came over with the band to the Giltrap camp. As Eddy Spence remembers: "I'm not entirely sure of our reaction when the idea was first suggested to us. I mean, I know we all wanted to do it, because we all wanted to work!

Graham, however, was always a bit less invested in it as a long-term arrangement than the rest of us, because Strange Days was his 'baby' in a way, with him writing all of the material. He was a very skilled songwriter and lyricist so that's understandable. Thankfully we were able to have the best of both worlds for a while, with Strange Days acting as support on those early shows".

Following these 'double shows', which were at modest venues such as the smaller halls on the college circuit, Gordon received the offer to tour the UK as support to Renaissance. This was a follow-up to a three-act 'package tour' affair he had previously been invited onto, with Renaissance headlining and Audience (who had a sizeable success with the album *The House On The Hill*) in the middle. That tour had been a success, with Gordon remembering all three bands getting on well together, especially Renaissance singer Annie Haslam, who he recalls as being "really fun to be around. A beautiful lady but one of the lads in terms of her sense of humour and a Northern lass (Haslam hails from Bolton). Everybody loved Annie!" Needless to say he grabbed the opportunity for this new support slot with the band with both hands and it provided a significant boost to his profile. Gordon was also invited to appear on *The Old Grey Whistle Test* with the full band. They played *Awakening / Robes And Crowns* and also *Lucifer's Cage* (footage of the latter can easily be found via a quick Internet search). The musicianship is exceptional, highlighting just what a tight and impressive unit they formed at this time. The arrangement of *Lucifer's Cage* is much tougher and fuller-sounding than even that on the *Visionary* album. Gordon chose to sit, rather than stand up, to play, and appeared perched on a stool with the band behind him — a decision that he later regretted.

"Looking back, I really wish I'd chosen to stand up to play on the *Whistle Test*", he says now. "Not only would it have looked better in terms of the music we were performing, but as it was it gave a sense of 'distance' between the rest of the band and myself, and that wasn't the impression I wanted to give at all. But I think I just didn't have the confidence to stand and play at the time. I could do it, of course I could; but it wasn't something I'd been accustomed to with my background, and that took a little while to come naturally. I do think it's a really good performance though — the band are on great form and thank God I managed to nail my solo bit in the middle! I remember concentrating pretty hard on that."

Eddy Spence also has vivid memories of that *Whistle Test* appearance because, as he says "it was the first time any of us, apart from Gordon, had been on telly. On top of that it went out live — we were playing it right then at eleven o'clock on a Tuesday night or something. I remember thinking when we finished 'That's it, I don't need to get nervous about anything ever again now that I've done that'! I know that we did *Awakening / Robes And Crowns* as well as *Lucifer's Cage*, but I can't for the life of me remember if we did anything else. I believe the *Lucifer's Cage* footage has survived because it was used later on another programme, called *Guitar Hero*, I think".

By this time, Graham Ward was beginning to get very restless about his, and the whole Strange Days, place in the set-up. His heart was in writing his own music and being master of his own art, and the discipline of playing someone else's material night after night in a 'backing band' scenario was making him more and more frustrated. Gordon himself remembers one occasion in rehearsals when Graham remarked "you know what, this really isn't for me". However, he, like the entire band, was nothing if not professional in his approach, and they continued to do an excellent job, which even to this day Gordon cannot fault.

Things appeared to be looking up just before the end of 1976, when Gordon and the band were invited to support Wishbone Ash on a European tour — the first time the 'Strange Days' Giltrap band had played outside the UK. Gordon, of course, knew Wishbone from his Miles Copeland days, but it was still a significant opportunity, and he knew it. Martin Turner, bassist / vocalist with Wishbone, still speaks fondly of their working arrangement: "I remember Gordon as being a marvellous guitarist — he reminded me of the Bert Jansch / Pentangle sort of English folk sound. It was always a pleasure to have him around; he was good company and a real gentleman, which is all too rare in this business". The tour began extremely well, with a series of dates in Germany, which were enthusiastically received. It wasn't a 'private-jet' luxurious affair, as all of the travel was undertaken by van, but it was nevertheless an enjoyable and successful time.

After the German leg of the tour, Swiss dates were lined up, beginning with a show in Zurich. The bands arrived in to the city and made their way to the hotel whereupon, having alighted from their transport across the street, Gordon announced he was checking in and that he would see them shortly. He set off across the street, only to be immediately hit by a car. It may have been caused by the traffic driving on the other side of the road to the UK, but for whatever reason, he did not see the car which hit him at all. He was thrown onto the bonnet of the vehicle and onto the ground at which point, clearly in shock and no doubt with a huge adrenaline surge, he got up to his feet straight away. Walking around in determined fashion, he informed everyone (who by now had rushed over to help) that he was fine, and unhurt, before his legs buckled under him and he fell to the floor unconscious. He had broken his collarbone — a lucky escape in many ways, but still enough to write off the rest of the tour and leave him unable to play the guitar for quite some time.

Gordon recalls little of the accident. "I remember being hit by something with a tremendous impact, an absolutely enormous blow — hard to describe the feeling. I don't remember anything about getting up, walking around or losing consciousness; that bit was just lost to me. The next thing I remember was waking up on the ground, with a cluster of people all telling me to stay still and wait for the ambulance to arrive. One thing I do remember very vividly was Graham leaning over me and saying, with a mischievous grin, 'I'm sorry to tell you Gordon, the gig's off!' — which shows the rapport we had between us I suppose, the fact that even in such a situation we'd be able to see the humour in it. Well, he'd be able to see the humour, anyway!" Martin Turner takes up the story, as he remembers how much the injury worried Gordon.

"Oh, he was devastated! He had to leave the tour, of course, but he was looking far beyond that. He was full of fear that he wouldn't be able to play the guitar again. I can remember him ringing me up and literally being in tears down the phone. I can't overstate how depressed and frightened that experience made him. I was telling him that it'd be all right, that it would heal and he'd be fine. I knew he would, but he just wasn't seeing it at that point. It was hard for me to see him so upset, and so down about things, and I kept trying to pick him up a bit, let him know it was going to be fine, but he really was fearing for his career. Of course, he did fully recover, but I do believe that was the last occasion we ever played together. At least there was a happy ending from his point of view, anyway!"

Gordon's playing relationship with Martin Turner and Wishbone Ash wasn't the only casualty of that fateful day as it would prove to be the end of the road for that particular configuration of Gordon's backing band. Shortly thereafter, Graham and Dave Ward, together with Phil Walman, left to return to a truncated Strange Days line-up, minus Eddy Spence who, having always been closer to Gordon and the music than the others, opted to remain. The other three went on to work under the name The Ward Brothers for a time, but sadly without any significant success. Strange Days never did record another album, and *9 Parts To The Wind* remains their sole, if quite impressive, legacy.

For Gordon, the healing process brought with it the next phase of his writing, and the next chapter in his musical and personal roller-coaster was about to begin, as he began to conceive the music which would form his most successful album, *Perilous Journey*.

10
Perilous Journey

As time went on, and 1976 gave way to 1977, Gordon's slowly healing collarbone began to permit him to start playing the guitar again. This was a massive relief to him as, although he knew logically that the injury wouldn't affect his movement in the long term in that manner, he couldn't silence the whispers of uncertainty in his head. As he says today: "Of course, the first thought I had was 'thank God I wasn't killed', but that soon gives way to fears about recovery once the immediate treatment is complete. Obviously a broken collarbone is a relatively minor thing, but when you're incapacitated with something like that, your mind tends to wander to the worst scenario. And there isn't anything they can do to hasten the recovery except to strap you up, and the convalescence is quite slow. In recent years, I was talking with Mark Knopfler, who'd suffered the same fracture, and his story of gradually being able to manage different guitars, starting with the thinnest electric and moving up in size as he healed, was almost identical to my experience!"

By early 1977, the enforced lay-off had resulted in a flurry of songwriting ideas building up in his brain, and as soon as he started playing with confidence again, they began to flood out. These were the building blocks — sometimes snippets, at other times almost fully-formed pieces — which would go on to form the framework of the *Perilous Journey* album. In contrast to the William Blake concept which fired his imagination for the *Visionary* album, Gordon had no such intention to follow that same route again, believing that to be a one-off creative inspiration which he had no inclination to follow up. With that in mind, he continued to work on separate, unrelated musical ideas. Jon Miller, however, had other plans...

When he became involved with the project, as it neared its creative focus, Miller was adamant that the *Visionary* template should be adhered to, and that such a discipline would not only prove a commercial boost, but also serve to focus Gordon's writing and make the end result hang together on a much more cohesive level. To this end, he suggested the book *Journey To The East*, by German writer Hermann Hesse. Gordon strongly disagreed with this, but rather than dig his heels in and risk derailing the creative process by being at odds with his production team, he reluctantly — and somewhat unenthusiastically — agreed to the concept. In truth, owing to his lack of engagement with the suggestion, he did little more than skim through the book, relying heavily on a summary provided to him by his wife, but he did nonetheless tie the writing, both musically and, more pertinently, in terms of the titles of the pieces, into the concept of the story.

For the uninitiated, *Journey To The East* concerns a German choirmaster known as 'H. H.' who is invited on an expedition eastward with a secret society known as 'The League', with the intention of finding spiritual enlightenment at the journey's end. However, along the way their initial harmony soon dissolves into rancour as the members of the expedition begin to find each others' characters increasingly intolerable. It is only years later that H.H., who had blamed the others bitterly for this failure, comes to a spiritual realisation of sorts himself, and the truth of the group's splintering. Much of the subtlety and fine detail of the work was lost on Gordon at this time, as he resisted the idea and therefore the work itself, but even the synopsis of the book was enough to allow him to take some inspiration from it as he admits now: "I think subconsciously I dismissed the idea of the album being thematically based and felt that I was being pressured by Triumvirate, and in particular Jon Miller, to turn the album into something that wasn't my idea in the first place, so it's understandable that the idea, or indeed the book, didn't move me at all. In actual fact it was a good idea, but I didn't see it that way then — I was a stubborn little person at times! I guess looking back now, if I had viewed Triumvirate as co writers and collaborators from the beginning, and that the albums were joint efforts (which I guess in all honesty they were), I may have got a different head on things".

Regardless of the concept, and how much actual inspiration it provided, the music continued to flow out of Gordon during the spring of 1977. In fact, thinking back to the creative process behind the big hit from the album (and still the Giltrap signature piece), *Heartsong*, Gordon can remember the initial idea for that emerging when he was busking around the chord progression from *Starting All Over*, from the *Testament Of Time* album. He was playing the descending chord sequence from that piece, and on improvising a little, changing it slightly and incorporating some fast strumming, the seed of *Heartsong* was planted, and his future was changed forever. As he says, "Where inspiration strikes you can never tell. On that particular day I didn't even have thoughts of writing a song, I was just practising, playing around — and there it was".

With the material all composed and sketched out on the guitar, it was time to begin the studio time, during which the first task would be to start the band arrangements for the material, which would be much fuller than the still occasionally sparse *Visionary*. These arrangements were, once again, done in conjunction with Rod Edwards and Roger Hand, who would also be credited on the album with 'additional music', such was the extent of their input. The core band for the album was the same as for *Visionary*, with John G Perry and Simon Phillips again joining the keyboards of Edwards. One regret that Gordon still has to this day was not using Eddy Spence more — he contributed the main keyboard solo to *Heartsong* but nothing else on the record — despite his remaining loyal after the remainder of Strange Days had departed. As he admits however, it was difficult to make that happen with Rod Edwards there: "I do wish we could have used Eddy more, but the thing was that Rod, along with Roger, had done all of the arrangements, and it didn't really make sense for him not to do the keyboard parts. Rod was a very solid keyboard player, particularly his superb piano work, very much in the Elton John mould, as you can hear on *Revelation* from *Visionary*. He and Roger did the arrangements, knew the sounds they wanted in their heads, so they didn't need to bring in another keyboard player when Rod could do it easier himself. So it was a shame for Eddy, without a doubt, but I can understand the logic behind Rod doing it, despite Eddy being a superb player".

In addition to the core band, there were a number of additional musicians used in the recording — not least the brass section of Henry Lowther, Martin Drover, Stan Sultzman, Jeff Daly and Chris Payne — and this addition of brass to the work is something which was entirely unexpected and unprecedented in Gordon's previous output. Nevertheless, he still stands by the use of it today — and, indeed, it is integrated into the arrangements in such a way that is complementary rather than obtrusive. The one exception to this ensemble when it came to the brass work was the saxophone in *The Deserter*, provided by Roger Ball and Malcolm Duncan of Scottish 'white soul' outfit The Average White Band. The way they came to make their contribution was courtesy of the Triumvirate guys who were able to persuade them to bring in their talents. Even now Gordon has marvellous memories of that particular session: "Oh, that evening, when we did that recording, was just magic — the kind of thing you could never hope to recapture again. Malc and Roger came in and brought their infectiousness with them along with their talent, and we got such a fantastic groove going, it was just incredible. One thing I do remember was that there was quite a bit of dope going around; I'd never been into that, especially when it came to people working, but on this occasion the music was just so great I didn't feel the need to say anything. It's not as if anybody was doing any hard drugs, it was all very mild, a bit of dope being smoked, and that was what went on at the time. The result was, as I said, an atmosphere and a magic in the air that you could never hope to recreate again, and I think that particular piece still works really well. I did the lead guitar parts that John doubled up on bass, and everything just seemed to work: a marvellous time".

Overall, the album certainly has a cohesiveness that, great as it was in its own right, *Visionary* didn't quite possess. On that album there had still been a sense of Gordon fighting for space against the band, taking time to get his solo acoustic parts in before the band were allowed into the space again. While this provided a fascinating contrast, and a very effective overall piece, it was indicative of the fact that Gordon was still at that time being coaxed into the full electric 'rock crossover'. The material had all been written by him with solo acoustic treatment in mind and so, while he liked the way the band arrangements sounded, there was still a sense of it going against his original vision, if you will pardon the pun.

On this occasion, all of that audible competition for space in the music was gone, replaced by a cohesive whole which unified the piece like nothing he had done before. While the music was written on acoustic guitar, it was done with one eye on how the band could approach it right from the moment of conception, and it shows. Indeed, if anything it is a rather keyboard-dominated sound, which showcases Gordon's solo playing less obviously or consistently than any of his previous releases, yet he is insistent that no egos were bruised during this process...

"Absolutely, and I'll tell you why. It was because these were my tunes, and I wasn't necessarily thinking of them from a guitar point of view; I could hear other instruments in my head. So, as long as it sounded great, that was all that mattered. I was listening to a lot of classical music at the time — the opening track *Quest*, for example, originated in part from a piece by Monteverdi — and it was all about composition, with the band acting almost like an orchestra in a way. If I was upfront in the mix then great, but it wasn't the most important thing. My head was finally fully in 'band' mode. I'd finally 'got it', and that's a big part of the reason that it works so well".

It is important to stress however, that although Gordon had the idea for the arrangements including the full band in his head, the actual written arrangements were done entirely by Rod Edwards and Roger Hand. The way the process worked was that Gordon would bring a piece in, they would work through it between the three of them, developing ideas, and then Rod and Roger would take it away to complete the arrangement — often at Rod Edwards' house in Mill Hill, North London, quite near to the Redan Recorders studio in Queensway where the recording was taking place. These arrangements would then be delivered, fully formed, back to the studio, right down to notes for when the drums, bass etc should come in and Gordon would overlay his original idea over the top. As a collaborative process, it worked, as Gordon puts it, "like a well-oiled machine", and the contribution of Rod and Roger was enough to earn them the aforementioned 'additional music' credit on the album. Indeed, Gordon notes it as being "very good of them" not pressing for co-composition credits, though these would come into place on some tracks for the following album, *Fear Of The Dark*.

One interesting thing about the construction of the album which Gordon attributes to the Triumvirate team, rather than himself, lies in the opening and closing tracks. It isn't immediately apparent on a casual listen, but the closing track, *Vision*, is in actual fact basically a reprise of, or at least a development of the theme of the opening track *Quest*. With the two pieces being separated by 35 minutes of all-instrumental music, it's easy to miss this similarity, until eventually finding the closing of the album naggingly familiar, and going straight back to the start to check it out. With an entirely different title, the listener's brain isn't wired to expect a reprise. On being asked why *Vision* did not have a more logical title — perhaps the obvious *Quest Reprise* or even *Quest Fulfilment* or some such idea — Gordon says "oh, without a doubt that would be them. I was still a little bit resistant to the whole conceptual idea, so they would have had free rein to run with the titles they wanted in that kind of situation".

Following on from *Deserter*, the third track *Pastoral* is a somewhat curiously named piece, in that it strays from the expected 'acoustic-based, pastoral' template that the title suggests, and develops into quite a big affair, with the brass instruments making an impression again. To the suggestion that the title is a bit of a misnomer in that way, Gordon describes it as being one of the foremost examples of the track being changed once he brought it into the studio, in that it originally did fall into the short, pastoral, acoustic mode, but once the arrangements were done, it took on a whole different life.

The original first side of vinyl closed with the track *Morbio Gorge*, which is in fact a reference to the gorge known as 'Morbio Inferiore' in Switzerland, which serves as the location for a crucial plot development in the Hesse book.[†] Gordon today admits that, while he was aware that it featured in the book, the full significance of its role was not of high importance at the time. Indeed he recalls the track having the nickname of 'Morbid George' among the musicians in the studio! Interestingly, the track was one of the few pieces which Gordon actually 'composed' in his head, away from the guitar. In fact, it was while he was doing the mundane activity of washing-up one day that the main theme of the piece came into his head. He carried on mentally refining it, until he was able to get to the guitar, at which point he figured out how to play the sounds he had in his head. The piece was a prime example of the influence of the arrangements developed in the studio, as it begins deceptively as a solo guitar piece, before the full band come in with what is certainly one of the most dramatic musical contrasts on the album, and propel the piece to its conclusion, ending the original Side One of the vinyl in some style.

The second side opened with the big centrepiece of the album, *Heartsong*, though as Gordon admits now, it was only ever envisaged by him initially as a necessary uptempo interlude providing some light relief in between the darker, what he saw as 'more serious' pieces — and which he himself took more seriously, as the darker, heavier material seemed to be where the real profundity lay as an artist. Indeed, as he says, it was only when *Heartsong* became a hit and, even more significantly, with the passing of the years, that he began to realise what a complex and clever piece it was...

"As I look back on it now as a 68-year-old still playing it, and still trying to play it as well as I can, it's only now that I fully realise just how much tricky stuff there is in the track. Things I was doing naturally as a young musician at that time, I now find I have to think more about, in a sense of 'okay, there's a little double hammer-on there, and at this point I have to shift up from the seventh to the eighth fret position to play that bit, and I have to hit a couple of harmonic notes there'; it was written from a place of pure adrenalin, which at that time would carry me through it, whereas that adrenalin naturally diminishes as you get a bit older, and playing some things requires a lot more thought and conscious effort to carry off. It's a piece which I'm more proud of now than at the time when it was first released, and I think I always will be".

One interesting feature of *Heartsong* is that it has an indefinable feeling of building towards a climax throughout, and particularly when

---

[†] At the gorge, a servant named Leo suffers a tragic fall, which leads to an allegorical loss of faith from the lead character, as the expedition is torn asunder.

the main theme comes back in after the mid-section with a more celebratory, uplifting quality to it — and as Gordon confirms, there is an explanation for that. He attests that if you were to put a metronome to the piece, you would find that it has subtle tempo changes throughout which might not be detected otherwise, but which do alter the mood of the piece, and before that main theme sweeps back in again toward the end of it, the tempo speeds up, and it is this which causes the extra energy and sense of joy that it embodies. It is overall the one piece for which he believes the stars truly aligned when it was recorded, as everything which was done to it — including the potentially 'cheesy' handclaps added by himself, Rod, Roger and Shirlie Roden — somehow worked to improve it. Even the strong melody contained in the chord progression was something he did not even consider until the arrangement, with the keyboard following it as a top-line melody, demonstrated what a strong tune it was; up to that point he had considered it more of a 'guitar piece' rather than an the infectious melody that it is.

The piece following *Heartsong* is *Reflections & Despair*, which was actually inspired musically by Gordon's double-neck guitar, which he was pictured with on the inner sleeve of *Visionary*. He had always viewed a double-neck as one single 18-string instrument rather than separate six-string and twelve-string guitars sharing the same body, and one thing he was therefore able to do was to shift from one key to another quickly; it was this key-change motif which was to form the basis of the composition of *Reflections & Despair*. Following this is the track *Cascade*, taking its name from the distinctive cascading theme which runs through it. The track was born out of Gordon's experimentation with half-speed recording, as he explains, "I'd become very interested in recording at half-speed and then speeding it up. I loved that really bright, clear sound it gives you. Of course, people had been doing it for years; Les Paul was doing that as early as the 1940s, and it gave him his distinctive tone. I recorded the *Cascade* motif on a tape recorder that I still have upstairs, actually. We had to keep that theme going throughout the piece, on repeat, with the guitar followed by the keyboards, so that was another one where we used a tape loop to get it perfect — I can still remember a thirty-foot loop of tape going around the studio floor, with pencils holding it up! It would be so easy with today's technology of course. When we played it live, we had to have that as a backing track, and we usually got away with it, but there were occasions when it came in at the wrong place and the band had no idea where they should start!"

As already stated, *Vision* provided a brilliantly effective way to close the album. On the recent CD reissue, however, there is a bonus track of *Quest* recorded with the Wren Orchestra[†] in superb fashion. It was the only track recorded with that orchestra. Capital Radio picked up on *Quest* as the theme for a show they had called *Operation Drake*, in which young people who wanted to travel around the world went on a brigantine two-masted sailing ship, called 'The Eye Of The Wind', and followed the route of Sir Francis Drake's circumnavigation of the globe, with their progress tracked by the radio show. This version roughly follows the original, but is significantly extended, with Gordon playing more electric guitar lines, especially toward the end of the piece. It was also intended to be played when the ship returned and arrived back in dock, though in the end a cut-down version just for brass was used for this purpose. He was also asked by the radio station if he would compose a piece especially for the Wren Orchestra, as they asked someone to do that every year. The previous year it had been Rick Wakeman. The result of this commission was the piece *The Eye Of The Wind Rhapsody*, which went forgotten for years until it was revived in more recent times — though there lies another chapter...

Hugely successful as the music was for the completed album, there was one fly remaining in the Giltrap ointment — that old curse of the album cover design! Inconceivable as it may seem, the same thing had happened as with *Visionary*. The album had been entirely based around the literary concept, yet the album cover entirely ignored this. The only oblique reference to the *Journey To The East* book is in small print on the paper insert, where a short quote from the book appears, simply with the credit 'Hermann Hesse' with no reference to the book title. Strange in itself, this becomes a baffling decision when one considers how Gordon was almost railroaded into following the concept.

The cover is again a very basic affair. There was no gatefold to the original vinyl issue, with the front cover showing a silhouette of a frock-coated man apparently hurtling through space, and the rear having just the song titles with a shadowy profile shot of Gordon. The insert offers little else beyond some musician credits and further small images of the cover man tumbling through the air (or lack of it if he is indeed in space).

The front cover image has become somewhat iconic in its way, but overall it was an underwhelming and ill-conceived design, which Gordon recalls only too well: "It was another example of Jeremy Thomas the label MD ploughing ahead with what he wanted to do without consulting me. I remember going up to the office to see the cover art for the first time. My first reaction was 'That's not it, is it?' — I was

---

[†] A now-defunct London based collective who were the house orchestra of Capital Radio.

incredulous. I'd been expecting to go up there to have a chat about what the album cover could be, throw around ideas, maybe with the Triumvirate guys as well. And there I was, once again faced with a fait accompli which I thought, frankly, was bloody awful. I mean, he's got a tail coat on in the silhouette there — what's the point of that? Is he Coco The Clown or what? I know it was successful, and it might have made a good image marketing-wise for adverts but I didn't think in marketing terms, I thought in terms of wanting a piece of art. And that wasn't it. It was a cheap cover and it left me feeling very short-changed and a bit betrayed once again. Thankfully, the next cover would finally get it right."

Indeed, despite the shortcomings of the cover design, it hadn't harmed the album's success — though one wonders about the lasting impact of it if the concept had been explained, as another layer of depth to the work would have been revealed. Nonetheless the album, especially after the single release of *Heartsong*, easily surpassed the sales of even *Visionary*, and the aftermath of that success led to Gordon's most unlikely career development yet; that of an unlikely pop star!

11
To The High Throne

Emerging in the Autumn of 1977 — theoretically a difficult time for anything of this musical ilk, with the tidal wave of punk having broken into the public consciousness in spectacular fashion that Summer — *Perilous Journey* nevertheless caught the momentum which had been generated by *Visionary* and built on it, selling strongly as soon as it was released. The next step was a single and *Heartsong* was the unanimous choice, albeit in a slightly edited form with a guitar section removed. Gordon himself was less than optimistic about its success, assuming quite naturally that it would merely sell a reasonable amount and act as a sort of 'trailer' for the album, but he was certainly in full agreement that it was the clear choice.

Backed with *The Deserter* on the B-Side, *Heartsong* emerged in the run-up to Christmas 1977 and began selling steadily if unspectacularly, nudging its way into the Top 75 before things slowed up over the Christmas period. Sales continued to slowly climb over the next month or so — partly due to enthusiastic airplay from several Radio One DJs, and the use of the song as a trailer for the news bulletins — until, with the record hanging nervously around the lower reaches of the charts like an uncertain house-guest outside a raucous party, Gordon was invited to perform on BBC TV's flagship chart-based music show *Top Of The Pops*, at the beginning of February, 1978. Things began to get really interesting as Gordon recalls today, "One of the big things that I remember about that first *Top Of The Pops* appearance was when the band were getting our photograph taken for the chart rundown at the start of the show. If you were in the studio they used to take the photos backstage on the day of the show especially for it. Anyway, I was in make-up for this photo-shoot and the make-up artist asked me where I was in the charts. I said we were hanging around the lower reaches, to which she replied 'Oh, well by next week you'll be much higher'. I was surprised by this and asked was she sure, to which she explained that it was just a given fact that if you appeared on *Top Of The Pops*, the record would go up. It was an acknowledged cause and effect. I'd never considered this, because I'd never taken the show very seriously, being more interested in the 'trendy, serious' shows like *The Old Grey Whistle Test*. But she was dead right, and sure enough that week it started selling in what, to me, were huge numbers! I'd get updates from Jeremy Thomas at the record company that it was doing up to 15-20,000 copies a day, which was extraordinary. I simply couldn't conceive of that amount of people every day going to the record shop and buying one of my records, it was mind-boggling."

The band which performed on the show that day was the touring one, which comprised the new rhythm section of Dave Barfield on drums and Dave MacDonald on bass, with both Eddy Spence and Rod Edwards on keyboards. Roger Hand did go out on the road some time later with the band to fill in on rhythm guitar, but he didn't appear on the show. Rod Edwards was resplendent in a pinstripe suit, *Old Grey Whistle Test* badge and a West Ham United football scarf, which he draped over his Yamaha electric grand piano; it was clear that the whole band were hugely enjoying themselves. Indeed Gordon confirms that, while they were miming, as was the norm on *Top Of The Pops*, they were able to pose to their hearts' content and generally have a good time for the camera, without taking the whole situation very seriously. Indeed, Gordon admits that at this time he didn't take the whole idea of singles as a whole particularly seriously — even including *Heartsong* and *Top Of The Pops* was treated in a very throwaway fashion until the big sales and the chart climb started — then it suddenly became a little more significant to say the least!

One man who was far from amused when he saw the footage of the completed show was Eddy Spence. To his considerable annoyance throughout his keyboard solo, which he had of course played on the record, the cameras remained focused on Edwards instead! As Eddy says now, admittedly without any real rancour, "Yes, I remember doing the show but it was only when I saw the footage years later on YouTube that I noticed that, not only did the cameras stay with Rod during that bit, but it looked like he was pretending to play my solo! I thought 'What's that about, you cheeky thing!' I don't mind too much really, because Rod really did some great work and he was invaluable to Gordon's records. But having said that, he didn't do that bit! It's the only part I did, I've got to hang on to that."

Gordon remembers the experience of actually filming their slot for the show as quite an eye-opener, after being used to the way it looked on the TV. "It was certainly a kick doing *Top Of The Pops*", he admits, "and we gradually realised just how important it was. It might not have had the kudos of the *Whistle Test*, but in terms of generating interest, and therefore sales, it was easily its equal if not more so. But the studio itself is much smaller than it seems on television. There were something like three stages, and the audience members were shuffled about by the producers between them, sort of 'right, go over here now, dance to this as if you're enjoying it' — and you could see them looking into the monitors because they were on the telly, without giving a toss about what you were playing! But it was great fun though."

The guitar that Gordon was playing on this appearance was actually a significant choice, being a Fylde acoustic, made by his friend of some years Roger Bucknall, one of the most respected guitar makers in Britain. Gordon had first encountered him in 1972, and he made him a superb 12-string — pictured on the cover of the *Giltrap* album — which he actually put together in his garage in Lytham St Annes, Lancashire, which served as his workshop! From then on, with Gordon's enthusiastic support, he went from strength to strength, with many of the biggest names in folk music going to him for instruments, and as demand grew he began using the Fylde name, after the Lancashire borough near to his base of operations. The Fylde instrument used on that *Top Of The Pops* appearance was also pictured on the inner sleeve of the *Perilous Journey* album, and Gordon still uses Fylde guitars to this day.

It's surprising to think now, with the extent to which people remember the piece, and associate it with Gordon still, that *Heartsong* actually only made it to number 21 in the charts, when a great many records which placed much higher are forgotten. This is largely due to the fact that the BBC selected a further re-edited version of the track as the theme tune to their long-running *Holiday* television programme — beginning with that year's *Holiday '78* right up to *Holiday '85*, after which point a new producer came in with the proverbial new broom and replaced it with a track named *Holiday Suite* by Simon May, composer of many well-known TV themes including *Eastenders* and *Howard's Way*. A somewhat frothy and insubstantial piece it proved unpopular with viewers and after a single year the programme went back to Gordon using his composition *Holiday Romance* for some time afterward. *Heartsong* is still the piece most closely associated with the show however and was also used for several regional programmes and a Radio Four programme called *Bookshelf* presented by the author Frank Delaney. The track is possibly unique in that it is associated in people's minds both with Christmas and Summer — stemming from the fact that while *Holiday* dealt with film footage of sunny climes it was nevertheless broadcast at Christmas time.

Looking back, the success of *Heartsong* should have been followed up with another instrumental single in a similar vein, but this didn't happen. There were no more singles released from the album, as it was felt that there wasn't really another good candidate as single material. Gordon didn't have anything else written in that mode which would have fit the bill. He could have written and recorded something to order but instead, in a decision he now refers to as "a ridiculous mistake", he recorded a version of the Fleetwood Mac classic *Oh Well*, complete with the first Giltrap lead vocals for several years. Needless to say, this ill-advised attempt at a follow-up hit bombed quite badly, and marked the end of the short Gordon Giltrap chart career. It was the last time he would record something unsuitable both commercially and in terms of the artistic direction he was going in, as a result of what he calls now "arrogance and wilfulness". Indeed, even had the single proved a hit, it is hard to imagine anything less representative of an instrumental musician and songwriter than a vocal-led cover version! As worthy as the record itself was in its own way, we will draw a veil over its contribution to his career.

With the success of *Heartsong* the inevitable boost to the album sales followed, with *Perilous Journey* making the UK album chart, achieving the highest position of 29. While that may not sound like a huge success, it was an excellent placing for an instrumental album — even in the halcyon days of the 1970s, such albums were normally a long way from the success of *Tubular Bells*! The album had been selling reasonably steadily since its release on the back of the success of *Visionary*, but it was without doubt the performance of *Heartsong* which allowed it to grace the Top 30.

Such is the lot of a suddenly prominent 'pop star' that other programmes were starting to covet Gordon as a guest. One of his biggest regrets is that he turned down the opportunity to appear on the legendarily anarchic Saturday morning show *Tiswas* — but at the time all he knew about the show was that it was made for kids and that it would entail having a pie thrown in one's face, so this decision can be understood! It was only later, when he saw people such as Iron Maiden, Robert Plant and Status Quo queuing up to appear that the penny dropped as to the show's enduring cult appeal. He did, however, appear on the 'other' Saturday morning show of the time, Noel Edmonds' *Multi-Coloured Swap Shop*, appearing with Keith Chegwin in an outside broadcast location, speaking to Edmonds in the studio. No music was involved and he didn't get to 'swap' anything, which was the loose premise of the show.[†]

[†] As an example, Rick Wakeman appeared on the programme in a similar outside broadcast capacity around that same time and swapped some white-label promo albums for copies of the *Just William* books (by Richmal Crompton) of which he was an avid collector, strangely enough!

One lesser known, and certainly less celebrated TV programme that Gordon appeared on was *Our Show*. It was hosted by kids, asking questions to a panel of celebrities, which on this occasion consisted of Gordon, sitting in between Kate Bush and Joanna Lumley, along with *Carry On* film veteran Kenneth Connor. A strangely eclectic mix, he recalls Connor as being a very soft spoken and pleasant man. He also recalls a conversation with Kate Bush, swapping compliments about *Heartsong* and the recently released *Wuthering Heights*. One very odd recollection he has is of his bass player Dave MacDonald having told him that Joanna Lumley was a friend of the family and would cut his hair for him, which he had always dismissed as a joke. But sure enough, when he asked Lumley, she replied 'Oh yes, that will be Dave MacDonald, he's a friend of the family. When I'm round at his house I do sometimes cut his hair', which left him somewhat astonished! He recalls chatting to both her and Bush during breaks outside as both women smoked — he can recall Lumley leaving a vibrant lipstick mark on the end of her cigarette, which oddly foreshadows her later *Absolutely Fabulous* role in a way. He remembers being quite entranced with Kate Bush, and her exuding an almost waif-like quality, despite being dressed in a greatcoat and smoking roll-up cigarettes! In particular he recalls complimenting her on a beautiful butterfly choker around her neck. As he says now "it seems hard to believe that she would end up as this towering genius so soon after that meeting, when she just appeared as a vulnerable young girl."

An inevitable offshoot of this TV work was that for the first time in his career, Gordon would begin to get recognised in public. Not on a daily basis as he still wasn't exactly 'a face on every billboard', as one might say, but enough. Sometimes these occurrences were stranger than others, as he recounts one memorable incident: "I remember I was on the tube, going from Charing Cross to Bayswater, for a rehearsal or a recording and this very bedraggled, dishevelled woman got on — almost like a tramp in appearance — with two carrier bags in her hands. She was mumbling to herself and she made her way to the seat opposite me, across the carriage and sat down. She started fumbling through one of the bags as if she was looking for something and still mumbling to herself all the while. All of a sudden she raised her head, looked straight at me and said very loudly in a broad Scottish accent — I think Glaswegian — 'Excuse me. I don't know if anyone's ever told you this, but you look just like Gordon Giltrap!' The whole carriage started looking. I was a bit taken aback and I didn't say anything; I just smiled. She continued 'Oh but I suppose you get told that all the time'. She began rummaging in her bag again so the moment had passed but when

I got up to leave the train I leant over her and said 'Actually, I am Gordon Giltrap'. Whereupon she looked straight at me, waved her hand dismissively and exclaimed 'Och, you're not!!' and went back to fumbling in her bag. She didn't believe me! That's always stayed with me, not just because it was such a funny ending to the encounter, but because it seemed so improbable that someone who just looked like this shambolic 'bag lady' should comment that I looked like Gordon Giltrap. It was at that precise moment when I really thought for the first time that fame had arrived!"

******

Another knock-on effect of the *Heartsong* success was to change the touring line-up of the band. After the chart action and the TV appearances, Gordon was starting to become a slightly 'bigger noise' and budgets began to increase a little. One day Jon Miller took Gordon aside and said "there's been a great opportunity that we can't afford to miss out on". He explained that Clive Bunker — the ex-Jethro Tull drummer — and John G Perry had become available on drums and bass respectively for the live work. Gordon was a little perplexed, protesting that he already had MacDonald and Barfield, who were doing a good job and that he didn't want to change them. But Miller was insistent that Bunker and Perry were on a higher level not only musically but also in terms of profile and that it was a change which could not be turned down. Reluctantly Gordon had to go along with it. He says now that the outgoing rhythm section did seem to understand why the decision had been made and that it had been taken out of his hands somewhat, but he still felt extremely uneasy about it. As he says to this day, if it had happened to him his nose would have been "seriously out of joint". Such was the reality of his new position in the rock hierarchy, things were inevitably changing.

One aspect of this change was that Gordon had attracted the attention of some heavyweight management representation in the shape of Harvey Lisberg who had managed the likes of 10cc, Herman's Hermits, Barclay James Harvest, Sad Cafe, Tony Christie and even for a time in the 1960s, Everton and England footballer Fred Pickering. Lisberg had a shared stake in Kennedy Street Enterprises and his was a significant reputation with which to be associated. With John Miller temporarily carrying out the management duties, Gordon signed up to become a part of the Kennedy Street stable — in the process gaining access to the very best PR men, photographers and the like. He was however, still deeply conflicted and confused in his view of his image and position in the business. He was being advised from all sides on the subject of his visual image and also of how he projected himself personally. The Gordon Giltrap that emerged from this process was, as he now readily admits, an unsuccessful amalgamation of everybody's input, including his own. He was pushed into wearing fancy shirts and white suits on stage and having his hair needlessly permed, while at the same time feeling uncomfortable with this because the people he had looked up to as his heroes in his folk club days — Jansch, Renbourn etc — were, as he puts it, "basically foregoing any such concession to image", preferring a drink and a relaxed demeanour to put their music across.

He was also advised by Miller in particular to affect an aloof persona on stage and not to talk to the audience, which went entirely against the grain of his naturally easy-going and open personality. It was only some time later that he began to eventually free up this repressed 'raconteur' side and turn it into an integral part of his act. The result was that he got into an unsatisfactory 'half-way' position and he now says that in hindsight he could have made a lot more of his image and the saleability of it, and injected far more into his career as a result.

Also contributing to this confused period was the inherent contradiction between his working life in which people who admired and respected him and his music surrounded him and his personal life, which he describes now as "a train wreck". Things had been deteriorating slowly but surely in his relationship with Maureen and he now points to one particular incident as representing a significant moment in his life at the time. "Basically what I remember is one particular evening when I appeared on *Top Of The Pops* and I was watching it with my Jamie on my knee. Maureen had gone out — she didn't want to be there and she certainly had no interest in sharing something like this with me. I can still remember, very clearly, sitting there with Jamie, watching myself on the TV and being unable to take any joy in it whatsoever. I knew that this was a moment that I should be sharing with the woman I loved, with my partner and I had the feeling that this would be something I would come to look back on as a low point in my life. I was right." They separated not long afterward, and finally parted for good a year later, in 1979, after nine years together.

If his personal life was going through a disastrously unhappy period, career-wise things continued to progress extremely well. When touring recommenced with the new line-up, the band found itself playing theatre venues which he could only have dreamed of a short time earlier — Manchester Free Trade Hall, Sheffield City Hall, Liverpool Empire, Leicester De Montfort Hall, Glasgow Apollo and the like. He can remember seeing the itinerary from Kennedy Street for the first time and being astonished at the fact that he was now appearing at the very same venues where really big bands were playing. He was supported on this particular Spring 1978 jaunt by John Glover and his band who had just released an album *Midnight Over England* on the same Electric record label. He recalls their particular input to the tour as including "a fair amount of booze and substances!" Indeed, it was at one of the early shows on this particular outing when an experience happened to really hammer home to Gordon both his new position as a 'star' and the impact of *Heartsong* in particular. When he came to start the piece the audience immediately rushed to the front of the stage. He remembers standing there playing, scarcely able to conceive of what was going on and completely taken aback by the sheer power and appeal of the song. It was without doubt one of his pivotal career moments.

Soon after this came the aforementioned unsuccessful attempt at a follow-up with the cover of *Oh Well*, but an interesting aside to that recording was a video filmed for the song by Hipgnosis, and directed by Storm Thorgerson. The company were attempting to branch out from sleeve design into video production and the *Oh Well* video was the first one produced by them. Gordon looks back at the filming now with mixed feelings: "It was an exciting thing to do, certainly; and especially with Storm filming it. As you would expect from Hipgnosis it was a typically arty, surreal production. I remember a shot where I had to knock a glass of red wine off a piano accidentally as I turned. As it fell they filmed it in slow motion and it morphed into another scene which was a fantasy sequence where I was running away from a pack of schoolgirl fans! We filmed that sequence at the old St Pancras station where there were a lot of corridors that I had to run along in this chase scene. Then there was another filming session in a pond on Hampstead Heath where I had to emerge from the water, wearing the same set of clothes that I had been running in. They insisted on filming me there at about six or seven in the morning. I had to submerge myself under the water then burst forth — it was absolutely freezing and when I got out they had to wrap me in blankets. I remember I caught an enormous cold from the freezing water and I also had a twisted ankle. On top of that I've never even seen it since! I don't even know if the footage still exists."

With the continuing success of the live performances it was time to start working on writing and recording new material. That meant another album, which would appear the following year in the shape of *Fear Of The Dark*...

12
Fear Of The Dark

As was the norm in those heady days of the 1970s, resting on the laurels of a successful album was a very short-lived option. Later in that same year, 1978, Gordon was back on the treadmill of writing material for a follow-up to *Perilous Journey*. Nowadays an act with a breakthrough album would be able to take three years on a follow-up without anyone batting an eyelid, but back then an album a year was the standard. Thoughts of a longer break would have management and record companies panicking about being forgotten and left behind — even Pink Floyd and Led Zeppelin didn't dare to have more than a two-year gap in that decade! This attitude wasn't without some foundation though to be fair, because the popular music scene and its attendant trends moved at a vastly quicker pace than it does today. It is incredible to think that the single decade from 1967-1977 saw the rise of psychedelia, progressive rock, country-rock, heavy metal, folk-rock, jazz-rock and punk, whereas a decade today in musical terms is more akin to a glacial speed of progression. Guns 'n' Roses took longer than that to make one album!

In any event the prevailing spirit of the times led Gordon to be already creating new music again, mere months into the world absorbing the last. Things this time were a little different however — for the first time he was going to be entering the studio as a major recording artist with four-figure audiences waiting for the next round of live shows. Gone — at least for the time being — were the days of playing new music to small and often unsuitable or uninterested audiences, which had been not uncommon during the earlier years of the decade. Indeed one such memorable evening had him directed to a show at a working men's club with the instruction to 'look for the giant rabbit on the roof, you can't miss it' before being introduced on stage with the confident declaration of 'Ladies and gentlemen... please welcome, Lenny Giltit'! There would be no such incidents now since 2000-plus capacity theatres rarely had to rely upon giant rabbits to be located and names tended to be spelt and pronounced with somewhat greater accuracy.

So it was a confident Gordon who began work on the new material with a clear idea of how his guitar and the band arrangements should work together on what was to become probably his best-realised and most fully rounded release to date. The first piece he worked on would become the title track, *Fear Of The Dark*. He can still remember that he was trying to work on what one might call 'virtuosic' riffs and phrases. It was this approach that produced the legato, flamenco-influenced opening theme to the piece, which he remembers requiring a lot of left-hand finger strength to perform live, without recourse to any backing tapes. The track was later to be redone in shorter form and released as a single but without quite the commercial success of *Heartsong* sadly.

Following on from this the next piece to be written would become the opening track of the album, *Roots (Parts 1 & 2)*, which begins with a very strong 'hook' in the shape of a 'twiddly' double hammer-on / pull-off guitar lick; it was in the 'drop-D' tuning which had been favoured many times by Gordon's hero Bert Jansch and used by him on pieces such as *Black Water Side* and his arrangement of Ewan MacColl's *The First Time Ever I Saw Your Face*. So interestingly it sees these influences continuing to exert their pull on his playing even with the entirely different musical environment he was now working within. It was written at home since, as he makes clear, he was writing very little while on the road and doing most of it after the touring had finished. It was put together in the house he still shared with Maureen in Heather Road, but he doesn't remember much in the way of encouragement at a difficult domestic time.

Paradoxically, despite personal relationship problems, Gordon still looks back fondly on the time spent living there, since, as he puts it, "I'd written *Visionary*, *Perilous Journey* and *Fear Of The Dark* in that house and seen my career blossom to a level I never dreamt possible. Above and beyond even that I'd had two wonderful children there, which I still reckon as the most important thing I ever achieved. I was fulfilled artistically and commercially and I counted myself a fortunate man at the time. I still do, to be truthful".

There is a rich irony that began to unfold during the writing and recording concerning the question — so contentiously addressed with the tribulations of the last two records — of a 'concept' for the work. This time out it was decided early on that there would be no preconceived conceptual framework to base the writing around and that it would just be a collection of musical pieces to stand alone. However — and this is where the irony manifests itself — that very lack of a conceptual idea gave rise to a loose concept evolving itself as a natural process during the conception and writing of the material. As such it ended up being the most satisfyingly natural, conceptual theme he had yet addressed, born out of a rejection of the very notion! As it evolved the theme threading through the album became a loose concept about fear, in a similar fashion to the way that Pink Floyd's *Dark Side Of The Moon* dealt with the theme of madness and its triggers in society. The pieces on *Fear Of The Dark* dealt with such issues as childhood fears (literally, of the dark), fear of the unknown and even nightmares (in the piece *Inner Dream*). Perpetuating the irony is the fact that after two albums of coveting their very own 'Pink Floyd' through the unsatisfactory sleeve designs of those records, the record company finally had 'their very own *Dark Side Of The Moon*', achieved through their very forbearance from pushing it in that direction. One can only imagine how delighted, yet possibly surprised, they must have been by this unexpected development!

Another departure from previous albums came when it was suggested that Gordon, Roger and Rod decamp to a base in the countryside to work on writing and arrangements for the recording — an approach that Gordon initially baulked at: "I was dead set against that idea at first, in the stubborn way that I had about myself at the time. I had this streak in me, whereby I resisted doing anything that seemed to be the norm, or the fashionable thing to do. I'd read so much about bands like Traffic 'getting it together in the country' as it used to be called, that I wanted nothing to do with the idea. Plus I probably had it in my mind that disappearing off for weeks like that wouldn't help what remained of my marriage either! Still, I went along with it and my God it worked! I was so glad I'd been persuaded, because we got so much done and it was such a conducive working environment. It was a place called Peasmarsh in East Sussex, very near to Paul McCartney's farm interestingly enough — though we never saw him. Every day when we finished working we went into the village to a pub called the Wagon And Horses, where they did this huge mixed grill called The Gannet's Grill. Despite me being so thin I used to demolish those! It was such a good time that when John Miller came down at the weekend to put his two-penn'orth in, Rod actually said to him as soon as he walked in 'Now don't start! We've done so well here we don't want you sticking your nose in and ruining it!'"

The finished album would have for the first time, songwriting co-credits on some tracks for Rod and Roger and these tended to be the ones for which a lot of musical ideas came up at the Peasmarsh sessions. The tracks *Weary Eyes* and *Night Rider* were two such pieces that were worked up almost from scratch there, with the latter being one that

Gordon remembers very much as being put together as an ensemble piece. This shows in the resulting finished track as it manages to combine the basic compositional origin on the acoustic guitar with a finished sound, which is very much of an integrated 'band', with quite a Celtic feel running through it as well.

Inner Dream was, as mentioned above, conceived with the idea of the 'nightmare' in mind and the piece certainly conveys this. Shirlie Roden's virtuoso wordless vocal combines with the instrumentation to conjure up an undeniably unsettling air, leaving the listener slightly uncomfortable and 'on edge' without quite being able to pinpoint why. It's a very clever trick, made all the more fascinating by Gordon's revelation that he conceived the piece with Kate Bush in mind for the vocal part! She had proved herself eminently capable of pulling off the eerie, unsettling effect on things like *Wuthering Heights* already. Having met her on the television programme and having the idea from that meeting that she would be ideal, Gordon even went so far as to contact her management with the request for her to do it. However, unfortunately it was blocked straight away — a decision that leaves Gordon even today wondering if she would have done it had she been made aware, while simultaneously understanding the policy of shielding her from the sheer volume of requests which must have been coming in at this time, as she began to become really famous. One thing is without doubt, however — he could not imagine anyone delivering a better performance than Shirlie as she echoed her similarly exceptional take on *Revelation* from the *Visionary* album.

Weary Eyes is a notable piece in the Giltrap catalogue for two reasons. Firstly, it was the first piece to have actual lyrics since the Phonogram album some five years earlier (albeit just the phrase 'Rest my weary eyes tonight' sung repeatedly) with Shirlie again taking up the mantle here. The line was coined by Roger Hand at Peasmarsh when he started singing it spontaneously, it fit so well that it was swiftly incorporated into the piece. Secondly, it contained some significantly overdubbed electric guitar from Gordon. There was electric guitar playing throughout this album, but the amount of overlaid parts in *Weary Eyes* made it noteworthy. He remembers vividly "when I went back to the studio from the pub one evening with engineer Roger Wake we began working on the guitar overdubs, just the two of us and it came together perfectly. It was such an exhilarating experience that, having missed my last train, I remember half-walking and half-running all the way from the Bayswater studio to my home in South East London without stopping for breath" (a distance of some ten miles in fact). Everyone loved what they had done when they came in the next morning and the only regret Gordon had about the piece was that the overdubbed parts made it extremely difficult to play live.

The track following this, *Fast Approaching* is significant because like *Lucifer's Cage* on the *Visionary* album, it is a rewrite of an earlier piece — in this case from his very first album. It was suggested that there should be a faster-paced track on the album and Gordon was asked if he had any up his sleeve, so to speak. He hadn't got anything in that vein freshly written but this song came into his mind and he gave it a new treatment. It was an extremely successful makeover and is a massive improvement on the original in every way, in terms of playing, texture, songcraft and instrumentation. Coming in at a much longer five minutes it begins with an opening section right out of the typical Gordon Giltrap drawer with hammer-ons and pull-offs on the acoustic until, when the band come in and the main body of the piece starts, he carries the top line melody on the electric guitar. As with *Weary Eyes* and several other tracks here, he was clearly growing in confidence.

"I just gravitated to playing the electric more, partly because these songs all seemed to have such strong top lines and it made a change from the keyboards carrying so much of that top line melody as they did on *Perilous Journey*. I'd practised a lot and was getting pretty comfortable with valve amps, mic placement, sustain — all of those things which come with the electric guitar and I was enjoying it. I think I was using a Yamaha SG2000 for all of that album and it was only when I got a Les Paul a little later, with those marvellous humbucking pick-ups that I started to realise just how much sustain I could get and how much it bolstered my electric guitar playing all round."

Following this is *Melancholy Lullaby*, a shorter, acoustic guitar-based piece with cello accompaniment, which again taps into the 'childhood dreams and nightmares' area of the concept then leads into what is in many ways the album's *piece de resistance* in the shape of the seven and a half minute title track. If ever there was a piece that showcased the development of Gordon's songwriting, this multi-faceted composition, going through multiple changes was it. A few short years previously he was still very much locked into the idea of the guitar having to carry everything and fill in every hole in the music, but now he was becoming increasingly adept at manipulating multiple instruments and combinations thereof into the whole mix. He credits the whole Triumvirate team with the inspiration for this because, "they taught me to think orchestrally".

Finishing the album is *Visitation*, another of his pieces to follow the model of commencing as if it is to be a solo guitar exercise, before the instrumentation builds up to a climax, with the electric guitar leading everything to a triumphant conclusion. A superb way to close an album which was widely regarded as a step forward in terms of both arrangements and songcraft.

There were other interesting tales surrounding the album and some of the characters involved in it. One of these was Tony Carr, who was credited with percussion, alongside the drums of Simon Phillips. Already in his late forties at the time, Carr was an accomplished bongo player. However, the thing Gordon most remembers him for is that he was allegedly one of the first men in Britain to have a 'bell tree' — a percussion instrument consisting of vertically nested inverted metal bowls, from the largest at the top to the smallest at the bottom — it looks a little like a doner kebab spit, sculpted from metal! Having this dubious honour, Carr would actually charge a higher session fee because of the bell tree — he would walk in carrying this bizarre creation, and announce apologetically that he was sorry, but he was forced to charge extra "because of the bell tree".

Aside from this percussion sideshow entertainment the presence of Simon Phillips was a massive addition to the sound. Even now he is regarded as one of the most influential British drummers in the history of popular music, having played with a veritable 'who's who' of the great and the good in the last forty years. Gordon remembers one incident when, ironically, as a guitarist who did not even use a drummer for his first three albums, he was approached after a show by a man who credited Gordon as inspiring him to become a drummer! This inspiration was Phillips — and specifically his playing on *Visionary*. As one of the first regular jobs in his long and distinguished career he still speaks fondly of his time in the Giltrap fold.

Another track recorded but not used on the album, was *Smiler*, which eventually saw the light of day as a bonus track on a CD release of *Fear Of The Dark*. An extremely strong piece with the electric guitar pretty much exclusively used it is described by Gordon as "my Wishbone Ash phase" and the comparison is a not an unreasonable one. The reason it was left off the album, he believes now, is precisely because it did not feature his 'core skill' as an acoustic guitarist at all, but in hindsight it would have still made an excellent addition to the record — and indeed a possible single. It was not to be however and it lay buried for almost four decades until its digital resurrection.

One thorny issue remained and it was one to which Gordon was hypersensitive this time around; namely the artwork and design. After the disappointments of the previous two covers, there was no way on this earth he was going to allow that to happen again. He ensured that he had full visibility and approval of the artwork before anything was finalised. On this occasion he needn't have worried as it was obvious from the first unveiling of the design how strong the image was. The front cover showed a stark image of a pair of dark glasses, in reflective silver, while inside the gatefold (yes, a gatefold at last!) there were photos of all of the musicians and engineers involved in the recording process with a shot of Gordon staring broodingly with the dark glasses. The back cover, as dark and unadorned as the front, showed Gordon's head and shoulders, side-on, in silhouette — a massive step up from the previous covers, and one that Gordon still loves today. Not only for the effective image of the dark glasses and the fact that they reflected the person looking at the cover, but also that they could represent a blind person's dark glasses, which went hand in glove with the album concept. This time out he had the whole package; the music, the concept and the artwork. Now, it just had to be unleashed onto a waiting world, and translated to the stage...

13
Indomitable

By this time the confidence to put the new material on the road was at an all-time high. The bigger venues used on the previous tour had all been well attended, the audiences enthusiastic and the band were bedded in and tight as a live unit. As soon as the album came out in late 1978 plans were put in place for extensive touring throughout the following year. The album sold well upon release and hopes were high that it would generate good size crowds, which in turn would lead to more sales. A usual though there were some tweaks to the line-up of the touring band.

The core of Gordon, Rod Edwards and Eddy Spence remained but a new, exciting rhythm section was drafted in. Arriving on drums was Ian Mosley who had played with ex-Curved Air man Daryl Way's band Wolf and also appeared on an album by Dutch band Trace. He would go on to work with Steve Hackett, both on stage and on record, before joining Marillion in 1984, where he remains to this day. On bass was the highly respected John Gustafson, a veteran of Quatermass, Roxy Music and The Ian Gillan Band. Studio collaborator Roger Hand also joined the band on rhythm guitar, to fill out the sound somewhat, but this was not until midway through the tour.

Another significant arrival was Shirlie Roden who had of course provided such memorable performances in the studio on the tracks *Revelation* and *Inner Dream*. Put forward for the role by her then-partner John Miller, Gordon admits today he had some reservations initially about her joining, wondering whether there would be enough of the mostly instrumental set to which she could contribute. These fears were allayed, however, as not only did Shirlie's vocals, whether lead or backing, add to the pieces considerably, but she also contributed keyboards and percussion.

As she remembers now: "It was interesting, because one stipulation Gordon had was that he didn't want lyrics adding to the pieces so I had to develop a wordless style whereby I would use my voice as an instrument, which was quite an unusual approach at the time. I did write some lyrics of course to the songs *The Deserter* and *Fear Of The Dark*, which I performed on stage but that was all. I did write a lyric for *Lucifer's Cage*, but Gordon wouldn't let me use that one! I think that track was already too special to him as an instrumental to change it."

The new line-up and the addition of Shirlie's vocals certainly gained some plaudits with one notable review in the *Melody Maker* of a London show noting that Gordon was now able to share his songs with 'four great musicians and an astounding girl singer' — a clip which Shirlie has unsurprisingly saved to this day!

"Yes, I was quite taken aback that he called me 'astounding' but I suppose what we were doing was a bit different," she recalls. "I wasn't singing all of the time though. As well as some percussion, I also played some keyboard parts, bringing the total to three keyboard players on stage during those parts! I did have a brief spell in a little more of the limelight as well when I had to stand in for Rod Edwards for a while. He'd had an accident when he fell and hit his head so he was advised not to play for a few shows. I had a session one morning with Eddy Spence going through the parts and then it was in at the deep end. I knew the songs of course but there was quite a bit to pick up. It was pressure but I really enjoyed it. *Nightrider* in particular was a song that I loved playing. I was actually quite sad in a way when Rod came back because I'd felt such a key part of the band at that time and I had to go back to being mainly the singer. I think one of the things people forget or overlook about that time was the strong visual impact of the band; Gordon was there in the middle, surrounded by all of these guitars in different tunings and I remember a special lighting rig was built which shone white light on him. It was an amazing time, really".

Shirlie was also the opening act in the same way as Strange Days had themselves opened shows on the *Visionary* tour. She received some excellent reviews and went down well with audiences but as she admits it didn't do anything to raise her profile too much as she did not have much in the way of available recorded music to promote. Eddy Spence is another who points to her arrival as a positive development saying that it made things "more interesting, and gave the music another dimension. She was great."

During the tour the Oxford Polytechnic show was recorded for live release although the resulting album *Live At Oxford* did not surface until two years later in 1981. Meanwhile, continuing on from the time following the *Perilous Journey* album there were more TV appearances although these became less common — especially on 'pop'-related programmes — as the chart visibility of *Heartsong* began to recede. One such appearance which did come along was on ITV's children's show *Magpie* — their challenger to BBC's massively popular *Blue Peter* — and this time Gordon did actually play some music; as far as his memory serves with his twin-neck acoustic guitar.

"I remember playing, I think, *Roots* and there was that guy Mick Robertson who looked a bit like Marc Bolan and also Jenny Hanley who was the daughter of the actor Jimmy Hanley and Dinah Sheridan and she was extremely beautiful. In fact I can distinctly remember her saying to me 'I don't wear perfume, I like to wear men's after shave' which for some reason has stayed with me! Anyway, we recorded the appearance about two hours before the show went out. I was with my publicist at the time Bernie Cochran and we didn't get home in time for the show being broadcast. We wanted to see it, so we stopped off in the Old Kent Road and went to a television shop — it was closed, but they used to leave the TVs on demonstrating them, so we ended up watching through the window, watching my own appearance! We couldn't hear it of course. Thinking about it now, if anyone else had come along and looked at the TV through the window at that point they might have done a bit of a double take when they saw me watching myself, standing on the street!"

Within the live band, while they were presenting a stronger and more cohesive unit musically than ever before, there were one or two tensions beginning to bubble beneath the surface. Eddy Spence, the ever-dependable keyboard man who had been a part of every touring line-up since *Visionary* was somewhat perturbed to discover that some of his band mates were now being paid substantially more than he was. As he comments now, "I have to stress that Gordon didn't know anything about this, it was purely a management thing but I did find out at that the new players were getting paid more than me, without me being told, which left me a little bit put out. So after I played my last gig with this line-up in August 1979 and another job came up, I took it. Which is a shame, really. I know how it happened; they came in, as 'name' players with their price tag attached, as it were, and of course my price had already been set and it was lower! It's just the way these things went back then, and I'm sure they still do." He is keen to stress that he never had a cross word with Gordon, who he describes as having "an honest, down-to-earth, genuine quality which is sadly too rare in the music business" but alas, business dealings are all too often the cause of friction and have been since time immemorial in the world of showbusiness.

Away from the business of life on the road a single had to be plucked from the album and the choice was a shortened version of the title track *Fear Of The Dark*. However, rather than simply editing the album track down, it was decided to re-record a truncated version using the live band on it, making this the only studio recording that this particular line-up appeared on. There was to be a 12-inch picture disc release of the single (the first of its kind in the UK), limited to a pressing of 15,000. A special photo-shoot was arranged, at which the band were descended upon by a small army of make-up artists, assuring the somewhat reticent musicians that this was necessary to highlight their features for the shoot and that it would not be noticeable in the finished result. Such was not however the case as Gordon recalls: "She told us we had to have the make-up on because as it was printed on the vinyl record our features wouldn't be plain enough otherwise — it would just make us look as we were normally, which was total rubbish! I was in the middle, white suit, all of that, with Shirlie and the rest of the band on either side of me in a sort of pyramid shape and you could see the make-up clear as day! We looked like Roxy Music or something. I remember thinking 'God, what are my acoustic friends going to think about this?' I thought I'd never be able to speak to Bert Jansch again!"

Nevertheless the 12-inch single did come out with that picture proudly displayed on it. In truth, it isn't quite so bad as all that — while the make-up certainly is evident it is a rather striking shot with the bottom half of the disc showing the band reflected as if in water. This was actually reproduced on the B-side (featuring *Catwalk Blues* and *Inner Dream*) — the A-side featured the sunglasses from the cover of the album. A regular 12-inch picture sleeve also appeared with a different band photo. These promotional efforts did not achieve quite the effect that was hoped for however. While it did earn the band one more appearance on *Top Of The Pops* the single quickly slid out of the charts, without causing much of a stir. Mind you, it did coincide with a strike by BBC cameramen which resulted in *Top Of The Pops* being off the air for several weeks which helped to blunt the impact of the record.

With all of this positive career development going on it was a bolt from the blue when Gordon took a phone call which bore some tragic news. It was his good friend Roger Bucknall the Lancashire-based guitar-maker who had been such an influence personally and professionally over the past few years. Roger delivered the shocking news that his daughter Alex had passed away unexpectedly at just four years of age. Roger was understandably distraught and Gordon wasted little time in going to his side to offer any support he could. He attended the funeral in Roger's home base of Lancashire where he did duty as one of the coffin-bearers on what he describes as one of the saddest and most difficult occasions he has ever been at. Not too long after this crippling blow, Roger parted company with his then-wife Ann and to this day Gordon believes he has never fully recovered from that tragic loss in 1979. He has, partly as a result of the bond they forged at that dreadful time, remained very close to Roger to this day.

******

Returning to the musical front, despite the disappointment of the relative failure of the *Fear Of The Dark* single, Gordon doesn't feel as if it made much of an impact on the direction of his career since he had already turned his restless musician's eye towards a return to the simpler, acoustic-based material again. Despite his pride in the whole of the *Fear Of The Dark* album, he felt as though too much more of the same might result in diminishing returns as the formula would begin to sound ever more stale. For this reason he embarked on a series of shows towards the end of 1979 with a trio with the dual keyboards of Rod Edwards and Laurence Harvey (from the recently disbanded Gryphon) who also contributed woodwind and percussion. The tour was a one-off but a show at the Magnum Leisure Centre in Irvine, Scotland, on 29th November was recorded for radio — Gordon had assumed this to be long-lost, and therefore was amazed to receive a copy of the recording some 25 years later, in 2004. So pleased was he with the result that the show was shortly thereafter released as a live album entitled *The River Sessions* (the show had been broadcast live on Radio Clyde, hence the 'River' portion of the name).

It is easy to see why he was so pleased as the performance is not only excellent but in some ways revelatory. As the only known recording of this particular trio, it demonstrates a previously undocumented 'half-way house' between the full band performances and the solo acoustic Giltrap shows which were to become more of the norm in the years that followed. Anyone seeking to find an example of Gordon's acoustic guitar prowess, with added texture and colour similar to that which the band accompaniment provided, would do well to seek this recording out. The clarity is wonderful as befits a professionally recorded radio broadcast and the guitar tone in particular is rich and warm. It opens with a version of *Catwalk Blues* delivered at a blistering pace, which even now Gordon describes as 'definitive'. The show cherry-picks several highlights of the *Visionary* and *Fear Of The Dark* albums, expertly arranged for the trio format, while also airing some lesser-known and unreleased material. *Birds Of A Feather* was the B-side of Gordon's version of the theme from *The Waltons*; *Country Bluff* would resurface in slightly different guise on the *Peacock Party* album (as would *Birds Of A Feather*), while *Passion Fruit* and *Preludes* would remain otherwise unavailable. What is surprising is the absence of not only signature piece *Heartsong*, but indeed anything at all from *Perilous Journey*. Be that as it may there are splendid performances here, not least *Inner Dream* and *Nightrider*, which are brilliantly arranged for the instrumentation available and also *Lucifer's Cage*, which is uncharacteristically aired midway through the show. The encore features firstly an arrangement of Blake's *Jerusalem* in another thematic nod to *Visionary* and also a final number entitled *Jig*. A showcase for the outrageously talented multi-instrumental skills of Richard Harvey, the piece can best be described in this way; if you have ever thought 'well, acoustic guitar recitals are all very well, but there has always been far too little *Captain Pugwash* for my liking', then this is the number for you! Enormously fun, it provides a perfect closer for a highly significant snapshot of a pivotal career juncture.

At this point Gordon, whether he knew it or not, was at what would prove to be a crossroads, both in his career and personal life. The family embarked on a significant house move, while musically the trio tour had crystallised in his mind the idea that he had to move on artistically to a slightly different focus. While the next album, *Peacock's Party*, would certainly not abandon the electric guitar and band arrangements entirely, it was a fact that, for the time being at least, the collective known as The Gordon Giltrap Band was no more. New challenges were around the corner...

14

Gypsy Lane

By 1979 Gordon's marriage to Maureen was on shaky ground, but it had brought them two children and a lot of good memories and neither of them were willing to let it go without a fight. It was to this end that the couple elected in late 1979 to move out of London — the only home Gordon had known — and relocate to the more idyllic and rural location of Wokingham in Berkshire. As Gordon reflects now, "I'm sure a lot of people have done the same thing when trying to rescue a marriage, make a significant life change in the hope that it will give the situation a fresh start. Sometimes it might be having another child, or even something smaller like a new kitchen, but always a landmark gesture to signal a new beginning. For us it was a change of scene even though moving away from my family and my work contacts was a big wrench".

In actual fact it was an American acquaintance of Gordon's named Carl who had planted the seed of leafy Berkshire in the couple's mind, as Carl was very vocal in his suggestion for them to have a look at the beautiful surroundings where he lived. Finding the location extremely inviting they managed to locate a dormer bungalow which overlooked open fields — a far cry from the South London environment Gordon had been raised in, though ironically it actually looked out at the fields over a railway line — an odd echo of his happy childhood in Elverson Road, with that disused old railway embankment at the back of the house. For a while they were so settled there that Gordon even had a music room built on to the house. "It wasn't anything massive, but I had enough money to afford it then and I really thought I would be based there for the long term. It wasn't what you'd call a 'rock star mansion' by any means — in fact, it was quite modest — but it was very nice indeed, peaceful and reflective and I thought I would be happy there. The move had certainly been more of my wife's idea in the first instance but at the time I'm certain that we both really thought we could find a future there."

Most of Gordon's working musical life was still based in the capital so he was faced with the most obvious drawback to such a move — the lengthy commute! But he does remember that the travelling was not particularly onerous and was certainly something he could cope with in return for his desirable surroundings. All the while that this was going on, musically speaking Gordon was experiencing a similar period of transition. The 'Giltrap Band' format was starting to wear a little thin for his ever-wandering musical boot-heels and he was already mentally looking out for a slightly different challenge. As it happens, this challenge was to present itself from an unexpected direction...

******

Some years before, cartoonist and children's illustrator Alan Aldridge[†] had produced an adaptation of the 1807 William Roscoe poetry cycle *The Butterfly Ball And The Grasshopper's Feast*, with new verse provided for the project by contemporary poet William Plomer. The book, published in 1973, was famously turned into an album (1974) and a stage production (1975) by Deep Purple's Roger Glover, featuring a star-studded cast of musicians. What is less well-known however, is that the Triumvirate team of Miller, Edwards and Hand had worked on an adaptation in their own right, which also came out as an album in 1974, with narration by Judi Dench and Michael Hordern and music by themselves with such guest musicians as Gerry Conway, Bruce Lynch, Morris Pert and David Cross. Indeed, despite the relative obscurity of this version, Aldridge was known to harbour a fondness for it over the more well-known adaptation and in 1979 he came to the Triumvirate team with a new work he had produced as a sequel, entitled *The Peacock Party*, wondering whether they might be interested in bringing their talents to bear on it once again.

The Triumvirate Trio told Aldridge that they envisaged this as a perfect fit for Gordon. Knowing of his desire to break away from the pattern of his recent releases and with Aldridge's agreement they met with Gordon (who interestingly never met Aldridge personally) to discuss the project. In another of those moments of synchronicity that had from time to time informed Gordon's career, this proved to be the ideal catalyst to fire his compositional imagination and it metaphorically fell right into his lap.

Enthused as he was by the challenge of adapting the book, there was

---

[†] Famous for such works as the brilliant *Beatles Illustrated Lyrics* book; the *A Quick One* album by The Who and later in the '70s, Elton John's ambitious *Captain Fantastic And The Brown Dirt Cowboy*.

one more immediate hurdle to negotiate; namely that of a record company. Since the release of *Fear Of The Dark*, Electric Records had ceased trading as a label, so once again Gordon found himself without a home for his recordings. Offers from larger labels would certainly have been forthcoming, given his recent successes, but in the end he chose to go with PVK Records, another smaller label. He is quick to point out that he was impressed with the way they went about their business and promoted his work so they certainly appeared to be a good choice, but there were a couple of other reasons which helped steer him in that direction. Firstly there was the legacy of his 'major label' dalliances before, when both MCA and to an even greater degree, Phonogram, had neglected the publicity and distribution of his recordings in favour of more established or commercial artists on the roster and he wanted to continue in the Electric Records vein of being "a big fish in a small pool" as he puts it. There was another, less logical reason for his attraction to the PVK label — namely that his hero, Peter Green, had signed to the label and had recently released his 'comeback' album *In The Skies*. Not only did this idea of sharing a label with Green appeal to Gordon, he also admits that he harboured the idea that he might get to meet the great man! As he says now, "That was typical Gordon Giltrap thinking at the time — think with my heart rather than my head! I tended to do things for bold, romantic reasons rather than business sense; It's not really a sound base for choosing a record company to work with, is it? Thankfully though, they were excellent and did well for me. And I did go on to meet Peter Green!"

With the decision taken to do the album, the next question was the direction that the music would take. Gordon had already decided that he wanted to take a step away from the formula of the last couple of albums and the 'Giltrap Band' touring machine. He had been enthused by the stripped back sound of the trio tour, but for all that the music he began writing for the project did not stray too far from the familiar in terms of the overall sound and arrangement. By now he was entirely used to hearing bass and drum accompaniment in his head when writing, so it continued on this endeavour. There is acoustic-flavoured material among the album's eventual twelve tracks, certainly, but for the most part it is a full band arrangement — and in fact, paradoxically, Gordon probably plays more electric guitar than on any previous album. The difference here was in the shorter duration of most of the tracks and more upbeat feel to the music. There are no dark meditations on the human psyche as on *Inner Dream* or *Fear Of The Dark* for example. Nor is there any room for examining the tortured musings of William Blake. No, what was produced were twelve self-contained pieces with titles pointing to a 'country-folk' direction, which was often quite misleading. Titles such as *Magpie Rag*, *Turkey Trot*, *Jester's Jig* and *Party Piece* abounded. There were also a good deal of 'bird' references to tie in with the conceptual 'party' of the parent work, such as *Tailor Bird*, *Birds Of A Feather* and *Dodo's Dream*. By virtue of this change of compositional approach and deliberate lightness of conceptual touch, Gordon had successfully created an album which managed to introduce the name Gordon Giltrap as a solo idea again and a perceived shift from the band, while still retaining enough of that familiar approach to avoid alienating those who had come on board during the recent 'rock' albums. Considering that demographic probably made up a comfortable majority of his audience at the time this was quite the deftly-executed trick.

Assembling the cast of musicians presented an interesting challenge as there was no restriction on who, and indeed how many, could be present, owing to this being an avowedly 'non-band' project — though on the other side of the coin there were certain people with whom Gordon felt very comfortable and familiar and were therefore extremely tempting to fall back on. In the end, the result turned out to be a middle ground between these two ideas. While there is an extensive list of players credited on the album — far more than any previous Giltrap release — there is a bedrock of the familiar underpinning the project. Rod Edwards again provides the majority of the keyboard parts, while John G Perry handles bass on all but two tracks and Ian Mosley completes the rhythm section, playing drums throughout. Away from this 'core band' as one could call it there are some interesting faces. The loyal Eddy Spence makes his first appearance on a Giltrap album since his keyboard solo on *Heartsong*, while Gordon's regular 'live' bassist John Gustafson handles the bass duties on the tracks *Birds Of A Feather* and *Party Piece* — his first studio work with Gordon, who says now that the reason for this was because the two bass players, while both superb players, had markedly contrasting styles, with Perry's subtler, sympathetic style ideal for conveying studio nuances, while Gustafson's more powerful and aggressive style was superior in terms of projecting the music on stage. Elsewhere, violinist Ric Sanders (now a Fairport Convention stalwart of many years) makes the first of several appearances in collaboration with Gordon. Peter 'Bimbo' Acock, who would also work with Steve Hackett, Mike Oldfield, Godley & Creme and Renaissance among others, contributes sax, flute and clarinet; percussion veteran Morris Pert (of jazz rock band Brand X) provides some 'tuned percussion'; Richard Harvey, from the *River Sessions* trio appears with some wind instruments; and finally and certainly not least, virtuoso Soft Machine guitarist John Etheridge crops up with some lead electric guitar work on the track *Party Piece* — something of a rarity for another guitarist on a Giltrap recording. Jon Miller handled the production duties with Rod Edwards and to a lesser degree on this occasion, Roger Hand providing the string arrangements. All in all it forms quite a stellar array of talent.

One of the strongest pieces on the record and certainly one which was guaranteed to appeal heavily to the 'rock' demographic of Gordon's audience is the majestic and sweeping opener *Headwind — The Eagle*, which belies its relatively brief three minute duration to pack in a lot of progressive rock influenced twists and turns, driven by some of Gordon's strongest and most confident electric guitar playing to date; an early statement of intent that this would not be any sort of frivolous acoustic-country work. Further examples of this electrified and powerful rock approach are found scattered throughout the album on such pieces as *Black Rose — The Raven, Birds Of A Feather, Party Piece* and the climactic *Dodo's Dream*. Elsewhere aficionados of Gordon's distinctive and virtuosic acoustic playing are catered for in plentiful supply with *Magpie Rag* and *Turkey Trot — Country Bluff* in particular showcasing some dizzyingly intricate playing. *Gypsy Lane* is a delightfully elegiac piece, evoking the serenity and tranquillity of the new Giltrap country residence in exquisite fashion, while elsewhere there is plenty of opportunity for the keyboards and wind instruments to shine. Closing out this varied and satisfying collection is the piece which has retained the highest profile from the album, the aforementioned *Dodo's Dream*. Over the almost four decades since the album first appeared this has evolved into a live tour-de-force of effects-driven wizardry as Gordon builds a tapestry of sound using sampling and delay technology, culminating in what can only be described as a one-man 'guitar orchestra' performed in real time. It's an astonishing performance to be sure, but that fact should not denigrate from this original interpretation, which is a triumphant album closer in itself. Gordon tends to downplay this version today comparing it unfavourably to its later incarnation while voicing criticism of the guitar sound — though in truth, to the outside ear as it were, it's hard to see why. Utilising acoustic playing along with electric building up as the piece moves towards its climax the powerful string arrangements combine to make this a different, yet no less successful piece than the one it metamorphosed into over years of live experimentation. All in all the album is a cornucopia of delights each evoking Aldridge's stunning illustrations and characters beautifully and a triumph after the 'Triumvirate Trilogy' and the lower-key *River Sessions* trio work.

With recording work completed in 1980 the wait was on for it to be released the following year. Other events were to come devastatingly into play before that happened as the eighties began with no let-up in the often topsy-turvy world of Gordon's life and fortunes...

15

Wherever There Was Beauty

During the latter part of 1980 with recording of the *Peacock Party* album effectively finished, Gordon took a little time off to embark on a series of shows with Ric Sanders and Eddy Spence in the trio format he had come to favour so much. These outings would prove to be an enjoyable and fairly successful diversion but this was soon to come to an end when he returned home only for Maureen to deliver the devastating news that his mother had been taken into hospital, diagnosed with cancer and given only three weeks to live.

This was a shattering blow, not only because of the incredibly close bond he had shared with his mother growing up but also because, with his father in increasingly poor health, she had always been the parent he subconsciously thought of as being there forever. Maureen immediately advised him to return to London to be with his father and support him through this time, which he did without a moment's doubt. But even this was to conceal a further unpalatable truth: namely that his marriage was finally crumbling beyond his power to shore it up. While urging him to go and be with his father, Maureen also suggested that it may be an opportune time for him to spend some significant time away, allowing them to seriously start thinking of separation. This had been coming for a while, but it was no less disorienting a situation, as Gordon faced both of the most significant women in his life drifting away from him simultaneously. As it happens, when he left his beautiful Gypsy Lane refuge for that trip back to London, he would never return on a permanent basis.

He does recall one particularly traumatic incident when he visited the house, wanting to see the children whilst knowing that the family unit was breaking asunder before his eyes. He was strumming away at a beautiful Fylde Orsino guitar on the sofa with the children on the floor when he suddenly felt a wave of anger and frustration wash over him, as if giving him a realisation that while music and his success had given him this good life with a family and a lovely home, it had in fact, in his mind, given him nothing as he was about to lose all of those things. In an almost unconscious 'lashing out' at the situation he started ripping the fully-tuned strings completely away from the body of the instrument. As anyone who has felt the strength and tension of a tuned guitar string, this is no simple feat. The strings broke along with the skin on his hand, resulting unsurprisingly in blood on the instrument as he went on to drop it onto the floor and kick it across the room. The unconscionable act of treating a guitar in this way gives a particularly stark glimpse into the dark corners of Gordon's mind at the time.

This was pushed to the back of his mind when thrust into the maelstrom of his trauma with his mother's health. The news initially was good as she underwent chemotherapy and almost miraculously returned home having been given a tentative 'all clear'. However this was to be a very brief respite as she quickly worsened again and was re-admitted a week later. Olive Giltrap finally passed away at Christmas time 1980 and was cremated in South-East London, the area she had always called her home. She was 58 years old.

******

With the *Peacock Party* album finally emerging in early 1981, after an understandable delay, the plans for a tour to promote it were drawn up. Gordon seized this as a vital way to gain some distance from the traumatic shock he still felt after the funeral, the burial and his father's understandable troubles dealing with the tragedy. The album was fairly successful; garnering some excellent reviews, but did not repeat the chart successes of the previous three albums.

Prior to this however there had been one more musical diversion with the unlikely entrance into proceedings of K-Tel Records, purveyors of numerous budget compilation albums of somewhat variable quality. They had an idea for a Gordon Giltrap compilation and they made it clear that they believed that putting one new recording onto the album would make it sell much better — a cynical marketing move, which has nonetheless proved depressingly successful over the years with 'new unreleased material' becoming de rigeur for quite some time whenever a compilation would hit the shelves. It was decided that Gordon should tackle an unlikely cover version of the theme from wholesome family TV show *The Waltons*. Gordon was actually quite enthusiastic about this suggestion, finding the tune (by veteran US film and TV composer Jerry

Goldsmith) to be an enjoyable and well-written piece, and very much in keeping with his style. In addition to the album, the track was released as a single, backed with *Birds Of A Feather*, but it failed to trouble the charts.

When the album appeared the marketing became even more bizarre as it appeared sporting a cover photo of Gordon on stage, seemingly in mid-show and given the title *Performance*. The effect of these two factors was clearly to make the album appear to be a live recording, which could easily be seen as yet another less than overt attempt to sell more. Despite these efforts the album didn't sell as well as the record company had hoped and it has faded into the shadows of history somewhat. One unfortunate side-effect of this has been that the *Waltons* adaptation has become rather difficult to track down as the K-Tel licensing has prevented it being swept up on subsequent compilations and even online searches for the piece tend to come up frustratingly dry. In a way, it has become Gordon's 'lost' piece though he does tell of one interesting occurrence during a flight a few years ago when the plane was coming in to land and lo and behold his *Waltons* adaptation began playing over the sound system, for some unaccountable reason!

Returning to the more significant release of the *Peacock Party*, it appeared in early 1981 accompanied by some excellent Alan Aldridge artwork on both the front and back covers. The whole thing conveyed the idea and atmosphere of the poem cycle extremely well. In fact, there was more than one cover design used, albeit both featuring Aldridge artwork on different pressings. It was a little disappointing however, that the album did not receive the benefit of either a gatefold cover or a printed inner sleeve design as the whole package could have been magnificent, showcasing much more of the wonderful illustrations and one would imagine, selling more copies in the process.

Nevertheless the album sold respectably if not spectacularly and did receive some positive press reaction. PVK Records were as good as their word; putting what promotional weight they had firmly behind the release with full-page advertisements appearing in many music periodicals of the time. In one of these advertisements Gordon was pictured holding a particularly prized guitar from his collection: "It was a beautiful Gretsch 6120 Chet Atkins style guitar [hollow-body electric with f-holes] which I had actually got from Andy Powell of Wishbone Ash. He had swapped it for my old John Bailey acoustic, which I wasn't using any more. Foolishly I later swapped it back with him, which was a stupid thing to do! It was a superb instrument and I'm certain it would be worth a lot of money now".

The band that went on the road to promote the album was a rather stripped-down affair compared to the large contingent for the *Fear Of The Dark* shows. The four-piece comprised of Gordon, Clive Bunker on drums, Rod Edwards on keyboards and the new addition of Bimbo Acock on saxophone, flute and additional keyboards. They elected not to use a bass player as it was decided that Edwards could cover that side of the sound on the keyboards, especially given his very percussive piano style. Stripped-down or not the band played a string of very successful UK shows, mainly in similar small theatre venues to the previous tours and were an extremely tight musical unit. The typical set showcased the *Peacock Party* material very prominently along with a selection of tracks from the three previous records. Gordon remembers one performance in particular at a London venue called simply, The Venue, where they went down an absolute storm and were at the peak of their powers. Overall it was a very effective way to distract him from the unravelling strands of his personal life but sooner or later the tour had to end and the reality of what to do next and how to deal with things, had to be addressed...

******

Upon his return to London after the tour had concluded, Gordon found himself in a very different world from the one he had known only a few months earlier. Not only had he lost his mother and to all intents and purposes his wife but he had also traded the rustic retreat of Gypsy Lane for a peripatetic existence back in the capital where he found himself essentially homeless. He had no property in London any more, his father was now in a tiny single bedroom flat and he began a period of shuttling between friends' houses, sleeping in spare rooms or on sofas. It was as he freely admits a big culture shock and one that affected him more than he would admit to at the time.

During the 'chart years' of the Triumvirate albums, when he had encountered a genuine brush with mainstream fame and recognition, Gordon had always resisted the ephemeral allure of the 'rock star' lifestyle, seeing it as an illusion rather than a real existence with any substance to it. Consequently he had spent all of that time as a moderate drinker, strongly against drugs and putting all of his energies into trying to keep his marriage together. Now however, with what would be described as 'real life' crumbling like sand beneath his feet there seemed less of an attraction in keeping those same feet anchored to the floor and he began to succumb to some of the temptations which he had previously turned away from. Ironically just as he began to retreat from the pursuit of rock stardom, Gordon allowed himself to fall into that very lifestyle; a shadowy existence of heavy drinking and dalliances with the fairer sex. It was the beginning of what we might term his 'Lost Weekend'.†

One notable woman to crop up in his life at this time was oddly enough one for whom his designs went resolutely unrequited. He had gone to do a radio interview with Bob Harris on a regional BBC station after which he went back to Bob's house and, as he puts it "went on to get exceedingly drunk and threw up all over his carpet! Though he was very patient, God bless him". While in the studio he met this "blonde vision" as he puts it and was instantly smitten. Her name was Kathryn Andrews an extremely talented artist. She had two brothers who he remembers as being a "sort of semi-gypsy family with the attendant lifestyle" and had a recording studio in Buckinghamshire which was rather successful. Kathryn would have none of his advances as she had a boyfriend; none other than Simon Hayworth who had produced Mike Oldfield's landmark *Tubular Bells* album along with Tom Newman. Despite there being a great many available women around at the time, as is often the case in these situations, Gordon lost his heart to one who was unattainable and his professions of love led him nowhere. He had a few dalliances but nothing really serious and his life was clearly a non-sustainable and somewhat hedonistic one for which he was patently unsuited. Of all the things that Gordon Giltrap was, Keith Richards or Lemmy were not among them!

Gordon had a couple of semi-permanent bases around this period with a friend in Croydon named Chris — a church minister no less — putting him up for a while. But Chris had his own issues that he was going through and though Gordon did have a room in his house this was not a long-term arrangement. He also stayed with the owner of PVK for a short time as well, interestingly, in the lovely house that he owned in Berkshire, and that was a relatively stable period. There had been a half-suggestion of him going back to try again with Maureen at Gypsy Lane but although he had been reluctant to make the break in the first instance he found now, having had the removal from the situation and the ability to look at it with some perspective, that he really could not see it working. While he had initially suffered somewhat from leaving the security and familiarity of his home and family he had been forced to develop the confidence to live outside that 'bubble' and now saw it as an irreparable situation.

---

† John Lennon separated from his wife Yoko Ono in 1973 and began a relationship that lasted more than 18 months with May Pang who had previously worked for Lennon as a personal assistant and production coordinator. It was a period that Lennon later referred to as his "Lost Weekend", most probably taking the description from the 1945 film of the same name.

So it was that Gordon made the final decision not to return home and admitted to himself that his marriage was finally over. As he sums it up now it is a time he will look back on with a great deal of pride and affection for the children he had with Maureen and the massive career developments which occurred alongside this, but also a very difficult and confidence-draining experience as things drew to their close. His marriage finally ended as the saying has it, not with a bang but with a whimper. At 33 years old new chapters were ready to open up...

16
Airwaves

It was clear at this point in 1981 that something would have to happen to allow Gordon to regain some stability. He was as he readily admits not cut out for the hedonistic, rootless 'rock star' existence. He was a man who craved and needed a solid foundation to build his life upon. For a while this duly arrived in the shape of Lesley Cowley who he met — coincidentally — while doing another radio appearance, this time for Radio Kent. Lesley was connected with the radio station via the presenter's wife and was emerging from a bad relationship with her husband, from whom she was separated (her maiden name was Ford). She immediately bonded with Gordon, perhaps in some way initially due to their shared experience with the end of their troubled marriages.

They quickly fell in love and moved in together in Kent in a shared house. At first things were extremely settled and compared to the previous couple of years, almost idyllic. He managed to settle down again, cut down his drinking and abandoned his wild existence and even started thinking about music again. Not for the first time Gordon's life had been changed by a woman — this time, fortunately, for the better.

A slight spoke was about to be thrust into this arrangement however and would prove to be an early test of the strength of the relationship they shared. Having met a new partner in her life, Stephen, Gordon's wife Maureen dropped something of a bombshell when she announced that they intended to go away for a lengthy period to travel the world. An understandable desire in a way as she was undoubtedly finding herself as keen to underline a new chapter in her life as was Gordon, but what it did mean was that Jamie and Sadie, would have to live with their father, for the duration of their absence at least.

For Gordon this was no problem as he had missed the children enormously and for the first time since then he found himself with a home base in which he could house them. For Lesley however, this was a very difficult situation. While she got on with the children very well she had, understandably, fallen in love with Gordon and that was what she had 'signed up for', as it might be termed. Now, with this unexpected and sudden turn of events, they had been left, both literally and metaphorically, 'holding the baby' and to make things worse the cause of it had been the wife of her new partner. By anyone's standards this was an awkward situation to be thrust into.

To Lesley's enormous credit, she put such feelings aside for the moment and embraced the arrival of the new 'ready-made family' and their new Kentish life together continued on an even keel. For Gordon the presence of his beloved children was on one hand an enormous tonic after the last few months and he adored having them there but he remained extremely sensitive to the feelings of his new partner on the matter and deeply appreciative of what she was doing.

"The thing is", he says now, "that even though I know it wasn't my fault — and I knew that then, as well — I still felt a degree of guilt for the way my kids had been 'upskittled' from their life and sent off to be with me. I did the best I possibly could but I was trying to be a father and a mother to them in a way, because obviously they couldn't see Lesley like that, however good she was. I'd grown up with a very loving mother who I was very close to and I was finding it hard to reconcile them suddenly being without a mother figure, because it was something I'd always had. I know they don't blame me and they didn't back then in truth, but nevertheless I'm sure the situation did them some harm. My son more than my daughter probably, because of the age he was at the time, when it's particularly crucial to have stability in your life, he was getting uprooted, which was the exact opposite. So it was a very difficult time not only from the physical point of view of having to take care of them and for Lesley to have to come on board with that as well, but also mentally in terms of the damage I was afraid would be done to them. I loved them and was so happy in one way to have them, in a selfish way if you like, but I was also very sad about the way things had affected them."

The other side of the coin as regards the close mother that the children were missing, for all his good relationship with his own mother, he had always had a father who was quite distant and remote from him emotionally, so his own children gained on that side of things. Away from all this however, some new music was on the horizon, and Gordon was about to get to work again...

******

The band which had toured to promote the *Peacock Party* album had proved to be a strong unit and Gordon elected to retain this line-up to record the next album, albeit with the addition of bass player Chas Cronk, who had recently parted company with The Strawbs after seven years. Cronk had in fact joined Gordon for his appearance at the Glastonbury Festival that year with a line-up also featuring Acock, Bunker and Edwards along with Eddy Spence making another appearance on keyboards. Remembering this today Gordon admits that he was initially a bit cynical along the lines of, "Playing on the Pyramid Stage, I thought, what a load of old tosh! But I was so wrong because playing there as the sun went down was one of the most magical gig experiences of my life. It was incredible — I just wish somebody had recorded it".

When rehearsals and writing commenced for the record, material was being produced by all of the band members as opposed to Gordon alone, with some tracks coming in fully formed without any Giltrap writing input at all. Only Cronk did not have any involvement in the writing process, but then he is listed as an additional musician rather than a full band member in the final album credits. Given this more democratic writing and creative process, it was decided to credit the album to The Gordon Giltrap Band — the first time this had been done for a studio release.

Before this a low-key album *The Band Live* had been recorded for radio but was not released until years later. It was the set list from the previous tour performed by the same band in the same arrangements live in the studio. The material is interesting, but the occasionally drastic rearrangements of some of the material meant it would never be as definitive as *Live At Oxford* (finally released this year to some acclaim, two years after it was recorded) in the hearts of most fans. It is a shock at first to hear *Heartsong* with the top line melody carried by the flute instead of the keyboards, while the heavy use of saxophone sits a little intrusively on *Revelation* and *Lucifer's Cage*. There are successes with *Nightrider* in particular being well-served by the new instrumentation, but overall it sits best when regarded as an alternative look at these tracks. The *Peacock Party* material suffers from less of this effect as the instrumentation is not quite so drastically different to the studio originals, which had not had time to become as well-loved and in some cases, almost sacrosanct by the hardcore fans. Some would say those original arrangements had of course been reinforced in the minds of the listeners by the ill-timed release of *Live At Oxford*, which through its popularity only threw the direction into sharper relief for those resistant to the change.

This change in instrumental make-up would also influence the new recording, especially with the writing being spread more throughout the band. The biggest factor in that change was without doubt the arrival into the fold of Bimbo Acock. While a brilliant musician the introduction of someone playing saxophone and flute — both entirely new to the Giltrap sonic repertoire — was unavoidably going to create a whole different emphasis on the sound and move the resulting work further from the heartland of Gordon's traditional following, both of his acoustic work and the band material. Nevertheless, recording began at the Redan Recorders studio in the latter half of 1981.

In actual fact the album was originally intended to be a 'library recording' —a collection of music intended for use on TV, film, radio or other non-commercial release and not for general sale to the public. As the music began to come together however, it became clear that there was a cohesive feel to it and the decision was taken to release it commercially. Thus early in 1982 the album appeared under the title *Airwaves*, credited to The Gordon Giltrap Band. As Gordon says about the process: "It was indicative of me at the time. I just wasn't as prolific a writer as I had been, because I was still recovering mentally from what had gone on over the previous twelve months. Hence the writing became much more shared out. To be absolutely honest I think it lost some of its distinctiveness because it just didn't have enough of my character in it. There is some good music there but there are parts which don't sound enough like recognisably 'Gordon Giltrap music' and that hurt it I think".

When the album was eventually released it did not sell particularly well in comparison to the last few releases, though there was much to admire on the record. It opens strongly, with the lively *Black Lightning* notably being an Acock/Edwards/Bunker composition — even on a democratically-written album, opening with a non-Giltrap piece did appear to say something about the change in focus and direction. Nonetheless it is a musically appropriate beginning to the record without doubt. Following this the Giltrap composition *El Greco* is much more familiar territory with acoustic strumming patterns reminiscent of *Heartsong* contributing to a little of the 'classic' Giltrap sound.

There was despite Gordon's reservations plenty of the album that did have his stamp firmly on it. *Haunted Heart* for example or the superbly crafted *Rainbells*, where the guitar gives the impression of raindrops on a windowpane and evokes an acute sense of melancholy. There is also the band-composed *Sad Skies*, possibly the outstanding track on the record, where Gordon provides some superb electric guitar playing and contributes some descending runs which are marked '100% Giltrap'. "That was recorded using a 1970s Strat, using a whammy bar — I still thought my finger vibrato was a bit weak, so I did like using the whammy bar. I loved how it sang like a woman's voice. I can still remember when I was recording that track though, the emotions which were going through my mind. 'I wonder how the kids are; I wonder how Lesley is doing'. There was so much going on with me emotionally at that time".

Elsewhere though it must be said there were issues. The band-composed *Heroes* despite its quality seems to owe as much to Mike Oldfield in the guitar and flute sound, while the title track, courtesy of Acock and Edwards pushes things a bit too near to Dire Straits with its funky bass line in particular sounding out of place on a Giltrap recording. *Dream Teller* and *Reaching Out* are a little heavy on the sax and flute respectively while *Lost Love* sees the saxophone becoming a little intrusive, despite the excellent electric guitar work, which is reminiscent of Camel's Andy Latimer. Gordon did contribute a trademark multi-part acoustic piece in the shape of the closing *The Snow Goose Parts 1-3* (coincidentally sharing a Camel title). But it is tantalisingly brief and sounds under-developed. Gordon recalls that many of the titles of the pieces and indeed the somewhat misleading album title itself (which give the erroneous impression of radio play and commerciality) were decided upon not by himself but by the KPM Music Library who commissioned the work in the first place, leading to even more of the fragmentary and disjointed feel of the result.

All In all the album is best described as an enjoyable entry in the Giltrap catalogue but far from definitive. When it appeared (again on the small PVK label) clad in a striking if bizarre sleeve showing an orange sky with a giant hand emerging holding a plectrum it would turn out to be the last Gordon Giltrap album for some five years — a time which would see yet more upheaval, trauma and ultimately, some stability in his personal life...

My handsome dad in the army.
I have his eyes.

My gentle-souled mum.

My maternal grandmother hop picking.

Mum, dad and me on the way to
London Zoo about 1953.

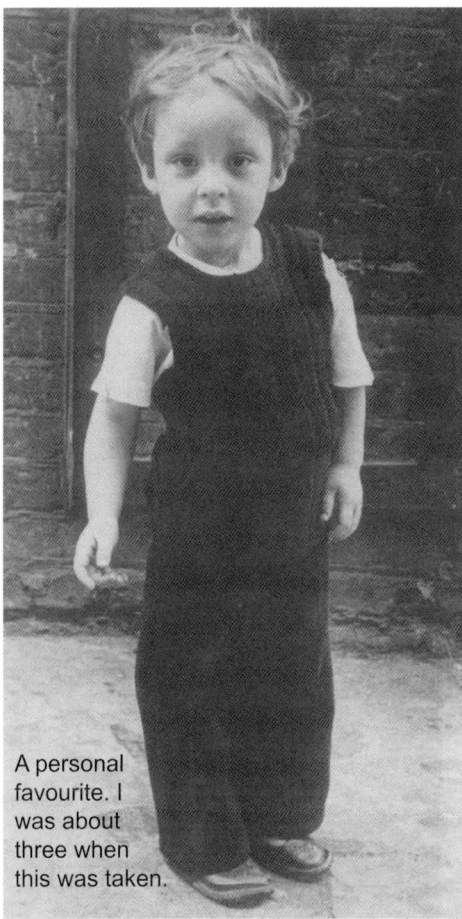

A personal favourite. I was about three when this was taken.

My first great guitar. The John Bailey used for many years.

With Jamie.

One of the photos taken for the 1973 Giltrap album.

With Cliff Richard after I did an interview with him for *Guitarist* magazine. He is holding the Tree of Life guitar that I gave him.

From a photo session with Derek Brimstone. My Fylde Tree of Life guitar being hugged!

My favourite photograph of Hilary and I. Taken by the late Mark Hadley.

Taken by the brilliant photographer Mark Hadley after I interviewed Bert Jansch for Guitarist magazine. This photo was later used on an album.

With the great John Entwistle taken at a London guitar show. Where did I get that shirt?

My big hair period during Heathcliff (*Alan Mills*)

With my first major guitar influence, Hank Marvin. I interviewed him for the Hofner book.
(*Hilary Giltrap*)

This photograph was used for the *On A Summer's Night* album.
Rob Armstrong looks proud of the guitar he had just built, and bought by Alvin Lee.
Taken at the then home of Joe Brown.

With Martin Taylor.
Don't we look smart!

With Sadie and Jamie.

With Steve Howe and
Bill Bruford of Yes.

With Maggie Weedon, Jim Marshall and Bert Weedon.

With Brian May after his session for me at the Workshop Studios in 1993.

With Cliff and Del Newman at the *Troubadour* recording sessions.

With Jimmy Page outside St Martin-in-the-Fields at John Entwistle's memorial service.

The Pedrazzini violin bought at a car boot sale for £20!

From the session with Rob Jewel for this book with my beloved wife Hilary.

17
The Long Road Home

For the first time in a while following a Giltrap release, there was to be no tour promoting the *Airwaves* album. In truth, neither artist nor audience had engaged with the work sufficiently for there to be either inclination on behalf of the former or demand on behalf of the latter for such an undertaking. The band were still an excellent unit, of that there can be no doubt, but the impetus and the cresting wave of enthusiasm following the release had temporarily departed, owing in equal parts to the nature of the recording and the massive shift in terms of the focus on Gordon's personal life — though it was an unassailable truth that one of these had impacted the other, with personal upheaval and worry clearly and understandably detracting from the complete immersion in the writing and recording of new material.

This is not to say that live work ceased — indeed, on the contrary, there was quite a sizeable number of concert appearances throughout 1982 in various permutations. The practicalities of life meant that he still had to play to earn a living. There were solo concerts in a range of small theatre venues that displayed his undiminished ability to perform unaccompanied. The intimate and entertaining side of his stage banter with the audience blossomed as it had not been allowed to within the restrictive band format. Audiences would find themselves being drawn into the show by the thoroughly engaging onstage manner that Gordon was increasingly cultivating. Other relatively low-key shows were being performed at the same time in a duo format with the versatile Bimbo Acock — surely a dream partner with his ability to switch between instruments to complement Gordon's guitar as the song demanded. These shows were proving successful and bringing in enough income to get by but towards the latter part of the year there were also an occasional series of full band shows although these never coalesced into a formal tour.

Rod Edwards had by this time departed, taking with him the final link to the 'Triumvirate Trio' of albums. Clive Bunker still occupied the drum stool with Acock covering a range of instruments, but entering the fray on keyboards was Matt Clifford.[†] Stepping in on bass duties was an acquaintance of Clifford's names Ken Boley, though Bimbo did play bass on some occasions. In this format the Giltrap band made quite a number of appearances when scheduling of all involved allowed it, but did not coalesce into a stable touring outfit. Gordon remembers that he felt profoundly grateful that he had begun his career as a solo performer so that he had no trouble stepping outside of the band environment to undertake unaccompanied shows, whereas a musician brought up and schooled in a band environment would find it far more imposing to step out of that familiar 'bubble' into the spotlight alone. The one thing that Gordon had acquired by this point more than at any time previously was versatility and it served him well.

******

Meanwhile, away from his musical endeavours, Gordon's personal life had taken another turn. After a few months away, Maureen had returned from her extended travelling period. "This upset and confused the kids a bit but at the end of the day it was their mother coming back, so it was important for them. We'd just got them settled into a new school in Kent though, so the timing was far from great".

The upshot of her arrival back into their orbit was that while Jamie stayed with Gordon and Lesley Sadie returned to Berkshire to live with Maureen and her partner. She sold the Gipsy Hill home and moved into a new place not far away where the three of them lived for some time. As Gordon remembers, "It was tremendously upsetting for me to lose Sadie again, after having her with me; it really broke my heart. But I can truthfully say that any decision we made was what we believed would be in the best interests of the children and their happiness."

In this way life went on in a reasonably stable fashion with Lesley until in 1983 Sadie ended up returning from Berkshire and coming back to rejoin them and Jamie in Kent. This was a source of joy to Gordon but it was also tinged with worry for the effect this further upheaval would have on Sadie and also the fact that Lesley was having to once again adjust to another addition to the household. This concern was well founded as the situation was beginning to take its toll both on Lesley and on the couple's relationship. "We'd started to argue", says Gordon. "Every day after the kids went off to school we'd start having these huge

[†] Clifford went on to work with the Rolling Stones around the turn of the 1990s as their onstage keyboard player but also did studio and live work with Jon Anderson and the short-lived band of Yes alumni; Anderson, Bruford, Wakeman, Howe.

rows which we hadn't had before. It was at this point when the relationship really started to destabilise, I think".

Meanwhile Gordon's father was starting to give real cause for concern. He was still living in the small single-bedroom flat and was not dealing at all well with life there and being alone, together with his own increasing health issues. "He was getting more and more depressed," says Gordon looking back. "I wish I'd been there more for him but I was trying to juggle keeping my relationship with Lesley and the kids on a relatively even keel, with getting back to London to see dad. I know now that I didn't get over to see him as often as I could have or perhaps should have done. Whenever I did go it was a bad situation. He'd be going to the pub every night with his dog (an aging black Labrador named Tina), getting drunk and coming home. He wasn't eating properly and it was obvious he wasn't in a good place physically or mentally. He'd lost the will to live, in a way".

With his musical career still needing a guiding hand on the tiller as it were, despite the temporary hiatus in recorded work, Gordon became conscious of the desirability of a new manager to help sort out his business affairs. One such opportunity presented itself when towards the end of 1983 he travelled to London to meet Peter Vernon-Kell in order to discuss the possibility of joining his roster of clients. At this time Vernon-Kell was managing Sky, the instrumental rock band formed by acclaimed classical guitarist John Williams and also featuring the considerable talents of keyboard player Francis Monkman, bassist Herbie Flowers, drummer Tristan Fry and electric guitarist Kevin Peek. This was a high-profile management role at the time and unfortunately Vernon-Kell elected on balance to pass on the opportunity to represent Gordon as he did not believe he could devote the time to do the role the justice it deserved.

On the way home, Gordon elected to pay a visit on his father and stopped off at his flat. Having knocked on the door and received no answer he was informed by a neighbour that his father had been taken into Lewisham hospital. It transpired that he had taken an overdose of pills in an attempt to take his own life.

Heading straight round to the hospital in a state of shock he found that his father had come round to a state of consciousness again, having had his stomach pumped, but he made no secret of the fact that he had lost his desire to live. When Gordon reached his bedside he turned his head towards him and simply said, "I'm sorry kid, but I'd had enough". It was a desperate state of affairs but it was at this point that Lesley came through with a timely and vital intervention, managing to find a retirement home for him to move into. He had only to return to the flat for a short time before moving to a place called Darenth Grange in Dartford, Kent, not far from where Gordon and Lesley were living.

During his hospitalisation the neighbours had looked after the dog, but when he came out it became apparent that he was unable to shoulder the responsibility of looking after her any more. Getting on in years and not a well dog the decision was taken that she had to be put down. It was desperately sad as she had been his companion during some dark times but for the sake of both dog and owner it was the only truly kind course of action.

When he moved into Darenth Grange things improved for a while. "It was quite a heartbreaking time really with everything from his overdose to his words to me in the hospital right through to his companion Tina having to be put to sleep but that home really was his salvation for a while. When he moved in there it was really good; he had company, he was being looked after, he was taking pride in himself again and it was so good to see him back to his old self". Sadly however this was to be short-lived as after a while his health deteriorated again and he was taken into Gravesend Hospital, where he died of heart failure.

Leonard Giltrap was 66 years old when he passed away, on Valentine's Day, 14th February 1984. He was cremated and interred in Kent. He had survived the loss of his wife by only a little over three years.

******

After his father's passing Gordon felt that his final link with South-East London and the family had been severed. It was no longer somewhere he thought of as 'home' and his roots had essentially been torn up. He was still together with Lesley in Kent but this also was coming towards its natural end.

Remembering it now, Gordon says that he feels he knew around early 1984 that his relationship with Lesley had been eroded to the point where it was irrevocably damaged. "Not through any fault of hers", he insists. "It was just the constant pressure of the situations she was thrown into with the children and I suppose with my dad as well. It was ultimately too much for the relationship to sustain. It was quite understandable because she had fallen in love with me initially and then I just brought so much unavoidable baggage along that, even though she loved the kids and really did her best, it couldn't carry on forever".

The couple finally went their separate ways in 1984 and Gordon felt very strongly that he would be destined to relocate and make a new home and a new life for himself elsewhere away from London and away from the ghosts of his past.

He had bought the house that he and Lesley had shared in Kent but when he left he signed it over to her so that she could keep a roof over her head. "The way it was, she had left her home to move in with me, so I felt that it was important she should not be left in any trouble in that way. I had to get away and get the kids out of such a stressful situation — which was not, I must emphasise again, of Lesley's making — so I signed the mortgage over to her and told her that the house was hers as long as she could make the payments. I suppose if I'd been a bit more financially 'savvy', I could have said that the house was in my name and that I needed the money — which I did — but essentially I was on the verge of a nervous breakdown by this time. Everything I had known had been pulled from under my feet. I had the kids with me and I desperately had to get away".

As it happened he had a cousin Pat with a house in Solihull in south Birmingham. She offered that he, Jamie and Sadie could come to stay there while they found their feet and thus ended the first phase of Gordon Giltrap's life. The London Years were behind him, his previous life was behind him, the stress and heartbreak of the previous years was, he hoped, behind him and the West Midlands was to become his new home, as it remains to this day.

He may not have realised it at the time but on the day he left in the Summer of 1984 to all intents and purposes Gordon had come home...

18
Shining Morn

The lifeline offered by Pat was a crucial one. It allowed Gordon to exercise his desire to move away from the capital with all of its past associations and old ghosts, while giving him the opportunity to do so by 'dipping his toe in the water' in case things didn't work out. It was fortuitous as he had already been thinking about the Midlands as a good place to relocate, central to the country as a whole and not a million miles from London for the odd business travel requirements, yet still crucially far enough removed from the metropolis in his day to day life — even his rural idyll of Kent had come with its own set of issues.

As happy as he was at Pat's he only stayed for around three months until he found his feet completely. She had disability issues and Gordon was aware that, while she did not attempt in any way to oust him or the children from her home, their presence was giving her a little extra responsibility which he did not want to burden her with any longer than was necessary. With no property to sell he was free to start house-hunting and make a new location a permanent home.

It didn't take very long as Gordon planted his newly found Birmingham roots by purchasing a house at 21 Tysoe Close in an area of Solihull called Hockley Heath. He and the children settled in there very quickly but little was he to realise this house would be his home for quite some considerable period of time. The Gordon Giltrap who had spent his life seemingly bouncing from one location to another in and around the capital had gone: replaced by a man older, more settled within himself and ultimately, not weighed down by as much of the mental and spiritual baggage that he had carried, sometimes unconsciously, for a rather long time.

Still, there was to be another important change to his life in the offing. One which was going to provide the biggest and most positive impact on him since the birth of his children and the career-changing release of *Visionary* — meeting the woman who was to become his second wife to this day, Hilary...

******

Throughout this period Gordon was still playing solo gigs, though he had left the band behind when he relocated. He had also hooked up with Ric Sanders again as Ric lived in the Birmingham area and the pair became good friends. Gordon had first met Sanders back in London in May 1980 when Ric had a band named 2nd Vision along with guitarist John Etheridge, keyboard player Dave Bristow, drummer Mickey Barker and ex-Gryphon bassist Jonathan Davie. Originally going by the names Surrounding Silence and then 20/20 Vision, the band were in the jazz-rock mould of Etheridge's other band Soft Machine and they launched their sole album *First Steps* by playing a four-night residency at Riverside Studios in Hammersmith from 7-10 May. The twist to this was that a different guest joined the band each night with Gordon being one of the four (along with ex-Fairport Convention man and solo artist Richard Thompson, folk singer June Tabor and Jethro Tull's David Palmer). In an incredibly unfortunate accident of fate most of the UK's music papers chose that precise time to go on strike for several weeks with the coverage being accordingly nonexistent and the album sank like a stone, hastening the group's demise.

However, it did yield the seeds of the Giltrap / Sanders partnership, which led to a number of recorded collaborations and gigs over the years. Unsurprisingly some performances with the two as a duo began to happen now that the West Midlands was their joint stomping ground.

Towards the end of 1985 Gordon had been booked to play a solo show at the Birmingham Guitar Club, a compact venue popular with largely acoustic performers at the time. In the audience that night was Hilary Logan who had been persuaded to come along with some friends on the recommendation of some of evening's organisers. She was unfamiliar with any of Gordon's music but he had come highly recommended. According to Gordon's recollection she said that she had enjoyed the show but that it was a little loud, as she had and continues to have, sensitive hearing. There was also a raffle on the night, which her friends were helping to run with Hilary selling the tickets. In a bizarre coincidence which thankfully did not have the patrons crying 'Fix!' she actually bought a winning ticket. With the laws of chance once again smiling upon this potential union, she actually won a copy of the *Peacock Party* album! She thoroughly enjoyed it and to this day it remains one of her favourites in Gordon's catalogue — partly, of course, due to this memorable and pleasant association.

After the show she approached Gordon, who had already taken note of her as someone he found extremely attractive, and she asked for his autograph. This was in itself not unusual but the slightly bizarre thing was that she asked him to autograph a postcard. Understandably intrigued he asked who she was planning to send it to, to which she replied that she liked to send postcards to herself and that was her plan for this particular one. Gordon's reply was somewhat understandably to ask in confusion 'Are you some kind of nutcase?' While this may not resonate quite like the balcony scene from *Romeo And Juliet* or the station in *Brief Encounter* as one of the Great Romantic Meetings, it nevertheless did its job as they were now aware of each other, even though they didn't really give a thought to meeting again at this point.

In January 1986 Gordon got the call to play at that same venue again, this time in support of a local singer/guitarist's first gig on the 23rd of January who he wanted to help out, even if only as 'moral support'. In the end he suggested to Ric Sanders they go down and actually play a few songs to which Ric agreed. As fortune would have it Hilary was in attendance again — she had no idea Gordon would be playing while he had no clue whatsoever that she would be there; indeed, he didn't even know her name.

When he arrived he noticed her across the room and instantly recognised her. He remembers thinking to himself "Hang on, isn't that the attractive woman I met here a couple of months ago, who had the strange postcard hobby?" — though this time he mercifully stopped short of enquiring as to her sanity or this romantic plot might be considerably shorter! As it happened, after the show they got talking downstairs, where there was a late night bar and they simply talked and talked for hours. They were both divorced and both had children and they found they were soul mates from the word go. It was clear to Gordon that something had 'clicked' right away and he knew they had something special between them. Ric Sanders even commented later on how much time they had spent together with Gordon replying, "I would be proud to be seen anywhere with that woman". Unsurprisingly, after this remarkable chemistry they began seeing each other and it wasn't very long before Hilary moved into the house in Tysoe Close.

After what would certainly qualify as what one might term a 'whirlwind courtship' the couple were married only four months after that second meeting on the 22nd May 1986. Hilary was 46 and Gordon 38 at the time and the idea of settling down again appealed to both of them.

The wedding was a small affair at Solihull Registry Office with the reception being equally low-key, taking place in a Chinese restaurant in the village of Dorridge within the Solihull area ("we didn't have much money, bless us", says Gordon). Far from a big 'rock star' affair it was the way they wanted it. Ric Sanders was Gordon's best man, while Bimbo Acock was also invited, along with Gordon's (short-lived) then-manager, Jeff Watts. Both Jamie and Sadie were in attendance of course, along with Hilary's mother and sister and her three children Rachel, Ruth and Simon from her previous marriage. Despite the small scale of the affair — or, in a way, even because of it — Gordon has a very fond recollection of the occasion, which he describes as "a beautiful day. A lovely day with some wonderful memories".

In line with the modest theme of the wedding, the couple did not have an official honeymoon as such, just taking a quiet few days away. They spent their first day as a married couple visiting the historic town of Chapel-en-le-Frith in Derbyshire, a picturesque place often known as 'the capital of the Peak'.[†]

After this charming and picturesque start to their married life they headed north to meet up with Gordon's old producer and friend Bill Leader before travelling up to the Fylde coast to visit Gordon's long time friend and legendary guitar-maker Roger Bucknall, whose 'Fylde Guitars' company was still based in the area. This enabled them to spend some time with two of the people that Gordon wanted to share the occasion with but could not attend the wedding itself. While visiting Roger, Gordon actually made it a sort of 'Busman's holiday' by playing a floor spot at a local club!

Returning from this short but extremely pleasant trip the couple settled into married life back in Solihull along with Jamie and Sadie. They were very happy but could not have guessed at the time that they would spend the first seventeen years of their marriage there. It reaffirmed this new start with new roots for Gordon as he was based here for longer than any other house he had ever lived in. They did not eventually move from the house until 2003 by which time a lot of water and a lot more recordings had flowed under the bridge. Soon after the wedding Sadie returned to live with her mother again, much to Gordon's regret, but Jamie elected to stay with him and Hilary.

With his personal life now on the most settled and even keel it had been for some considerable time the hour was fast approaching to return to the world of songwriting and more specifically, recording. The time was long overdue for the unfocused and transitional *Airwaves* album to be followed up, and so it would be the following year.

[†] Referring to the Peak District national park even though most of the town lies outside the boundary of the Peaks. The name of the town actually means Chapel In The Forest deriving from French and the middle-English word 'Frith' meaning 'Forest'.

19
Elegy

In the years since *Airwaves* Gordon had not been idle when it came to live performance, maintaining a gigging schedule as indeed he had to from necessity as a source of income. There had even been one final roll of the dice with a Giltrap 'Band' in 1985, getting together with a new group of musicians including bass player Ken Bowley and singer Barbara Deason, both of whom had recently spent time as members of progressive rock band Solstice[†]. This new Giltrap band line-up did some recording with vague plans for an album that never materialised. This is something of a shame as the material they did put down on tape featuring — unusually for a Giltrap band — an actual full set of lyrics, showed promise. They did contribute a track to a charity album called *Action!* in aid of a Birmingham children's hospital charity along with other local bands and musicians such as UB40, Level 42 and Jeff Lynne, but that proved to be their only officially released recording at the time. Three tracks which survived from that abandoned album session, entitled *Gold*, *Solitaire* and *Gemini*, eventually surfaced on the 2000 CD reissue of Gordon's 1987 album *Elegy* — more of which below...

With the abortive 1985 band now in the rear view mirror once again a serendipitous set of circumstances provided the catalyst for Gordon's next career reboot. With no recording contract to his name at this time he had understandably slipped into a sort of holding pattern of simply going from gig to gig, keeping his skills sharp and earning a crust. There had always been far more to Gordon Giltrap than simply a jobbing 'song and dance man' however and new material was essential if that creativity was to resurface. Some new music had been composed during this period, but only as and when inspiration saw fit to strike, and certainly not enough for an album.

[†] While neither Bowley or Deason made any studio recordings with Solstice they can be heard on the bonus disc included on the deluxe CD reissue of the album *New Life*, by way of some live material.

As fortune would have it Gordon developed a friendship with Colin Blaney — builder by trade and part-time drummer. Blaney had a keen interest in home recording and had installed a rudimentary home studio of sorts in his house. With an eight-track tape set-up and an AKG-414 microphone it was certainly enough to record more than passable home demos on. With this being literally a two-minute walk from Gordon's front door it fired his creative juices again and he set to recording his recent compositions. He also found himself with the impetus, so often born of a target to aim for, to write sufficient material for a full album. For the resultant record, *Elegy*, which was to appear in early 1987 on the small Filmtrax independent label, Gordon played every note on the record himself, all of it on guitar. In several places on the record it appears very much as if there are violins and other strings present, or at least a mellotron or some similar keyboard device at work, but these are all produced via electric guitar, using an assortment of effects units such as volume and chorus pedals. Gordon played mainly acoustic six and twelve string guitar on the material but there is a good amount of quite subtly rendered electric guitar playing as well in addition to some bass guitar where required. One of the main instruments used on the album was a Fylde 75 acoustic guitar with a tree of life design inlaid into the fretboard. Also used on the recording of *Heartsong* and one of Gordon's most beloved guitars, this beautiful instrument was later given as a gift to Sir Cliff Richard, who loved it when he first set eyes on it and is still the proud owner.

When the album was released Gordon was about to step out onto the wider public stage once again, albeit in a far more restrained and unadorned way, musically speaking, than anything he had released since the *Giltrap* Phonogram album, back in 1973.

******

In many ways the purest 'Giltrap' collection of material since *Visionary* over a decade earlier, *Elegy* might well have seen Gordon returning to the essence of his musical raison d'être but it was nevertheless a hard sell for the audience raised on the Giltrap Band albums, for whom the idea of a solely guitar album must have been a challenging step to take. In fact with the first four albums, pre-*Visionary*, all having featured Gordon's vocals, *Elegy* represented the first purely instrumental solo Giltrap album after almost twenty years of recording! Nevertheless, perhaps indicating the wait there had been for new material, the album sold respectably and indeed extremely well for the slightly niche genre it represented.

Opening the album is *In Unison* a fairly upbeat piece to get things underway with an interesting story behind it. Possessed of a strong instrumental 'hook' this previously written piece had come to the attention of Yorkshire Television in 1984 who had used it as the theme music for a children's programme called *Benny Comes To The Common*, also sometimes credited as *Benny On The Common*. Telling the story of a dog named, unsurprisingly, Benny who lived on Midsummer Common, Cambridge, the show may have faded into the shadows of television obscurity but the piece remains a fine one, and a perfect album opener.

The following *A Christmas Carol* initially comes as something of a surprise as it has no relation to Christmas carols either in direct reference or even by way of the mood of the piece. It is by contrast a slightly sombre, reflective piece, borne out of Gordon's belief that Christmas, while it may be a time of joy for many, is by no means always the case. This juxtaposition of mood versus title subverts the listener's expectations in a subtly effective way. The piece is in the non-standard DADGAD guitar tuning, which is also used for, among other things, *Kashmir* by Led Zeppelin.

The Mariner's Tale is another piece with a story behind it. Not directly inspired by any specific seafaring reference, it was actually written for Gordon's friend Bob James, a guitarist who he had met, once again, through the Birmingham Guitar Club scene. A talented player who in Gordon's words "lived to play — it was his life, basically", he suffered a car accident which, in a shattering blow for such a dedicated player, cost him the tips of the middle two fingers of his left hand. Gordon often used the first and fourth fingers quite heavily on the fretboard with the little finger handling hammer-ons and pull-offs. He wrote this piece based around the fretwork of those two fingers. The hope was that it might encourage Bob to see that there was light at the end of the dark place he found himself in and spark him into trying to play again. "I haven't seen him since that time", says Gordon now, "But I really hope it did help him in some way and that he still plays. He was a lovely man, very self-effacing and a little insecure and it was such a shame what happened."

The following piece, the somewhat moody and sombre *Blue Lady* has another slightly unusual genesis as it was actually inspired by the very guitar used to record it. One of Gordon's favourite guitars was his Gibson J45 acoustic. Such was the quality, especially of the bottom-end tones, that Gordon felt driven to compose this piece, which he felt showcased the instrument in its best light. All good material but still there was a danger that too many laid-back acoustic pieces back-to-back could see the listener's attention wander if they began to blur together.

A masterstroke of sequencing sees the album's most upbeat track, *Lucky* coming at just the moment it is needed to jolt the listener out of their reverie and sit up to take notice. The top line melody is extremely memorable, which can be unusual for a purely acoustic track and is quite reminiscent of the Small Faces' *Lazy Sunday*. This was another piece born out of a commission for television, this time for an adaptation of the well-known Roald Dahl story *Danny, The Champion Of The World*.

The title track is without doubt the centrepiece and the longest piece on the record. It features the acoustic guitar augmented by the electric through the compression and swell effects, sounding remarkably like a string accompaniment and can best be described as 'lush'. It was a very personal piece for Gordon, as it came directly from a poem written by Elizabeth Barker who was none other than Hilary's mother.

"She was a wonderful lady, and very sadly missed. She wrote this amazing poem, *Dear Love* in the form of a love letter. It's about a love that never was, which is what made it so sad and tragic. The first line was 'dear love that never was, where are you now' — oh, it's a real tearjerker and I found it profoundly moving. So what I tried to do — and this is something I've never done before or since — was to write the music to fit the metre of the poem. There are no vocals but if there were the poem would fit perfectly. It was an unusual approach but it worked. I can still remember the first time I played it to Elizabeth in my living room in Tysoe Close and Hilary and her sister were also there. Elizabeth thought it was so beautiful that she actually cried. I told her then how it was inspired by her poem and she was moved beyond words. I'll never forget that moment. I didn't title the piece after the poem because I thought it had such an elegiac feel to it that *Elegy* fitted it just right. I never thought at the time of putting vocals on there with the poem being sung but looking back that could have been very interesting, so perhaps I should have. Hilary could have sung it actually — she has a lovely voice. I think I was intent on staying instrumental though. I know the whole 'new age' thing was taking off at the time, and I had been advised that I could maybe get some success from that sort of thing but that didn't happen. Sometimes it really doesn't do to listen to people, well-meaning though they may be, because there are always these carrots being dangled in front of you and so often they come to nothing".

The track has gone on to a second life now because as early as 1987 Gordon was working on a suite of tunes inspired by the Pre-Raphaelite Brotherhood. When thirty years later it finally saw the light of day on the *Last Of England* album as *The Brotherhood Suite*, *Elegy* reappeared in another guise as *Elegy (Chatterton)*. Indeed, the following track on *Elegy*, *Spring Dance*, made its way into the *Brotherhood Suite* by way of a different tuning and a change of title to simply *Spring*.

Following this comes another upbeat track, *The Poacher*, which uses the same tuning as *Roots* from the *Fear Of The Dark* album. Another well-placed track giving a much-needed tempo boost at just the right time, it is notable for a fairly intricate guitar figure driving the piece, which manages the trick of being simultaneously complex yet catchy; a tricky thing to pull off. This leads into yet another piece of television-inspired music with *Sallie's Song*. Gordon had been contracted to write the incidental music for a TV drama series called *Hold The Back Page* starring the acclaimed actor David Warner who has appeared in everything across the board from *Titanic* to *Time Bandits*.

"It was actually shortly before I met Hilary that I had been offered the chance to write the music for this major 10-part drama series. I wrote all of the music for it — what an opportunity! I was sent the 'rushes' of each episode after they were filmed so I was able to watch it and compose the music directly from that, which was a tremendous way to work. I absolutely loved doing it and it gave me quite a good income as well as invaluable experience. The way *Sallie's Song* came about was that David Warner's character, Ken Wordsworth was a sports journalist who had split up from his wife Sallie. They got together and were reminiscing about what had gone wrong in their marriage and *Sallie's Song* comes from the music I composed for her character on screen. The director of the series was a hugely talented man called Adrian Shergold. I actually ended up writing music for a couple of other productions he was involved in. He was quite edgy in the subject matter he chose. I remember one of those things I wrote for was called *Will You Love Me Tomorrow* about the infamous child killer Mary Bell. It concerned a fictional story of her escaping for a weekend from prison with another inmate, ending up in Rhyl and meeting two young men, one of whom falls in love with her. Joanne Whalley played Mary Bell and the two male actors were Ian Glen and Phil Daniels. The next thing that he commissioned me for was an even more controversial work called *Close Relations*, which was about incest of all things! So I wrote quite a lot of stuff for TV at that time, but most of it never got released because it didn't really work away from the screen to be honest".

Another feature of *Sallie's Song* is the delay effect that Gordon uses to great effect and for which he was inspired by the work of Brian May. It was an effect that he had only recently started using and he remembers an anecdote from around that time connected to this...

"I remember the first time I'd used the digital delay pedal was when I was demonstrating it for Rose Morris, the instrument retailers who specialised in Ovation guitars, at the Olympia in London. I was playing in this booth, nothing too grand and Roy Harper walked in with another chap. I knew Roy, but I didn't really look up at them in any detail. Anyhow this other fellow pointed at the pedal and said 'What's this then?' and I said 'It's a digital delay pedal'. He asked 'What's it do then?' to which I went into demonstration mode. I said 'Oh, it's really great. You click this button here, you see, and you turn this knob to the right for the length of time you want it to delay before it repeats...' and went through all of this explanation of it. Anyway, I looked up then and it was Dave Gilmour! He was winding me up and I took the bait hook line and sinker!"

A couple of relatively low-key pieces, *Storm Brewing* and *Downwind* follow before the closing track *Sleuth*, which was inspired both by Gordon's 'love of the word Sleuth' and also the fact that he had seen the play, which was later filmed starring Michael Caine, and it had made quite an impression on him. He describes it now as a 'finger-buster' to play. Interestingly, it was misspelled on early pressings of the album as 'Slueth'! This closed the original album, though as already stated the later CD reissue added three tracks by the last Giltrap Band incarnation. These tracks are both enjoyable and historically significant, but this may not have been the best way to release them, as their sound is jarring and out of place when put against the album material itself.

In keeping with the history of disappointing Giltrap album covers, it was initially released with a somewhat bizarre, and frankly under whelming, illustration of a green diamond or prism of some kind, resplendent against an oddly brown and orange skyline and horizon. Thankfully this was rectified on future releases of the record when this oddity was replaced in favour of a painting by artist Sue Martin depicting a random arrangement of musical notes spread across a background of musical manuscript paper. To be honest it still isn't one of the best Giltrap cover designs, but it does at least fit the concept of the album better than the original aberration and has gone on to become the generally accepted cover design for future releases. Sales of the record were understandably not in the same league as the albums from *Visionary* through to *Peacock Party* but given the nature of the recording it performed extremely creditably and made enough of an impact to announce the 'return' of Gordon Giltrap while also signposting the direction he would look to take from this point on. New partnerships would however, shortly be afoot...

20
One To One

Following the artistic and relative commercial success of *Elegy* a small tour was put together to promote the album. Gordon was headlining a triple bill with support coming from a duo of Brian and Irene Hume — who had formed two thirds of the band Prelude, most famous for a hit version of Neil Young's *After The Goldrush* in 1973 — and Phil Thornton, who performed a set of new-age-like keyboard material. It was a strong line-up but Gordon, performing solo this time, was the main attraction. The tour went well, though Gordon does remember a run-in he had with one of the other musicians — who shall remain nameless — when he caught the person responsible smoking dope in the dressing room. Always vehemently anti-drugs, Gordon proceeded to tear this unfortunate inhaler off a strip to say the least. As he says now "Oh yes, I really did get very angry over that. I even threatened to leave the tour if it happened again, which in retrospect was rather self-righteous of me I think as it wasn't any hard drugs or anything like that. But I'd been brought up very much with the idea I'd never liked it myself, even the smell of it and I just thought 'I don't need this' and got a bit stroppy!"

The tour carried on, notwithstanding this slight bump in the road and by the end of it Gordon felt more buoyant about his prospects than he had for some time. The audiences had been appreciative and crucially, were not calling out for a band. He was being accepted once again as 'Gordon Giltrap, Guitarist', which was where his heart had always lain in truth.

Following this burst of activity after so long on a virtual hiatus, 1987 continued to see yet more activity as another album appeared most unexpectedly just before the end of the year. Unexpectedly also with regard to its theme as the *A Midnight Clear* album turned out to be a collection of traditional Christmas songs and carols, rearranged for guitar and occasional accompaniment and performed instrumentally. The album came about through Filmtrax by Tim Hollier who floated the idea of the recording to Gordon. The budget for the recording was very small — no more than a few hundred pounds — but Gordon readily accepted as it was something which he relished the idea of having a crack at. He started running through lists of tunes, trying out different arrangements, before settling on a final list of twelve (plus a reprise of the opening *We Three Kings Of Orient Are* to close the album).

He enlisted the help of two old friends in the shape of Bimbo Acock and Ric Sanders to provide accompaniment on a few tracks. There were also some basic sequenced keyboard parts programmed by Gordon himself. Hilary even popped up on parts of the album, playing such diverse instruments as the bodhran and the medieval psaltery! For all this it was a sparsely arranged album in the main with the most effective moments often coming when Gordon's guitar is the primary focus and the inventive rearrangements can be most readily appreciated. Ric Sanders' accompaniment is generally very unobtrusive and sympathetic to the guitar, consisting largely of the violin being plucked rather than bowed. This is more successful than those occasions when Bimbo's flute takes the lead as the brain tends to hone in on the over-familiar melodies to the detriment of the subtleties of the arrangement. A particularly effective inclusion is the slightly lesser heard *Past Three O'clock*, also recorded on their own seasonal albums by Linda Ronstadt and Chris Squire. Based on the traditional tune 'London Waits' it is a fairly popular Christmas piece but not overplayed on the same level as such other entries as *The Holly And The Ivy* or *God Rest Ye Merry Gentlemen* for example and in a way the better for it. Another lovely treatment is that afforded to the almost-title track, *It Came Upon A Midnight Clear*, while the arrangement of *I Saw Three Ships* is particularly well done. Overall, however it remains a lesser entry in the Giltrap discography though it at least comes highly recommended for when themed music is played at Christmas time as the treatment of the pieces does lift it ahead of the regular pack.

Initially only a small run was pressed, although it soon got greater distribution. Once again the cover artwork changed with subsequent releases, with several cover designs adorning it at different times. The original pressing featured a snow scene, but as with *Elegy* before it this was later replaced by a Sue Martin design, this time a line drawing in white on black of a hilly landscape resplendent with traditional Christmas star. Interestingly a later cover featured this image closely replicated, right down to the placement and style of the typeface in the form of an actual photograph, with the same hills but the moon replacing the star of the original drawing. It's an interesting variant but does lose the charm of the starkly portrayed original scene.

The album was fairly successful in its way and remains one that

Gordon is very fond of with good memories of its creation, but more serious meat was going to have to be served for the next course — and so it would be a little over a year later.

As 1988 rolled around Gordon was to celebrate his landmark 40th birthday on 6th April and it was a memorable event. Through Hilary he had developed a profound fascination with the Pre-Raphaelite Brotherhood, a group of painters and poets founded in the mid-1800s by, among others, the artist Rossetti and had begun work on the suite of songs entitled *The Brotherhood* when making the *Elegy* album. He discovered that unbeknownst, he had grown up with a famous Pre-Raphaelite painting entitled *The Light Of The World* by William Holman Hunt, which depicted Christ preparing to knock at an overgrown door and carrying a distinctively ornate lamp. It was actually illustrating a verse from the book of Revelations, Chapter 3:20, in a symbolic way. A reproduction had hung on the wall in his Grandmother's house so he had grown up looking at the image, drawn to it without knowing its significance. He had spoken at length with Hilary about this when he discovered what the work actually was.

On the morning of his birthday, Hilary came into the bedroom carrying a tray covered with a tea towel as if bringing breakfast in bed. Assuming it was a cake although it was quite heavy, Gordon removed the cover to find to his astonishment a beautifully made replica of the lamp from the painting. To this day it sits in his house and also features proudly on the cover of his 2017 album *The Last Of England*. Friend Mick Dolby — a highly skilled metalworker who had a company making replica parts and ornaments from vintage cars — had made the lamp for them. Hilary had got a draughtsman that she knew to produce a scale drawing of the lamp to be used as the template. In fact, Holman Hunt had commissioned an original lamp to be made when he painted the work and apart from that original, the 'Giltrap Lamp' as we may call it, is as far as is known, the only other one in existence.

Gordon was deeply moved by this piece, which he still considers one of the most special gifts he has ever received and it has remained both a treasured memory and an equally treasured possession. The birthday party itself was another highlight as they held it at a venue dear to Gordon's heart: the Warwick Folk Club at the Globe Hotel, which he and Ric had frequented for years, both as performers and as regular attendees as it had a reputation for some of the finest acoustic entertainment in the country. With Ric in attendance among a host of other guests the party was the icing on the proverbial and astonishingly sumptuous cake.

******

During 1988 there were no new releases but Gordon continued a busy gigging schedule. As the year wore on he began to play some duo shows with Ric Sanders again and when their musical chemistry appeared to be coming together very successfully on stage, the idea of recording together began to formulate. Looking back it seems surprising the pair had not recorded much together and certainly not a full collaboration. However, as soon as the idea arose it seemed to be the most obvious thing in the world — after all they enjoyed and respected each other's playing enormously and had been such close friends, cemented when Gordon chose Ric to be his best man. It seemed like a partnership made in heaven and they began to draft ideas for a collaborative album, which appeared in early 1989 as *One To One*. However during the recording and the lengthy tour to promote it, cracks began to emerge in their relationship and after the tour was over the pair would not speak again to rekindle their relationship for some twenty years.

The two men look back on the album now with differing views. Ric regards it as a high point in his career, while Gordon, partly owing to some memories associated with the period, could not even listen to it for quite some time. One thing the pair do agree upon now is that the mix was too unbalanced with Ric's violin much more prominent for the most part than Gordon's guitar. "I love the album", Ric says now, "It has some marvellous material and playing on it and it sounded quite unique in its approach but looking back it could do with a remix, I agree".

The album is made up of thirteen tracks with six each contributed by Gordon and Ric and one slightly surprising cover; the Miles Davis piece *All Blues*, from his landmark album *Kind Of Blue*. Ric again: "That was definitely my idea, I think I had to talk Gordon into that one. It's something quite removed from his repertoire, whereas it is right in the middle of mine. It's odd in a way but despite my having spent decades playing folk-rock in Fairport and absolutely loving it by the way, my heart is still with jazz-fusion playing. I never even imagined myself playing music with vocals — I listen to vocal music of course from the Beatles onward but in terms of playing I always saw myself in the instrumental, jazzy Soft Machine type of role, which in a way was why Gordon's band material appealed to me so much, having that same approach but from a more rock direction. So yes, the Miles piece was from me as I'm a huge fan but I must say that Gordon found a most tremendously inventive way of interpreting the piece on the guitar and I love how it came out".

Elsewhere on the album three of the *Elegy* tracks made a return in the shape of *The Poacher*, *Spring Dance* and *A Christmas Carol*. There was also a rearranged version of *Heartsong* as well as *Roots* and another excerpt from the *Brotherhood* suite entitled *Work*. There are no other musicians appearing on the album and Gordon's playing is entirely acoustic, using a Martin guitar throughout.

From Ric's side came six of his own pieces, including *Portmeirion*.[†] Unique among these pieces was the seven minute-plus *PDC*, which stood for Pretty Damn Cosmic; a title which makes sense when one listens to the astonishing 'violin orchestra' created in real time through the utilisation of an array of effects, including delay, echo and reverb. Similar in approach if not execution to Gordon's own *Dodo's Dream* live showcase, it was described by Gordon as being — especially when executed live — "like Ric becoming a one-man Pink Floyd." Ric laughs at this description offering the rejoinder "Well, I've never been a particular fan of the Floyd but if you made it a 'one-man violin Jimi Hendrix' then I'd certainly take that comment!"

As stated there was some dissatisfaction on Gordon's part around the mixing of the album as he even recalls today an occasion when engineer Paul White jokingly remarked to him, "The guitar is just a bed for the violin really, isn't it?" However, as he says, there are always two sides to a story and he does accept the fault for not speaking out more vociferously at the time. As he says now "I think that it's a natural thing for any violin player to want to be mixed loud, because it is naturally a top-line instrument. The violin will tend to carry the melody and fiddle players don't tend to go out on their own to perform so much so they are used to playing on top of a band arrangement." Nevertheless, he does remember the atmosphere growing slightly strained.

The problems really intensified when a tour was booked to promote the record consisting of a gruelling forty UK dates on an almost daily schedule. As Gordon says now, "I'd defy any group of musicians not to feel the strain when placed in that sort of intense bubble for so long. It creates an artificial environment where every little irritation or disagreement begins to grate and become magnified. When we finished the tour we went our separate ways and sadly did not reconnect until a few years ago". For his part Ric does not remember these problems being so noticeable but he does freely admit that he was going through

---

[†] Named after the Welsh coastal village most famously used as the setting for the 1960s TV series *The Prisoner* starring Patrick McGoohan as the eponymous prisoner in 'The Village' — a track which has been performed many times over the years by Sanders with Fairport Convention to great success.

Portmeirion village was built and designed by British architect Sir Clough William-Ellis with work starting in 1925. Stylised on an Italian Mediterranean fishing village it has transcended that stated intention and is a tourist draw for a huge amount of people each year. Episodes of other TV shows such as *Doctor Who*, *Danger Man* and *Citizen Smith* have been filmed there and Noël Coward wrote *Blithe Spirit* while staying in the village.

some personal issues, which affected his demeanour and behaviour. It may well have been the unfortunate timing of when they were forced into such close proximity that led to their estrangement. Once again, Gordon accepts his own part in this admitting "I could have argued with the agent about so many dates being added and I think looking back I probably should have. It was too much and too much time away from home, but I went along with it. I went along for the quiet life in a way, taking the easiest path, regarding both the album mixing and the tour and that was probably a mistake. It wasn't the easiest time to spend a lot of time together with Ric as he will admit and it could have been avoided".

Away from that however, both men remember some tremendous shows with Gordon stating that while the album holds some negative memories for him, he looks back on the best of the gigs as being quite exceptional. "When we were on form, we were something special together", he enthuses. "The problems were away from that and something that I regret very much".

Happily the pair had a full reconciliation some two decades later when Gordon called Ric on the phone believing that it had just been far too long. Ric concurs with this absolutely: "Oh, me too! I was over the moon when he called me. I'd sent messages to him, passing my love to him via friends but to finally reconnect was wonderful. We met up in a cafe in Birmingham and honestly it was as if we'd spoken just the day before, never mind twenty years! I'll always consider us to be very close friends and I still nurture an ambition to play *Heartsong* with him on stage one more time someday! I still remember all of that stuff, because that's the thing about Gordon's material — it's very melodic and very memorable."

The album appeared on the Marco Polo label, which was set up by the pair's then-agent Mark Ringwood specifically for the album. When first released it featured a photograph of Portmeirion, which was actually taken by Fairport Convention bass player Dave Pegg. With Ric's piece of the same name appearing on the record, this cover image was a perfect fit.

As had been the case with the previous two Giltrap releases however a re-release of the album was accompanied by a change of cover design — in this case a radical one! The CD release on Terra Nova records ten years later had a new cover, which has become the more familiar one and it is truly bizarre. Described memorably by Ric Sanders as "A sort of cartoon version of *Game Of Thrones* after a session on the magic mushrooms" the picture depicted a kind of abstract seascape with the foreground taken up by a yellow-coloured giant carrying a small man on his shoulders while the rear cover has a gypsy-looking woman leaning out of a window in a tower clutching what looks like a rose and watching a fleet of ships sail away. The intention of the pictures or relevance to the record is difficult to define. While Gordon says that he doesn't mind the cover, Ric is more outspoken about it, expressing a hope that if the album is reissued again then perhaps the original Portmeirion design can be reinstated.

The album sold well as indeed did the tour promoting it with most of the shows being sell-outs ("Ric brought the Fairport crowd while I brought in my audience, so we couldn't lose in a way") and the album was sold at the gigs, boosting its sales considerably. Although the period is remembered somewhat differently by the two men, the ultimate outcome was a happy one and perhaps the last word should go to Ric, who wrote the following in the Fairport Convention Cropredy Festival Programme for 2017, remembering an appearance by the pair at that very festival around this time: "Now, speaking of great guitar players the only time I've ever done a whole set at Cropredy as part of a different act (rather than just being a guest) was way back in 1987 when I had a duo with Gordon Giltrap. We recorded an album called *One To One*, which is one of my favourite things I've ever done. Great cover photo of Portmeirion too, taken by Peggy... Gordon has, amongst other things, always embraced an orchestral approach to music and he writes such lovely tunes. He can rock too! I was so happy to have the opportunity to play again [on Gordon's 2017 album *The Last Of England*] with my old friend."

From Gordon's point of view after the *One To One* tour finished, with his relationship with his old friend soured for so long, he had no intention of playing in collaboration with anyone else for some considerable time. The experience had left him afraid to do so in case it led to rancour developing again, but as it happened, another 'star' collaboration was exactly what he was going to get, sooner rather than later...

21
The Price Of Experience

As part of the lengthy and somewhat arduous *One To One* tour Gordon and Ric found themselves performing in the relatively remote outpost of Ayr on the West Coast of Scotland, a little way down the coast from Troon — home of the famous golf course. Not exactly a much-travelled point of call for visiting rock bands nevertheless the Giltrap/Sanders caravan wound its weary way there. The show itself is lost to time and fading memory in terms of anything musically notable but it was to prove the catalyst for another partnership that Gordon found himself, against his prior instincts, drawn into. Ayr was, among other things, home to noted jazz guitarist Martin Taylor who played alongside the great violinist Stéphane Grappelli. Taylor attended the show and afterward Gordon and Ric spent some time with him drinking and chatting.

Not giving it another thought after this seemingly inconsequential if convivial evening, Gordon was surprised when some weeks after the tour had wound to its conclusion he received a call from Taylor suggesting a possible collaboration. Flattered to a degree and certainly taken aback at the idea, Gordon was initially quite reticent so soon after the somewhat upsetting end to his collaboration with Ric. He was also rather dubious as to why Martin with his jazz background should want to attempt a pairing with someone seemingly musically disparate, shared instrument notwithstanding. Assurances from Taylor that he believed it could work, by virtue of him having a high regard for Gordon's work and also their shared appreciation of Celtic music, left him musing over the possibility. He went to see Martin play at none other than the Birmingham Guitar Club, which persuaded him.

They recorded an album, which appeared in late 1991 under the title *A Matter Of Time*. Still highly regarded the album saw the pair tackle a selection of tracks written by each of them along the lines of the *One To One* template. Experimenting with the technology of guitar synthesisers, albeit quite subtly, the album is a deserved addition to Gordon's catalogue and he went on to perform some of his selections from it in his solo repertoire. The pair went on to tour successfully and even appeared on the BBC's *Pebble Mill At One* TV show in January 1992, performing the track *Collins' Meadow* to excellent effect — Gordon if anything taking slightly more of the lead in impressive form.

During 1992 the pair even took a trip to Ghana to play although this ended in disaster when Gordon ill advisedly drank water from a bottle in a hotel fridge, assuming it was safe. This sadly was not the case and the ensuing bout of dysentery cut short the tour and forced him to return home, thus missing a further leg of planned shows in Cameroon.

A more successful venture came with Gordon becoming involved as a partner in a video filming company called Starnite, which put out a series of hour-long music instructional videos. Gordon did the first one, *Giltrap On Guitar* with Martin then doing one on jazz guitar. From there Gordon recruited friends and associates to do more of these, including Steve Howe, Danny Thompson and even Rod Argent on keyboards and composition. Sadly the company folded in the end as this series of videos was their only real success with their planned corporate work never really getting off the ground.

Bizarrely with plans for further recordings by 'G & T' — as the Giltrap/Taylor partnership was known — not only mooted but also in demand from their audience, Martin took the somewhat artistically questionable decision to abort the partnership, claiming that they had gone as far as they could. A strange call to be sure but nevertheless the short-lived if quite exciting collaboration was no more and this time Gordon would stick to his instincts as regards entering into a 'muso' partnership. It would be some time before he elected to step out of his solo world again in such a way.

During 1992 he was certainly anything but idle with further recordings appearing. In the summer he appeared at the Warwick Folk Festival at which he played a set of quite notable intensity, spurred on by — as he admits — the presence of someone there to whom he felt he "had a point to prove". Unbeknownst to him the performance had been recorded by producer Graham Bradshaw. Indeed the first he heard of it was when he received a phone call from Bradshaw suggesting that they could perhaps put it out as an album. It appeared soon afterwards on Music Maker Records, which was affiliated with Music Maker Publications who published *Guitarist* magazine among others. The album is an impressive listen, as what it may lose in precision it more than makes up for in attitude and excitement. The adrenaline and pent-up anger of the performance is almost tangible, particularly during the delivery of *Lucifer's Cage* as Gordon tears through what may well be the quintessential recorded version of the piece. Interestingly, it was this album that first brought Gordon's playing to the attention of Ritchie Blackmore who went on to be a self-confessed admirer of his technique.

There were two other recordings put out during this hectic year. The first being a low-key cassette only release of the Birmingham Youth Orchestra performing an orchestral arrangement of Gordon's composition *The Eye Of The Wind*, written as we have seen way back around the time of *Perilous Journey*, but having lain dormant for years. Previously only attempted live in unsuccessful fashion during Gordon's troubled period in the early 1980s this version was recorded at a showcase concert at Birmingham Town Hall; Gordon played a short set beforehand but the main piece which makes up the cassette release was performed by the orchestra only.

The other recording to come out that year under Gordon's name was *The Solo Album*, a strange hybrid of compilation and new recording. The album came about from an idea Gordon had to revisit many of the tracks he had put out on previous albums with arrangements for other instruments but to perform them stripped right back and played unaccompanied to bring out the flavour of the original compositions, which had of course been done on the acoustic guitar. Booking himself into Workshop studios in Redditch he recorded the 19 tracks in sessions he describes as "quite difficult" as many of the pieces were quite challenging to perform solo in real time. When the album came out it was, like *A Matter Of Time* before it, on Prestige Records, whom Gordon had encountered through A&R man Keith Thomas, and who had reissued some of his earlier albums on two-on-one CDs not too long previously. Obviously by definition of containing no new material it was a relatively minor entry in the Giltrap catalogue but it is an interesting one, showcasing as it does the bare bones of the compositions. Adorning the front cover was another Sue Martin illustration, depicting a sort of collage of three pictures of Gordon performing, arranged in such a way that two of the 'Giltraps' as it were almost appear to be looking over the shoulder of the third in the centre. A striking illustration to be sure, if somewhat ironic in its depiction of three men on the cover of a definitively 'solo' recording!

******

There was one more project commenced in that busy year of 1992 but this time it was far removed from his usual field — this time it was a pen he chose to wield rather than his guitar as he began research with a view to writing a book about Hofner guitars. He had always had an affinity with Hofner instruments right back to that very first Hofner Verithin that he owned in his teenage years. By this time it was possible to pick up Hofner guitars for very reasonable money as they were far from in vogue and were viewed as more of a nostalgia piece than a cutting edge instrument. "I always loved Hofner guitars, they made some absolutely beautiful models and at that point they were fairly inexpensive to buy, considering the quality. I remember I actually bought one at a shop near Liverpool after I'd done a gig up there. It cost me about £250 for this beautiful Hofner Committee in Bird's-Eye Maple. I started looking around to see where I could get information about them and there was just nothing out there. After thinking that someone should write a book I turned to the idea that it might be down to me! So I started buying up all these guitars — all for the right kind of money — and I had the idea of interviewing other guitarists about their experiences and knowledge of Hofners. I had a head start because I knew such a lot of these people and I thought that they might be willing to open up to me about it as a fellow guitarist. I spoke to a lot of people in person like Hank Marvin, Joe Brown and Roy Wood. I managed to get interviews over the phone with the likes of Ritchie Blackmore, Justin Hayward and David Gilmour. In fact, I remember getting back home from the supermarket one afternoon and the phone rang as we walked in and it was Gilmour, saying 'Hi Gordon, I believe you wanted to talk about these Hofner guitars' to which I replied 'Oh yeah, just let me put the shopping away', which I did and he was still on the phone! All I had was a cassette recorder and this suction pad thing that you stuck onto the receiver. I did Paul McCartney as well but that wasn't direct — in that case I sent him the questions and he sent the answers back on tape. Hilary diligently transcribed all of the interviews for me, and my co-author Neville Marten — who was editor of *Guitar* magazine — then edited it all into something very readable".

When the book eventually appeared the following year it was published by International Music Publications as a 100-page hardback and titled *The Hofner Guitar: A History*. Out of print for a long time and with used copies sometimes fetching very high prices, the book was re-published 20 years later in an expanded form with an extra section — written by guitar expert Paul Day — covering the newer post-1993 Hofner models, by the Hal Leonard publishing group. A major selling point was its lavish selection of photographs as Gordon recalls. "When it came time for the pictures a photographer friend, Neil Cope came round to my house to photograph all these guitars. I remember for props we had the beautiful lamp from my 40th birthday and also a plaster Buddha which Martin Taylor had given me — he was a Buddhist and I must admit I was very interested in the whole Buddhism thing at the time, I found it fascinating. So we had the lamp and the Buddha with the guitars around them and it really worked as a sort of home-made studio. David Gilmour gave me a couple of photos that had never been published including one with his first band in Cambridge where he was playing a Hofner Club 60. We reproduced some pages from the old catalogues with these wonderful guitars in there and the whole book really was chock full of nostalgia. To this day, it still is widely regarded as the 'go-to book' about Hofners, and it was pretty much single-handedly responsible for putting the price of Hofners up as it raised their profile and reminded people of how good they actually were. I admit to benefiting from that myself when times got a little harder and I had to sell many of those guitars. I loved doing the book though and I'm very proud of it still".

Writing the book took up much of the latter half of 1992 rounding out a very busy year — more so than people might imagine given that there were no 'major' new albums released in the period. One unexpected knock-on effect from the book was from the interviews, which Gordon says he had enjoyed enormously in terms of talking to these people about their guitars, which was the main love they all had in common. On the back of this he was approached later by *Guitarist* magazine to conduct a semi-regular series of 'celebrity interviews' for them wherein he would talk to various players about their favourite guitars and their guitar collections for inclusion in the magazine.

So while it might have appeared that the abrupt ending of that promising partnership might have ushered in a period of inactivity quite the reverse happened. Before long however, much bigger projects would come into Gordon's life, giving his career another timely and welcome boost.

22
In Unison

Much of the first half of 1993 was taken up with the execution of an idea which had come to Gordon during a conversation with his agent about *Heartsong* and the fact that it was fifteen years since the original recording. As he puts it now, "a light went on" in his head and he began to think of a way to commemorate the anniversary. The plan was to record a new, 'all-star' version of the piece with a selection of guest musicians from his circle of friends and acquaintances. Once the idea had taken root he began getting in touch with people and soon had an enviable cast lined up who had agreed to appear on the track — Brian May, Steve Howe, Rick Wakeman, Midge Ure and Neil Murray were all pencilled in.

The way the piece was approached was to keep Simon Phillips' drums and Gordon's original guitar as a baseline, along with Eddy Spence's iconic keyboard solo (though the rest of the keyboards would be redone). There were early experiments with a new drum track but none of these worked anything like as well as the great Phillips original. As luck would have it Gordon was in possession of the original two-inch master tapes. A year or two earlier he had received a call from Jon Miller informing him that they had been given notice to leave Redan Studios where all of the Giltrap masters from the Triumvirate period were stored and that everything unclaimed would have to be thrown away owing to a lack of storage space. Gordon unsurprisingly drove straight down there and rescued all of his master tapes which he still retains to this day. Keeping only certain tracks of the original would have otherwise been impossible.

The recording took place in Workshop Studios where *A Matter Of Time* had been recorded. A tiny little studio located in the basement of what used to be a needle factory in Redditch about 15 miles south of Birmingham. It was so small that it didn't even have a toilet on the premises. As Gordon recalls if you wanted to answer a call of nature you had to go down to another unit in the development and use theirs!

Nonetheless it had a good reputation acoustically and the owner, the late Dave Morris was regarded as an excellent engineer. The first recording session was on 7th April for Midge Ure, who Gordon remembers turning up at his house in his old mini for the drive down to the studio. After that came bassist Neil Murray — formerly with Whitesnake and Colosseum II among others — on 30th April. Then the following week on 6th May came Rick Wakeman who put down new piano parts replacing the original keyboards either side of the Eddy Spence solo. On 18th May came Steve Howe of Yes, who drove up from Devon before the biggest recording day of all on 29th July when Brian May came to record his guitar parts.

Throughout the recording, Gordon took a deliberately 'hands-off' approach, preferring to let the musicians do their own thing without his input. As a result he remembers not engaging with some of them as much as perhaps he might have done. However the Brian May visit was something else entirely as it had a whole different feel to the other sessions, as everyone was struck by how high profile he was. His guitar and two Vox AC30 amps arrived first before he did, delivered by his then roadie. This guitar was of course his famous 'Red Special', which he made with his father when he was a teenager out of the wood from an old fireplace and which he always played with the milled edge of an old pre-decimal sixpence to get his signature sound (the Royal Mint used to actually mint a small amount of copies of the coin specifically for him to use, which underlines his standing as a musician quite starkly).

As Gordon regales, "I remember thinking I'd better lay some food on for him and I knew he was a vegetarian so I got all of this vegetarian food, but as it turned out he wasn't hungry and didn't touch a thing! I'd already gone to the studio and he turned up at the house in his chauffeur-driven limo, so Hilary came down to the studio in it with him. I remember him coming down the stairs and walking up to Dave Morris saying 'Hi, I'm Brian'. Of course we all knew who he was, that goes without saying, but that was just the way he was. He's a genuinely humble sort of guy and it was lovely really although of course he must have known that he was one of the most famous guitarists in the world. Such a nice chap, he gave us a couple of his sixpences in little presentation cases. The thrill of being able to hold that guitar was so exciting for me although I didn't play it. That's one of my things, actually — I won't play someone else's guitar because I find it a little disrespectful. I don't really like it when people ask to play mine, because it's a very personal thing for a guitarist, it sort of has your DNA in it. I once got to hold Hank Marvin's original Stratocaster that he used on those early Shadows tracks and believe me there's no way I'd have tried to play that, I was in awe just holding it. So yes, that session with Brian really was the icing on the cake, an amazing day".

Quite bafflingly considering the array of talent on the recording, there was actually very little interest from any record companies to release it and it would be some two years until it finally saw the light of day on an album. This is all the more surprising when a listen reveals it to be of excellent quality. With 'all-star' projects such as these there can be a tendency for a 'too many cooks spoil the broth' situation with everyone jostling for position and the music being swamped. But in this case it works extremely well with everyone clearly respecting the piece and egos happily not clouding the issue. It will never be the definitive version, or threaten to take over from the original *Perilous Journey* recording but it does its job as a very entertaining and credible alternative arrangement and period piece, capturing as it does a moment in time for an array of great musicians.

In a connection to this recording, 1993 also saw Gordon taking part in Midge Ure's solo tour, away from the Ultravox banner, called the Out Alone Tour. He and Gordon had written a song together called *Feel So Good*, which eventually came out on a compilation of unreleased Midge Ure tracks called *Little Orphans* in 2001. Gordon would join him on stage each night to perform the song. There was another unlikely pairing that year when he played guitar on a session with guitarist Jan Cyrka. Heralded as a massive new talent and even referred to as 'The English Steve Vai' in some quarters, Cyrka released an album of soaring instrumental progressive rock entitled *Spirit* that year for which Gordon contributed guitar on a track called *After School*, with the pair having become friends at the time. A somewhat unsung and undeniably atypical Giltrap session it is by the same token arguably among the finest pieces he has guested on.

Away from the studio there was a tour of Germany with the legendary guitarist Albert Lee and his band Hogan's Heroes which in effect Gordon undertook for nothing. He describes the tour as "rather a waste of time, sadly" and he was astonished to see some audiences as low as around 15 people. Lee was, like Gordon to an extent, a 'guitarist's guitarist', with luminaries such as Steve Howe, Ritchie Blackmore and Eric Clapton (with whom he worked) all being avowed admirers, but a reputation among one's peers — no matter how heavy those peers' names might be — does not necessarily translate into public profile and audience numbers as was demonstrated at some of those shows. Gordon does remember that in some cases, however, Lee would not do himself any favours as to audience perception...

"The thing about Albert was that he just saw himself as a jobbing musician and he really undervalued himself. To me, he's still one of the finest electric guitar players I've ever seen but after a show finished he wouldn't even go off stage. He'd just get a carrier bag full of T-shirts and CDs and start selling them off the front of the stage! I remember saying to him one time 'Albert, you shouldn't be doing this! You're Albert Lee, you shouldn't be seen to be selling your own stuff like that from a carrier bag!' — but that's just how he was. He'd be lugging his own gear in and all that kind of thing. It didn't help in terms of his image, I'm quite sure — but then again, listen to me saying it, I've been guilty of the same sort of thing on more occasions than I can count. I didn't like to see Albert doing that though, it wasn't right."

In terms of a personal experience the tour was very memorable. Albert was a mine of entertaining anecdotes, not least about Eric Clapton, with whom he had worked in the '70s and early '80s. He related that on the one hand Clapton was, during his 'heroin phase', very clearly in trouble with his addiction, reportedly not cleaning his teeth for years for example, but by the same token he never lost his humorous and generous spirit. One story he told was that when Eric had shaved his beard off everyone in the studio said how much they preferred him with it so he cut some carpet into the shape of a beard and stuck it on his face, to howls of laughter. Also on a more personal front, Albert remembered telling Eric one day about how he had a treasured Gibson Les Paul 'Black Beauty' guitar stolen from him and how he missed it so much, only for Eric to say "wait a minute" and walk out of the room, then return with an identical model Black Beauty guitar of his own, hand it to Albert and say "here, it's yours". Such stories would understandably stay with Gordon, as would the experience of playing with someone he respected and admired so deeply as Albert Lee but from a commercial and career viewpoint it was, as he put it, a waste of time. He made no money and no work arose from it either. His agent at the time had suggested to him that some overseas work might come from it, but it wasn't to be.

******

Playing and recording wasn't the only thing Gordon managed to turn his hand to during 1993 as he also found time to be heavily involved in the design of a revolutionary new guitar string. He had been using strings made by the company Albion Strings based in Derby, which had been bought by Malcolm Newton. Talking to Malcolm one day Gordon happened to ask the question as to whether there was a reason why a guitar string could not be made with a round core. As a general rule guitar strings are made by wrapping around a hexagonal core so that they grip when they are wound on. It had occurred to Gordon that if a round core could be used then it would be possible to get a greater range of gauges (that is, the thickness or heaviness of the strings) — a thinner core with a thicker wrap or vice versa for example. Malcolm took this suggestion on board and went away to have a try. As Gordon tells it, "He came back and said he'd done it and that he'd send me some samples. The way he managed this was to flatten the last six to eight inches of the string so that it would grip when you wound it on and when I tried them they were absolutely stunning. They had a beautiful tone and they also lasted longer than regular strings. I got back to him and told him 'This is the one. It's superb'."

At that point Malcolm changed the company name to 'Newtone Strings' as a play on words with his surname and a reference to the new design. From that day on all of the strings from the company have been made to that design. "Malcolm, bless his heart, was a lovely guy but I don't think he has ever given me enough credit for that to be honest and not many people to this day are aware that I came up with the design. To be fair to him he did pay me a royalty but they weren't expensive strings and it was so small that I just told him to plough it back into the company as long as he supplied me with free strings, which he did. I was designing the string packets for some time as well, doing drawings for them; I was very much an amateur artist but it was something I enjoyed doing. I did spread the word around about them and largely because of that people like Ralph McTell, Ritchie Blackmore and Joe Brown began using them. Eventually I had to stop using them all the time as he couldn't keep up with the amount I needed. He was an individual manufacturer, not a mass production operation and if I was going on a tour and needed 30 or 40 sets of strings, he'd only be able to offer me about six. I was approached by Picato shortly afterwards, with a view to doing a 'Giltrap Signature String' for them. I passed that over to Malcolm but nothing came of it. It was very difficult with him being a one-man operation, but I did feel a loyalty to him — and I loved the strings".

Some time after this matters did take an enforced change as Rotosound approached Gordon with an offer to use their strings in return for some widespread publicity — which they did deliver on, with Gordon appearing on posters and in trade advertisements. He still wanted to use Malcolm's strings as he liked them so much but he clearly had to be publicly seen to be using Rotosound to fulfil their agreement. He did go on using the Newtone strings but he feels strongly that something of a barrier had been driven between them and things wouldn't be quite the same again. In fact after a while when he left the Rotosound deal he went back to Malcolm and said he wanted to use the strings full-time again but offered to pay for them. Therefore, for a while, Gordon was paying for his own strings that he had designed with his own picture on the packet! After all that had happened he still felt strongly that he should support the business and in fact even financed some Newtone Strings posters designed by Sue Martin, which he gave to Malcolm as a gift.

With this fascinating yet ultimately less than lucrative venture behind him, along with the equally austere Albert Lee tour, it was clearly time for Gordon's career to ramp up a notch in terms of profile and importantly, income. There would be opportunities in both of these areas coming along over the course of the next few, highly significant, years...

23
A Hint Of Blue

One of the first opportunities to come Gordon's way in 1994 was a support slot on a UK tour by ELO Part II, the band made up partially of ex-members of The Electric Light Orchestra but without that outfit's leader and frontman Jeff Lynne. By the time this tour came about the band had recorded their second album *Moment Of Truth* and counted ELO alumni Bev Bevan (drums), Kelly Groucutt (vocals and bass) and Mik Kaminski (violin) among its members. Guitar and vocals were handled by a very talented singer Phil Bates who had interestingly enough been a member of a band called Trickster which had supported ELO on their mammoth *Out Of The Blue* tour in 1978. With keyboard duties being handled by American musician Eric Troyer, the band were achieving some considerable level of success considering the unavoidable Jeff Lynne-shaped hole in their existence and the UK tour was a success.

Gordon bonded in particular with Phil Bates with whom he became very friendly. During his support set he would invite Bates onstage where they would perform a blues number together. Despite the enjoyable nature of the tour and the exposure it provided there were significant elements of dissatisfaction behind the scenes, among which was the insistence of the band's American manager that Gordon had to suffer the ignominy of auditioning for the support slot. "I had to go along to meet him in a hotel in Solihull, and he said 'Okay, let's hear what you've got'. So I went into *A Dublin Day* and after a while he stopped me and said 'Okay, okay, that'll do. You've got the gig'. It was ridiculous — I realise that he didn't know who I was but someone should have told him that I had a bit more of a profile than having to audition for an unpaid support slot".

Therein lies another factor — namely that Gordon received no pay whatsoever for the tour — but worse than that was that he didn't even have his name on the posters or publicity material. Not only was there no financial reward but he had to pay for his own food from the caterers and relied on them giving him a discount, which seems a bizarre state of affairs. Understandably he felt that this was a slightly disrespectful way for him to be treated as an established and successful artist in his own right. "I don't know why they did that", he says now. "It might not have been many but I might have attracted a few people along. Certainly there were a lot of people who were visibly surprised when I came on and I was told later by a number of audience members that they were extremely surprised at the fact that I was playing unannounced. In fact, some even said they didn't even stay for all of ELO's set because they enjoyed mine so much — which may sound egotistical but I can only go on what they said! Certainly there used to be a cheer most nights when I was announced onto the stage so that side of it was great. I was just left quite disappointed that someone in the band didn't put their hand up and say that I should be on the poster at least. But still, it's water under the bridge now and the audience reactions made it very rewarding; plus the fact that we sold a lot of CDs at the shows, particularly the *On A Summer's Night* album, so I made something in that regard".

******

Gordon was also carrying out the interviews for *Guitarist* magazine with various celebrity musicians and one such conversation was with Cliff Richard. It was the first time he had spoken to Cliff since the 1970s. Indeed this was the occasion when Gordon gave him the beautiful Fylde guitar he had used on *Heartsong*. He had loaned it to him in the late '70s when Cliff was doing a stint at the Palladium and on the occasion of their meeting this time around he was again waxing lyrical about the exquisite Tree Of Life fretboard inlay and Gordon decided to present it to him. This meeting was significant not only for the fact that it rekindled their friendship again after a gap of so many years but it also planted a seed in Cliff's mind which led to a very important working collaboration.

Also during 1994 came Gordon's latest foray into the charitable world with his involvement as a patron in the Tracy Sollis Leukaemia Trust, an organisation with which he is still connected with to this day. Tracy was a schoolgirl from Evesham who was diagnosed with acute myeloid leukaemia in 1993 at the age of just 15. Gordon and Hilary got to know Tracy and were extremely fond of her, doing everything they could to help her and the Trust set up in her name. They were devastated when having undergone a failed bone marrow transplant she tragically lost her battle in February 1995. Even today Gordon finds it difficult to talk about her passing but takes enormous pride in the amount of good that has been done over the years by the Trust, which is her legacy to the world. His 1998 album *Troubadour* would later see a track dedicated to her memory.

Despite his aversion to collaborations following his prior experiences there was one such partnership in 1994, albeit short-lived and fairly low-key, when Gordon formed a duo with acoustic guitarist and singer Kevin Dempsey. While not a high-profile name in his own regard, Kevin had recently been in a band named Whippersnapper along with the great violinist Dave Swarbrick and also multi-instrumentalist Chris Leslie, a long-term member of the current Fairport Convention, who released five albums between 1985 and 1993. Some time earlier than this going back to the early 1970s, Dempsey and another Whippersnapper band mate Martin Jenkins had been in the 'psychedelic progressive folk' band Dando Shaft who are still celebrated as influential in cult circles today, despite none of their four albums causing more than a ripple in terms of sales and contemporary recognition. The Giltrap-Dempsey duo was a successful one musically with Gordon still speaking fondly about the time, and one which came with somewhat less 'baggage' than his higher profile partnerships. But while this made for an enjoyable and diverting time and some excellent shows, it gently fizzled out without any recordings taking place.

******

Away from the performing arena, one avenue which Gordon branched out into in 1994 was that he became involved in a music shop in Knowle, near Solihull, with his friend Neil Cope. Neil had got the offer of some space at the back of an existing music shop and asked Gordon whether he would be interested in going into the venture with him. Gordon immediately agreed, "It was an absolutely tiny space, just about big enough to put some guitars on a rack and that was it but I was really interested in giving this a go. I had a lot of guitars I wanted to sell, so when we first opened the shop it was just stocked with all of my old guitars! The shop was called Giltrap & Cope. Bert Weedon actually came up to perform the opening ceremony, which was great. It did quite well, actually — people I knew used to drop in and it all helped give the place a bit of a buzz. I got very hands-on with it I have to say; I used to go down there every day, I'd help out serving people and it was great fun, I loved it. People would sometimes come down to see if I was there and it definitely helped in getting the business built up. Neil eventually took over the whole shop and moved out of that back room and he was doing very well. He later moved to another shop, different premises, but eventually like a lot of smaller shops with the advent of the Internet and things like that the business dried up and he closed down. But it was great while it lasted and I'm really glad I did it".

As 1995 dawned another short set of dates with ELO II led into a few sporadic projects. There was an involvement with Stuart Ward who was responsible for developing the line of Award Session amplifiers with a new amp. Then there was a performance of the still-embryonic Brotherhood Suite with the Nottinghamshire Education String Orchestra at the Albert Hall, Nottingham. This latter show was recorded and put out to the public but only as a limited cassette-only release of some 300 copies. He also purchased a Taylor guitar, partly in a bid to get involved with an influential label called Acoustic Music Records, who were aligned with Taylor Guitars. Everyone who released an album on the label would play a Taylor and it was hoped that this would lead to some American exposure among other things. Managing to get a good deal, Gordon picked up a top of the range Taylor instrument, which he describes as "expensive at over £2,000, but then again it was about four and a half grand's worth of guitar, it was that good". Sadly, the involvement with the label and hence the US profile boost never came to fruition but at least a nice guitar had come of it!

There was an appearance on *Children In Need* which saw Gordon playing in the foyer of Broadcasting House, an interesting diversion if nothing else and a TV appearance, which is never wasted. It was also around this time that Gordon met Tony Iommi of Black Sabbath for the first time in very interesting circumstances. "Tony lived quite near to me", he remembers, "and I used to bump into him from time to time; he used a gym in Knowle near to the music shop for instance. I had the idea at the time that Sabbath, or at least Tony himself could do an incredible version of *Lucifer's Cage* so I approached him with the idea. Sadly, it never happened but we ended up becoming friends". Certainly the idea of a Black Sabbath metal assault on the *sturm und drang* of *Lucifer's Cage* is one to have the fans salivating so it is indeed a great shame that nothing ever came of this. The friendship between the two men continued to blossom however, as Gordon goes on to explain, "The thing was that, out of the whole 'Brummie' lot, the clique of musicians based around there at the time. Tony was the only one who really invited me in as you might say. I tried making overtures to some of the other musicians around there — including Bev Bevan, who I used to see in the local shops — about maybe working on some projects with them, but there was no interest. With Bev I actually think he was quite a shy character and he was most probably just naturally reserved — maybe I even seemed a bit pushy, I don't know. But Tony was great and there was some talk with his then manager Ralph Baker about Tony making an acoustic album. Black Sabbath were at quite a low point at the time and the thing about Tony that many people don't realise is that he has composed some beautiful acoustic pieces for Sabbath; he really is a man of taste. He owned a Taylor guitar as well! I remember him playing his piece *Laguna Sunrise* [from *Black Sabbath Vol 4*] for me and it was superb, really evocative. Ralph thought the time was right for Tony to branch out and do something different and he told him he thought he should team up with me as I could advise him about his acoustic playing and really bring out the best in him. Sadly it never happened in the end although I was certainly keen on the idea. I remember turning up at his house one day with a load of guitars and some ideas for us to have a try at working on them but he was out — I think he'd gone to the gym — so I just came home. I asked Ralph about it and it really surprised me when he said Tony was a little bit intimidated in a way by the idea and even by me. He said it just 'wasn't him' and he felt as if it was something he didn't fit with. I can understand how he felt because if I had been asked to plug in a Les Paul to a big stack and play some Sabbath material with him I'd feel like a total beginner. I'd have to start from scratch almost and I think I really would feel as if I was an imposter in his world, so I can see how he might have seen it, but it's a shame because it could have been really good; and I liked Tony. I haven't seen him for years now but he has always struck me as a really nice chap, honest and without any side to him. But it wasn't to be".

******

There was one other major undertaking before 1995 was out with Gordon's next album release, *Music For The Small Screen*. A sort of 'half and half' album straddling the line between being a new release and a grab-bag of previously issued material. It consisted in the main of pieces that Gordon had written for television shows. We have already seen that he had moved more and more into that area in the previous decade or so, yet only a small number of those compositions had seen the light of day on his albums. This was mainly because, with the instrumentation often being quite a full arrangement, they would not have fitted stylistically onto acoustic works such as *Elegy*. Much of this stuff was of great merit however and as such formed an extremely successful and coherent album when collated together.

The album opened with the first ever public airing of the 1993 all-star *Heartsong* recording, which was right at home on the disc as, even though it did not have the direct small screen link in itself, it was of course a reworking of Gordon's most popular and recognisable TV theme of all. It surely must have come as quite the surprise to fans who bought the record being previously unaware of this new interpretation, and the quality of the personnel taking part.

The following track *The Last Of England* was used in the previously mentioned Adrian Shergold drama *Will You Love Me Tomorrow*, concerning the infamous child killer Mary Bell. This edgy play also featured Gordon in a somewhat bizarre cameo role as a guitar-strumming newspaper seller! Forming part of the *Brotherhood* suite, this is a superbly evocative version with acoustic and electric guitars coming together with expansive keyboard textures to create a memorable piece of music. Also appearing elsewhere in Gordon's repertoire is *Shady Tales*, included here as it was planned to be used in a comedy/drama series of the same name featuring Adam Faith, in a role not dissimilar to his classic early '70s show *Budgie*. Unfortunately the piece remained unused owing to a change in the programme format. The show did emerge briefly on Thames Television but was shown late at night in short episodes and sank quickly without leaving so much as a ripple. One piece that was used was *The Lord's Seat* written for a BBC documentary about the working aristocracy entitled *Working Titles*. Reportedly a favourite of Ritchie Blackmore, the track was written in a deliberately Renaissance style and utilises a 'baby' guitar made by Rob Armstrong, which possesses an unmistakeably lute-like quality which emphasises that 'early music' style extremely effectively.

The association between *Heartsong* and the BBC *Holiday* programme is very widely known and remembered but what is perhaps often overlooked is that this was not the only theme music which Gordon provided for the show. After *Heartsong* was retired from the programme credits a piece of library music was used for a year. Gordon had presented them with a new piece entitled *Holiday Romance*, which appears on the next album. It hasn't retained the link or resonance with the show that its illustrious predecessor did but this is something of a shame as it is an excellent composition on its own terms and conjures up the 'summer holiday' spirit just as well, if not, as some might argue, even better than *Heartsong* — which was, lest we forget, not originally composed with that idea in mind. The appearance here of *Holiday Romance* is a timely and fascinating reminder of the fickle memories of the viewing public!

The controversial Adrian Shergold is the man behind the following selection *The Unbroken Promise*, written for another of his excursions around the limits of broadcasting taboos in the shape of *Close Relations*, a drama written around the wholesome subject of incest! This somewhat unpalatable theme notwithstanding the piece is a charming and beautifully melodic one, inspired by the work of the hugely prolific British TV composer Richard Harvey. Formerly a member of the medieval influenced progressive rock band Gryphon before entering the Giltrap orbit during his time as a session musician, Harvey got his first TV break with the theme to the long-running *Tales Of The Unexpected*, leading to his lifelong career path. Perfectly underpinned by violin and flute from virtuosos Susan Aston and Robin Hilary Ashe-Roy respectively, *The Unbroken Promise* is something of a hidden gem.

A series of full band-arranged pieces comes up at this point beginning with *Brutus*, as far away from the world of Adrian Shergold as it is possible to get, being used as the theme music for the *World Bowls* coverage! *The Carnival* is yet another holiday-themed piece, written as it was for an ITV show in competition with the BBC's *Holiday*. So at this point Gordon was representing both sides of the 'holiday wars'! Oddly enough this piece was the last of several which he submitted to the Thames Television 'selectors' and although it was the one which they elected to go for, it was in fact dashed off as something of a 'last-gasp' afterthought, which just goes to show that one never knows when inspiration might strike...

The drama series *Hold The Back Page* had already been represented on record with the inclusion of *Sallie's Song* from the *Elegy* album but here we have the actual theme music for the show, also composed by Gordon. A truly excellent and lively full-band excursion, it clearly would have disrupted the flow of *Elegy* completely had it been included therein but it provides an unexpected delight here. In a way, this track more than any other on the record exemplifies this album's appeal and worthy place in the Giltrap canon as it gives a late-period reminder of the rockier, electric material which was much missed by some older fans by this time and shows up in stark relief against the more reflective, acoustic material. This quartet of band-oriented pieces is rounded out by *Sunburst*, a track released as a single but never included on an album until this point. There is no TV connection here but it is a more than worthy inclusion nonetheless as it is full of merit with its lively melody and skipping rhythm somewhat reminiscent of *Heartsong* in places. Indeed, allied to a strong top line melody it seems surprising and unjust that the single sank without trace, as it surely deserved to be another chart contender.

Back to the more introspective material next for *Revelation Highway* a piece named for Gordon's much-favoured electric guitar of the time, the Hohner Revelation, whose whammy bar reminded him of the time he spent striving to emulate Hank Marvin all those years ago. This was also unrelated to his TV work as was the following *Indomitable*, the most powerful and aggressive track on the record with its driving percussive accompaniment; it had been written for a vocal project which had not materialised but is another strong piece thankfully curated here. The album is finally rounded out by two TV pieces previously released on *Elegy* in the shape of *In Unison* and *Lucky* — both favourites of Gordon's and written around the same time for separate TV commissions; he regarded them as something of a matching pair. Strong pieces, as previously discussed, they finish off the album nicely.

All in all, a very pleasing compilation of mainly unreleased material and probably one of the most overlooked items in the Giltrap catalogue. The album's sales and profile were probably not helped by a somewhat unimaginative cover design with a shot of Gordon playing the acoustic guitar accompanied by a stark font on a black background. Indeed, this image is rather misleading given the far from solo acoustic nature of the majority of the collection.

Still, excellent as this release was, there were bigger events about to unfold around the corner, an opportunity which was to come about courtesy of Gordon's old friend Cliff Richard...

24
Heathcliff

By the time 1996 came around, Cliff Richard had been harbouring an ambition for quite some time. He had been drawn towards the world of musical theatre and in particular the potential of the central character Heathcliff from Emily Brontë's novel *Wuthering Heights*, which had for many years been his favourite book. The dark, brooding nature of Heathcliff was one that Cliff had long believed would be perfect to be brought to life on the stage and he felt compelled to portray this wild, fascinatingly untamed character himself. As long ago as 1991 he had contacted lyric writer Sir Tim Rice about the idea with a view to producing an album's worth of songs and he had managed to get Rice on board with the idea. Australian musician and composer John Farrar was brought in to write the music. Farrar was a long-time associate of Cliff having been a member of both his backing band and also the Shadows for some time during the 1970s, as well as an excellent if largely unsuccessful vocal trio with Hank Marvin and Bruce Welch, simply named Marvin, Welch & Farrar. He had worked extensively with Olivia Newton John and written many of her hit singles including two number ones from the soundtrack to the film *Grease* so his pedigree was certainly unquestioned.

The original concept developed quickly but somewhat too quickly for practical purposes. While the show was intended to be staged in 1994 this was an untenable plan and the dates booked were instead used by Cliff for his *Hit List Tour*. The plans continued unabated however and by 1995 concrete ideas were forming with the release of the 'teaser' single *A Misunderstood Man* followed a month later by the album *Songs From Heathcliff*, consisting of ten songs which would later go on to be used in the stage presentation. John Farrar's old collaborator Olivia Newton John interestingly sang on five of these tracks, so there was a sort of 'family affair' feeling about the project.

Early in 1996 Gordon's manager Mark Hadley received a call from Cliff saying he was interested in having Gordon in the show. He readily agreed since, as he now says, "Cliff was part of my childhood, along with Hank Marvin and one of my boyhood heroes. Musical theatre wasn't something I'd nurtured any ambitions about in itself, but just to be up there on stage with Cliff and to be a part of the whole set-up of such a big production made it something I couldn't refuse". He was invited along to the first rehearsal, held at Cecil Sharp House, an award-winning folk music and dance venue and arts centre next door to Regents Park in central London. As he walked in Cliff was there with Frank Dunlop the show director along with some of the dancers. Gordon was welcomed by both of them but was told that they didn't actually have anything written for him as yet. Cliff had stated that he wanted him in the show as the 'Troubadour' character — the sort of musical narrator in a way — but that the part hadn't yet been worked out. He returned home without taking any part in rehearsals but one thing which did surface from this meeting was that since the role was technically designated an acting part he had to join Equity, the actors' union. A result of this was that he was therefore subject to Equity rates, which he confirms were much lower than those that the band members were receiving, even though he was to be playing the guitar onstage at every performance and was therefore a musician. He accepted this without any protest however as he regarded the whole experience as much more valuable than the rate of pay — much like the ELO tour in a way.

Whilst he was kicking his heels so to speak, waiting to find out how he would be incorporated in the show, Gordon took it upon himself to come up with a rewritten arrangement of that first single *A Misunderstood Man*. He describes the arrangement as "typical trademark Giltrap with all of those hammer-ons and things that I used". But he didn't do anything with it until one day he received a phone call from John Farrar to introduce himself, who was in California working on the music. He told Gordon that Cliff had passed him a copy of the *On A Summer's Night* live album, which he really enjoyed. He said that such was the appeal of Gordon's playing and in particular his use of the delay effect in that performance, that he was excited to have him in the show, but that he was unsure of how to best utilise him, as he hadn't yet written anything for his part. At this point Gordon asked him if he minded if he played his arrangement of *A Misunderstood Man* down the phone. When it finished, a clearly impressed Farrar exclaimed, "That's brilliant man. I love it! In fact, I know what we'll do — let's make that the Overture! You open the show every night playing that, just your guitar and some strings, and it'll be great!" And that was exactly how Gordon ended up doing just that. This was an excellent development, but it did come with a tinge of frustration when Farrar added, "I wish I'd known earlier that you could come up with stuff like that, because I'd have used you a lot more!"

A second round of rehearsals took place at Ealing Studios before the sheer scale of the production was made clear by the hiring of Earl's Court for the first set of full rehearsals, in itself an enormous expense. It was necessary in order to accommodate all of the lights, projections and what Gordon describes as "a small army of computer operators". There were such devices as a large rotating rock on the stage in addition to all of the lighting effects and other visuals, so this was a long way from your standard small theatre based show to say the least.

It was at this point that Gordon's role began to be expanded beyond that initial opening sequence, as he was asked to add extra bits of music here and there for other sequences. One of these was a piece called *The Picnic*, while another was *Isabella's Wedding*, which was originally titled *Beachcomber*: both of these (with *Isabella's Wedding* in expanded form) would appear on his next album *Troubadour*. Therefore when the show finally came to be staged Gordon had these three pieces to play each night. The Overture, opening the show was the only part he played in the first half of the performance but in the second half both of his other pieces were played. He also had to open the second half by miming to the Overture again of all things. As he says now, "I hated miming in one sense but in another way I quite enjoyed it because I got to pose a bit. I had a count in through my ear monitors, which alerted me to have my fingers ready for the music coming in. But as there always is, there was one night when this went wrong. The sound engineer had omitted to turn up the volume on my count, so when the music started I was standing there with my arms at my sides! I moved them pretty quickly of course — probably no-one noticed at the time".

The costume provided for him as this 'troubadour' figure was not a 'wandering minstrel' garb but rather a vaguely Edwardian suit of clothes in a grey pinstripe with velvet collar on a long coat. A collarless shirt completed this somewhat unspectacular ensemble with Gordon admitting it wasn't how he had pictured himself. "I must admit, I did hope they'd give me a cape", he says now. "I always fancied a cape, I think that would have looked rather good! But I suppose the wardrobe department had other ideas".

The show opened in Birmingham on 16th October 1986 at the NIA before transferring for a run in Edinburgh then Manchester before finally climaxing with a run of shows in London at the Hammersmith Apollo, ending its run in May 1987. Every night the show would open with Gordon entering onto a balcony, picked out by a spotlight as he played the overture piece live; an experience which he describes as being extremely nerve-wracking every single time from first night to last. However, these nerves failed to get the better of him as remarkably, he executed the piece in note-perfect fashion every single time — much to his own surprise in a way but certainly very much to his satisfaction without doubt. "I was really pleased that I got that right", he says now. "The thing was that there was something about Cliff that made you want to do your best for him, I don't know what it was exactly. He was such a nice bloke and more talented than people realise. He's got great musical ears and he's worked tremendously hard to get where he is and to stay there. The only thing I was a little bit unhappy about was that when the show was in London, Hilary and I had to stay with friends in Kent and I had to drive to and from London every day — I wasn't getting any hotel expenses, which seems crazy now, and after I'd paid my manager 15% out of my Equity fee I couldn't get near affording accommodation. Some people have suggested that maybe Cliff could have stepped in and seen to it that I got a better deal in that way but I don't blame him myself to be honest. I don't believe he's ever allowed himself to be drawn into that side of things — that's why he pays accountants and other staff to deal with the nitty gritty numbers stuff, he can't afford the time to get involved, which is fair enough I think".

A soundtrack album from the show appeared during its run and then toward the end of the final leg in London a DVD (or video as it was then) was filmed — although the odd thing about this was that, rather than simply film one of the regular shows, a performance was staged behind closed doors on one of the days off and it was shot without an audience. "I think that was a mistake", insists Gordon. "I suppose there must have been reasons behind it but the atmosphere at the live shows was tremendous. When you watch the one that was put out on the DVD it's so obvious that something just isn't there, some of the magic is missing. As I said, there may have been very good technical reasons behind it but for me it was a missed opportunity".

After that final run in London the show closed and never had another shot. Reviews had been absolutely scathing, with critics at the time referring to the production as, variously, 'wretched', 'withering' (as opposed to 'wuthering') and perhaps worst of all, the dreadful punning headline 'Living Dull'. Audiences had been much more forgiving generally than the critics but Gordon does acknowledge the flaws in the production. "To be honest, I thought it should have been better in some ways. Cliff took so much on with it and I think he could and should have had better advice. The music was great and it was an ambitiously-scaled use of the budget but it could have been tightened up quite a lot by the right experienced pair of hands. Maybe if Trevor Nunn or someone could have been involved there might have been just that extra sheen of perfection and professionalism that wasn't quite there in places but then again I'm no expert on musical theatre staging so I can't say, really".

When the show originally closed after that run the plan was always to go on with it. The intention was to take the production to Australia and indeed Gordon remembers Cliff coming into the dressing room one night towards the end of the run and asking him (along with a select few others) if he fancied a trip 'down under'. The plan was to take a few cast members who were considered critical and make up the rest of the cast and crew over there. This was obviously a very appealing offer (as long as it didn't include a commute from Kent!) but sadly it never came to fruition. Gordon asked Cliff about this after the trail had gone cold so to speak and he confirmed that they simply couldn't make the figures add up in order to make it financially viable so that was the end of *Heathcliff* in live performance. As Gordon remembers it now, it was an experience never to be forgotten with some truly memorable elements, if in the final analysis fatally flawed.

What the show did do was to cement Gordon's strong relationship with Cliff and this was demonstrated shortly after the production came to its end when Cliff's then manager, a tough, sometimes intimidating character named David Bryce did Gordon the favour of trying to get him a record deal with the prestigious EMI Classical label. Having contacts with the label and hearing what Gordon did in his performances, he thought it might be a good fit. To that end he arranged for a representative of the label to come to a Giltrap show to check him out. In the end the label declined on the basis that it didn't quite fit their brief but it was a good indication of the warmth in which he was regarded by Cliff and his organisation. Plus, even though that contract didn't come to pass, it did lead in a way onto the next crucial development of his career — the following year's *Troubadour* album...

25
Troubadour

As unforgettable an experience as the *Heathcliff* run had been, after the dust settled it was clearly time for Gordon to get back to what he did best: writing and recording original music. Although the attempted liaison between him and EMI Classical had failed to ignite, it nevertheless gave him the taste for recording again and led him to start looking for a label which might be interested in lending its support to a new album. As odd a fit as it may seem his mind went back to that compilation album *Performance*, which he had done with K-Tel Records some years earlier. He suggested Mark Hadley should approach the label, which he duly did and as it turned out they were very interested in financing and releasing the planned album. They were more widely known for budget-priced compilations of somewhat variable quality which they had put out over the years — often with the backing of similarly shoestring budget television advertising campaigns — but on this occasion the idea of a respected and musically serious, original release had appealed to them.

With a budget agreed for the recording to take place (not a huge one, by Gordon's own admission, but a budget nevertheless), the next stop for Gordon was without hesitation to approach his old friend and collaborator Del Newman to see if he would like to work with him again. The answer was an unequivocal agreement as Newman said to him at the time, "I turned down working with you on *Visionary*; I'm not going to make that mistake again!" As Gordon recalls it now, "Del told me that he had always regretted turning down *Visionary* and that he had vowed that if I ever approached him again he would accept the job whatever it was. He was true to his word. So much so in fact that he agreed to do the arrangements for half his usual fee, as long as he was allowed to produce the album, which he didn't charge for at all. He said he wanted to produce it to ensure that my guitar didn't get buried underneath the string arrangements, and sure enough he achieved that brilliantly".

The initial discussions had taken place during the final days of *Heathcliff's* run and when Cliff heard the planned record was to include a new version of *A Misunderstood Man*, Cliff actually approached Gordon and asked if he would like him to do backing vocals on the song — which he duly did. As Gordon remembers it, "The thing about Cliff was that he said he loved doing backing vocals; in fact he said he found it more enjoyable and creative than doing a lead vocal because he loved harmonies. He's such a great singer, which you realise when you work with him. His ear is just so good for melody and harmony, he's absolutely natural and true to his word, he did it. He came into the studio on 1st October 1997 at 11am, and just worked straight through without a break until the vocals were finished. It was a great session and a great day."

Not everyone was as clued-in to Cliff's talents as Gordon was, and one of these people was none other than Del Newman. He'd been out of the business for some time and he actually asked about Cliff: "Gordon, is he still in the business?" — which naturally received the reply, "He's never been away! Cliff's huge, Del". Del had never met Cliff personally and an amusing moment came when he first spoke with him in the studio and he committed the faux-pas of asking him whether he still played golf! Cliff's reply was a somewhat bemused "Er, no, it's tennis" but the pair got along extremely well once Del had fully sorted out who he was!

Looking at the album cover when it emerged in 1998, it is clear that it followed directly on the heels of *Heathcliff*, as it mines much of the same seam for its inspiration. While the title itself is a nod to his character in the show, the front cover depicts Gordon in full 'wandering minstrel' garb — and indeed, finally gives him the cape he yearned for! Three pieces from *Heathcliff* are included, albeit reworked, and the first edition of the album even included comments written by both Cliff and Tim Rice, making reference to their time together in the production. When the album was later re-released on Voiceprint Records these notes were removed as it was felt that they were no longer relevant, allowing the album to stand on its own two feet in a better way.

Many of the tracks which would ultimately be used on the album had already been recorded during a series of marathon sessions in Gordon's son's bedroom at home, after he had moved out. Taking this route entirely through financial constraints and recording directly to DAT he was using pickups on his guitar which had been designed by Mike Vanden. Later sold by him to Fishburn and becoming the very popular Rare Earth brand, these early Vanden pickups, excellent though they were, presented their own particular set of problems for the recording process. Being single coil they would by their very nature tend to hum when not facing the appropriate way and Gordon found himself in the decidedly unglamorous position of having to sit as still as possible facing a radiator in order for this irritating interference to be kept at bay! "I can still remember doing about ten takes of *Down The River* before nailing the perfect one. This was a seven minute piece and many times I would get almost to the end and make a fluff and had to start again. I had no editing facility, nothing! But in the end I got some pretty good performances. So many of these pieces were already in place for a possible deal with an American label started by Steve Vai, who incidentally liked the tracks but passed on them because I don't think they were 'flashy' enough for him. In the end it worked out okay but of course *Troubadour* by then was waiting in the wings so to speak. By that time I had a slightly better recording set-up but still no idea how to drop in, so all the pieces were still pretty much complete takes. Those DATs were the masters we used for the final thing and the guitar sound has its own quality of sweetness I think."

The album opens with the aforementioned rendition of *A Misunderstood Man* — played acoustically with only the superb Cliff Richard backing vocals supplementing the guitar and lush string accompaniment. The track segues into *Be With Me Always*, another *Heathcliff* piece and provides a stunning six-minute opening to the album. In fact, similar to the show, this almost seems to form an overture of sorts. Following this is *Rain In The Doorway*, a piece inspired by a long-ago moment of connection between the youthful Gordon and his father. "One day as a boy I was out for a walk with my dad and we got caught in a thunderstorm. Running for cover we took shelter in the doorway of a derelict house. That memory of standing there with him, watching the rain pour down is one of the fondest memories I have of him for that time. We didn't often share moments when I felt a closeness and emotional connection with him, but that day has always stood out as one. The piece was already written actually and I was searching for a title. It sounded very much like rain falling and two things came to mind; that incident and somewhat randomly, a book Hilary read once by Thorne Smith called *Rain In The Doorway*."

The book in question forms a slightly odd inspiration in itself, being a slightly risqué — for the time — 1933 novel, but the title clearly worked in triggering that long-ago fond memory, which is perfectly evoked by the piece. It was performed, curiously, on a guitar purchased from a car boot sale for the princely sum of five pounds. It was later retooled slightly to give it a sound unlike any other guitar Gordon had ever played and was known affectionately as 'the boot sale guitar'. The following *On Camber Sands*, a beautiful and subtly embellished piece is dedicated to the memory of Tracy Sollis, the young girl of Gordon's acquaintance who had so tragically died of leukaemia at the age of 15 who had fallen in love with the piece as soon as she had heard it. The Camber Sands of the title is actually a stretch of Sussex coastline where Gordon both visited as a child and then later took his own children and it evokes his memories of pleasant and warmly nostalgic days spent there.

Also taking its name from a geographical location is the following *The Lord's Seat*, which is named after a beauty spot in the Lake District in North West England and was in fact composed while staying in a house quite close by. It had previously been included on the *Music For The Small Screen* album and used in the BBC documentary series *Working Titles*. It was redone here to create a differently arranged feel to the previous recording and as such is very successful. The next piece, *Rainbow Kites* is titled very much because the sound of it conjures up the idea of kites bobbing and weaving in the air, but the most interesting thing in a compositional sense is that it was written and indeed inspired, by a delay effect that Gordon was using. By utilising a single second delay it rather effectively conveys the illusion of two guitarists playing together in a very tight fashion and gives the track a uniquely interesting sound for an acoustic guitar piece. Indeed this perfectly encapsulates a large part of what makes this album so successful, in that there is more inventiveness, ambition and contrast in the pieces than any of the previous non-band albums. It manages in this way to engage the interest throughout of those who might normally find acoustic guitar music bland or dull.

Following the introspective remnant from the Martin Taylor period with *Who Knows Where Tomorrow Goes* we are treated to another *Heathcliff* piece, *Isabella's Wedding*, which was developed from an existing theme into the new and complete piece heard here, before the interesting *Quest For Nonsuch*. This latter piece, written in somewhat Renaissance-period influenced style and based around the sound of the lute, is perfectly judged in terms of mood as the odd-sounding title refers to Nonsuch Palace which was built by Henry VIII before falling into decay and disappearing over the centuries. The title refers to the thus-far fruitless searches for the location of the legendary building which have been launched in recent times.

A Dublin Day is a piece which does 'exactly what it says on the tin' as it was written directly as a result of Gordon's first visit to the city, a place which he loves. It is extremely evocative as is the aforementioned seven-minute *Down The River*, which has a title drawn, not for the first time, from a book — this time the autobiography of H.E. Bates. Written in an open tuning shown to Gordon by an old friend, it is another nicely orchestrated piece and is followed by the third and final *Heathcliff* tune in the shape of *The Picnic*, which Gordon claims always gives him fond memories of playing it at a particularly dramatic juncture towards the end of that production. A touch of inspiration in the arrangement here is the sound of a flute evoking butterflies fluttering about the titular picnic and another example of the subtle charms of the album.

The album begins to wind to a close at this point with the quintessentially 'English' sound of *Daisy Chain* leading into the tricky *Nursery Chimes*, which utilises a technique known as 'harping', wherein the combination of plucked string and attendant harmonic combine to create a harp-like sound, to great and rather original effect. The track also notably features Del Newman playing keyboards for the only occasion on the record. Closing the album comes something of a rarity in the Giltrap canon; namely an arrangement of a traditional tune in the shape of *The Kerry Dancers*. Like much of the album — and unsurprisingly given the title perhaps — this shows a significant Celtic musical influence; it was actually Newman's favourite track on the album and it is easy to understand why. Using three Armstrong guitars in turn from a baritone guitar to a normal one and finally to the 'baby guitar' and taken at a slower tempo than the piece is often played at, the melody is highlighted extremely strongly and it closes the record with yet another stylistic about-face — unusually so for what is essentially a solo guitar album.

Garnering favourable reviews from the majority of the music press at the time on its 1998 release, the *Troubadour* album was a very healthy seller, aided by the publicity efforts which the record company had thrown into it. Like them or loathe them, K-Tel had put their money where their collective mouths were and the publicity machine generated allowed Gordon to get on such outlets as TV pop video channel VHS, where he sometimes sat a little uncomfortably alongside the 'hair metal' bands of the time such as Guns 'n Roses or Poison. Nevertheless, this exposure did his profile no harm whatsoever...

26
Janschology

By now in 1998, Gordon had finally been able to settle into a comfortable latter-period routine of sorts. The *Troubadour* album and to an extent *Elegy* before it, had provided a musical template for where his journey had led him to: namely, acoustic guitar music with some embellishments (strings, flute etc) but no attempts at full band arrangements and little electric guitar work. He had in effect, been able to assume a sort of position as an 'elder statesman' of instrumental guitar music and the ability to relax somewhat and plough this furrow was an enviable one. *Troubadour* had certainly sold well enough to bring in some welcome royalties, as well as the equally welcome positive reviews in the press, without ever threatening the sort of sales which might have brought him back into the mainstream public gaze — despite the efforts of K-Tel in the publicity arena, sometimes ill-focused as they may have been. The remainder of 1998 and much of 1999 were taken up with regular live work — but once again, nothing as arduous as lengthy organised tours, as most of his this was in the form of either one off shows or a short series of gigs. Now that he had no band to rehearse, pay and get onto the road together there was much more freedom, which was extremely welcome.

There was also a significant meeting at this time with Rob Ayling, the man behind Voiceprint Records, who undertook a quite extensive reissue programme of Gordon's back catalogue over the following few years. They would also, as we will see, become involved in issuing new material and would actually go on to become the longest running record label association of his career. Some journalistic work was also on Gordon's agenda as he continued to do some 'star interview' features for *Guitarist* magazine. As a related offshoot of this he got to know Fay Goodman, who was to become a close friend and who was aiming to produce a whole series of filmed interviews for DVD release. Having some experience in this area, Gordon took on the role of interviewer, talking to such luminaries as Tony Iommi, Albert Lee and flamenco virtuoso Paco Pena. He also interviewed Who bassist John Entwistle and spent the day at Entwistle's small mansion in Stowe-on-the-Wold being filmed with him. He had met Entwistle some time earlier, through singer-songwriter Ian Brusby, who had recorded an album produced by Entwistle's son, on which Gordon agreed to play. He later met up with Entwistle again at the Frankfurt Guitar Show where they proceeded to get along extremely well. On the basis of this acquaintance, Fay Goodman added this interview to the series.

John Entwistle's partner at the time, Lisa was also there and both Gordon and Hilary got on with her very well, although she was somewhat more ingrained in the 'rock and roll' lifestyle, having also previously been Joe Walsh's girlfriend for quite some time. It happened to be Gordon's birthday on the day they were filming in April 2000. While he and John were busy working, Lisa and Hilary went on an expedition to the local shops and returned with some cake to mark the occasion! As it happened, the material had not been used by the time John passed away in 2002 and the interview footage went to form a large part of a documentary film *Thunderfingers*, put together in tribute to him. One amusing fact to come out of this period is that Gordon almost ended up joining The Who, unbelievable as that may sound! John had mentioned that they were planning to start touring again and that they were on the lookout for an additional guitarist to play the rhythm parts as a member of the touring band and he asked Gordon if he would be interested. Overqualified as he undoubtedly was for this role, he nevertheless agreed in principle without a second thought. As a long time fan and with his own playing having been influenced so much in the past by some of Pete Townshend's work, John said he would go away and ask Pete about it, but sadly it came to nothing, most likely due to the aforementioned over qualification for a simple rhythm guitar role, though the thought of Townshend-esque windmilling power chords being performed on stage by an animated Gordon Giltrap remains the stuff of surreal imagination!

2000 also saw Gordon inducted into the Grand Order Of Water Rats, the prestigious showbiz charity organisation, which gave him enormous pride. Around this same time there was a short trip to the United States for Gordon and Hilary as he embarked on a short East Coast tour of sorts. Despite this trek being notable as his first time over there, the whole exercise was nevertheless, by his own admission, "nothing to write home about really". It was clear that the time was well overdue for some more recorded Giltrap output, and he already had an idea coming together in his mind as to what form it would take.

******

As we have already seen, one of Gordon's most revered influences was the great Bert Jansch, '60s acoustic guitar pioneer and founding member of the highly respected band Pentangle. Without a large amount of new material having been written at the time, Gordon hatched an idea to record his own tribute to Jansch, recording material famously written or arranged by him in a similar style to his original arrangements. Originally planned as a full album, time necessitated that the project ended up as a six-song EP, or mini-album as it might be termed, entitled *Janschology*.

Perhaps the most interesting thing to note about this release from a historical perspective is that it marked the first time since 1973 that Gordon's own lead vocal made an appearance, on the track *Running From Home*. He had done the backing track and he knew that for this particular piece the vocals were essential. He asked Hilary who she thought he should get to sing it. He was quite taken aback when her response was "Gordon, you've got to do it! You're the only one who can do this as it needs to be done". So, he duly went away and recorded the vocal which came out extremely well. As he remembers now: "I must admit, it did come out okay. It was just about the first time that I'd done a vocal that actually sounded like me, instead of putting on a sort of affectation as I used to do when I was young. Instead of trying to sound like someone else, I just sounded honest and it worked. I like the way I approached it musically as well, with some electric guitars in a kind of symphonic way — though God knows how I did it, I certainly couldn't remember it now, far too complex!"

Another fascinating track is the opening interpretation of the Ewan MacColl song *The First Time Ever I Saw Your Face*, made famous by Roberta Flack. Jansch had in fact first recorded his arrangement of the song on his 1966 album *Jack Orion*, some time before the Flack version and Gordon's interpretation follows the Jansch arrangement quite faithfully. While it may seem an odd tactic to use a song written by someone else on a Jansch tribute, it is easy to see why upon listening because the arrangement is incredibly clever. It takes the piece and by altering the tempo and embellishing the melody, it changes it in such a subtle manner that until some way in it is easy to be fooled into thinking it is a new composition. This demonstrates to perfection Jansch's genius for interpretation, which was central to his output, in the form of the many traditional arrangements he recorded both solo and with Pentangle. A further interpretation of another composer's work comes up next in the form of Davey Graham's *Angie*. Recorded using a Rob Armstrong semi-acoustic guitar, giving a slightly jazzy feel, once again the Jansch arrangement is followed as the template, but another strong reason for the inclusion of this track is the influence it had on Gordon's own early work — in particular *Catwalk Blues* which, despite using an ascending bassline as opposed to the descending one on *Angie*, has very much the same feel and is, by Gordon's own admission, very much indebted to the piece as inspiration.

The final two Jansch pieces on the album come in the form of *Chambertin* and the traditional *Blackwaterside*. The latter may seem familiar to many through the track *Black Mountain Side* on the first Led Zeppelin album on which fellow Jansch acolyte Jimmy Page drew direct inspiration from the Jansch guitar arrangement of the piece. Gordon's treatment is once again quite faithful. The Jansch original *Chambertin*, first recorded in 1974 on his album *LA Turnaround*, is a piece which Gordon actually revisited on his next studio album in expanded form, which we will come to shortly. In terms of this particular version, he admits now that he felt he never quite nailed the feel of the piece as well as he would have liked. It is a very difficult piece to master, requiring — as many Jansch compositions did — a lot of strength in the left hand on the fretboard. Another contributory factor to these difficulties was that the tablature that Bert had provided for Gordon was in fact done incorrectly. While it featured all of the correct notes, the fingering positions indicated were not in fact the ones which Jansch had used. As a result Gordon found himself having to painstakingly figure a lot of it out. Nevertheless, it is in itself a well-played and pleasing rendition.

The album was completed by the addition of Gordon's own piece *Roots*, first introduced on the *Fear Of The Dark* album. The reason for this surprising inclusion was to showcase the influence of Bert Jansch's work on Gordon's own compositions as he felt *Roots* to be one of his pieces which owed the most to Jansch in style and approach. As such it rounded off the 'tip of the hat' that the whole recording was intended to demonstrate the genius of Jansch.

The material was again recorded at Gordon's house but happily it found a label to give it a home as Voiceprint elected to diversify from their reissue programme. Even the cover was a result of a suggestion by Rob Ayling, using as it did a design which evoked very closely the iconic sleeve of the very first, self-titled, Bert Jansch release from 1965. It was not a direct copy as Giltrap and Jansch clearly looked very different, but in terms of the monochrome photo, looking into the lens holding a guitar, bordered in stark blue, it managed to call it instantly to mind for anyone familiar with the original Jansch album, especially by using the identical typeface. The same approach had been used by The Clash for their album *London Calling*, which evoked the first Elvis Presley album in very much the same way.

In the previous couple of years the Voiceprint reissue campaign was churning on with a great many of Gordon's back catalogue albums, along with the occasional compilation and live album to add to the pot. Many of these were simply straight reissues — though very often with different and sometimes improved cover designs. One exception was the cleverly thought out 2001 re-release of *Troubadour*, which came with a second disc containing the pure acoustic guitar of the original album, shorn of the orchestration and other instruments, for those who wanted to concentrate solely on the guitar work without what could be seen by some as distractions. One for the purist perhaps but an excellent selling point nonetheless.

Following the *Janschology* release, 2001 saw Gordon undertake another short East Coast US tour, but this time with more success. There were a couple of significant venues on the itinerary — not least the Cafe Lena in Saratoga, arguably the most prestigious folk venue in North America, and the place where Bob Dylan had played one of his first shows outside New York City. The list of artists to have appeared reads like a virtual 'who's who' of acoustic and folk music. There was also an appearance at a venue in Bethlehem, Pennsylvania called Godfrey Daniels, not far from the Martin guitar factory, which also had a high profile on the acoustic music scene.

Despite the successful gigging schedule at this time however, there had to be some new Giltrap material recorded soon and this would come in the following year with the album *Under This Blue Sky*.

27
Under This Blue Sky

After an intense flurry of activity by Voiceprint label with no less than 14 reissues, compilations and live albums appearing on the label in the three years since *Troubadour* appeared, their 'Giltrap production line' finally slowed by the beginning of 2002. Happily there was to be another significant Voiceprint release in 2002 with Gordon's *Under This Blue Sky* album — his first full length album of new material since *Troubadour*.

Once again recorded in a 'home studio' environment, the album was unusual in that, although a solo release, it credited another musician on the cover, which read 'Featuring the flute of Hilary Ashe-Roy'. While not made clear in the album notes, Ashe-Roy (his full name was Hilary Robin Ashe-Roy and he later adopted the name Robin) was an enormously talented flautist who had been taught by none other than James Galway. Gordon met him through Ric Sanders as he was very much a jazz-influenced player. He was so impressed that he was absolutely delighted to be able to enlist him on several tracks on this album.

The mood is sombre from the word go as the title track opens proceedings and is a piece with a tragic inspiration. Gordon's friends Sue and Mike Williams had a daughter Fay who was killed in a road accident in her late teens along with another girl, whilst abroad working for a travel agency. Gordon and Hilary both attended the funeral and he was moved to write the piece in her memory. It conjures up those feelings extremely evocatively, especially with Ashe-Roy's perfect flute accompaniment. This is the first of a two-part tribute to the memory of Fay as it segues directly into the next track, an arrangement of the traditional *Sing A Song Of Sixpence*, which was included to make reference to Fay's love for, and work with, children. This arrangement is noteworthy in that it follows the Bert Jansch trick of subtly changing the melody and tempo just enough to render the piece recognisable yet not intrusively so, and succeeds admirably in that aim. Towards the end of the piece an overdubbed second guitar emerges to carry a second melody as a counterpoint, which lifts it again and puts the icing on what is a very successful, if unlikely, reworking.

Another rearrangement follows this in the shape of George Harrison's *Here Comes The Sun* with a treatment for the Rob Armstrong Baby Guitar. Indeed, while Gordon admits to his regret at never having met George, he does take some pride in being indirectly responsible for George discovering the Baby Guitar and going on to own three of them. It is certainly an arrangement far removed from most other reworkings of the piece and as such benefits from a lack of over-familiarity. Gordon says now of his introducing George to the Armstrong guitars, "The connection with George Harrison came about via Joe Brown. We were visiting Joe along with Rob Armstrong. We took Rob along because we knew how much Joe loved guitars, handmade or otherwise. I had taken the Baby Guitar along with a few more guitars that Rob brought with him. Joe fell in love with the Baby Guitar and promptly ordered one as a birthday gift for George. George in turn fell in love with it and ordered two more as gifts for close friends. Also whilst on that visit we met another old friend of Joe's, the late Alvin Lee from Ten Years After who also purchased then and there one of Rob's larger bodied acoustics!"

Another original piece follows this in the shape of the lively *At Giltrap's Bar*, written to evoke the feeling of a busy night in an Irish bar where the Guinness and the 'craic' are flowing in equal measure. There is actually a real-life 'Giltrap's Bar' in Northern Ireland according to Gordon who says, "It's definitely there, for sure. I haven't been myself, but my daughter Sadie has. I should go, really — it will certainly have arisen from the same family stock, because the Irish Giltraps are all related somewhere down the line." The plan for the piece was for Ashe-Roy to double the guitar part on the flute, but when he listened to it he respectfully declined on the basis that the tempo of the piece would make it extremely difficult to make it work!

There are a couple of revisits to recent material next, as *Chambertin*, from the Janschology album, pops up, followed by a return to the *Heathcliff* piece *The Picnic*. *Chambertin* is notable for two reasons: firstly because Bert Jansch himself plays on it, and secondly because it is extended to around double the length of the *Janschology* version. As Gordon remembers, "It was a fuller version, because I'd managed to work out some parts that I hadn't been exactly sure about when I first recorded it, so it's more representative and true to the original. Better, I think. Bert recorded his parts over at his place — I sent it to him for him to do. It was under sufferance I have to admit: I had to bully him into it a little bit! But that was Bert. He wasn't comfortable with fame, or any sort of praise even. In the photo of him with me in the CD booklet you can see that he doesn't look overjoyed about the whole thing. But it was nice of him to do it all the same". *The Picnic* similarly justifies its revisit, as Hilary Ashe-Roy's flute is brilliantly evocative of butterflies fluttering in the air and giving a real impression of an actual picnic on a summer day — more than even the *Troubadour* recording did. Adding in the fact that the piece had developed over time when played live, owing to the use of digital delay, and it is clear that on this recording is a piece whose true time has finally arrived.

A brace of relatively minor pieces follow, in the shape of the nimble-fingered virtuoso composition *The Racer* (again in the DADGAD tuning), followed by *Pedrolino*, which takes its name from a comic servant character in Italian opera. Interestingly, the latter is dedicated to the comedian Joe Pasquale, who was a good friend of Gordon's at the time and a fellow Water Rat. The two of them were spending quite a lot of time together and with the piece having a comedic link, he felt it a nice touch to include the dedication. The next piece entitled *Kaz* was actually commissioned for Kaz Greenham by her husband Leigh for her 40th birthday. It was requested that the piece have an oriental undertone to it, to reflect the time that the couple had spent working in Japan. To this end Gordon enlisted the help of Fay Goodman once again who, aside from being a film-maker was also a songwriter, as well as an accomplished martial artist (one of the world's leading exponents of Iaido, the Japanese 'way of the sword'). Her arrangement fed by her immersion in the Japanese culture, gives the piece exactly the right oriental flavour. Sampled backing vocals add an extra edge to an already successful piece.

Much of the time Gordon's pieces are named 'after the fact', in that he will compose a piece and then title it after deciding what it is reminiscent of (he credits Hilary as being particularly gifted in this ability). It is less common for him to sit down with an idea in mind and compose a piece specifically to capture that particular thought or emotion. The next track on the album however, *Crossing The Border*, is an exception to that rule, being directly inspired by an event in Derry, Northern Ireland, where he was playing a show during the 'political and religious troubles'. He was talking with someone after the show about the difference between the North and the South and was struck by a comment made by this man to the effect that as soon as you cross the border 'everything is suddenly jigs and reels' and that the atmosphere lightens almost tangibly just by crossing that arbitrary line between the two areas. He set out to write a piece which gives the impression of the mood shifting from darkness to light and back again. He is abetted on the piece by second guitarist Kevin Dempsey, with whom Gordon had formed that short-lived duo in the mid-'90s and the piece gains much from the contrast between the two players, together with the flute of Ashe-Roy once again adding the icing as it were.

Leading towards the end of the album comes firstly a holdover from the *Troubadour* sessions in the shape of *Secret Valentine* (it had not fit the mood of that album so had been shelved at the time), followed by *Fell Runner*, which is another fine example of a title coming along after the composition, since the titular runner is conjured up by the propulsive, forward moving feel of the music. Gordon describes it as a piece he wrote simply by way of the idea "arriving at my fingertips and seeing where it would lead". Surprisingly, it has never been played live to this day.

Rounding off the album comes *Winterdance*, another piece with a literary inspiration. Gordon had read a book of the same name by Gary Poulsen about the unlikely subject of Alaskan dog racing. The Iditarod Trail Race is an annual dog sled race covering an incredible 1000 miles, from Anchorage to the Bering Strait, which has as its core intent the preservation of Alaskan dog culture and heritage. A truly marathon event, the book is described by Gordon as "Brilliant and descriptive, sometimes harrowing but often amusing: a fantastic book". Inspired by this, he composed the piece bearing the name that paints a picture in the imagination of long; snowy wastes, and finishes the album in grand style.

The cover of the album featured an 1860 painting called A Shepherd Boy, by German artist Franz Von Lenbach. Depicting the boy of the title lying on his back resting under, appropriately, a clear blue sky, it completes what is a classy looking package, living up to the standard set by its predecessors *Elegy* and *Troubadour*. Hilary was credited as 'Reluctant Executive Producer', referring not only to her invaluable role as 'sounding board' for the musical ideas, but also her unerring ability to come up with the perfect name for a piece at those times when it would be eluding Gordon.

******

The following year, 2003, saw a number of interesting, if lower-key-releases. Firstly there was another archive live recording, this time dating back to the Peacock Party band in 1981. It was discovered on one of the master tapes rescued from Redan Recorders. Certainly not as definitive as *Live At Oxford*, the album is nevertheless another fascinating period piece, looking at an era which by this time seemed almost a lifetime away. Gordon was also contacted by the Arthritis Research charity to put together for them an album of solo live performances through the years, which he duly did. It appeared on Arc Records titled *Fingers Of Fire*. This was later re-licensed and re-released through the Hypertension label in 2006, as *Captured From A Point In Time*, with the bonus track of *Dodo's Dream* — the first recorded appearance of the celebrated solo rendition using the electric guitar and looping effects.

Also appearing that year was an album of cover versions, entitled *Remember This*. It was not exclusively covers because there were outings for *Appalachian Dreaming, Isabella's Wedding and Down The River*. The latter two were included because they came from a BBC Radio 6 recording where Gordon was accompanied by Rick Wakeman. The songs on the album were selected partly for having been an influence on the youthful Gordon Giltrap. For example *Substitute* by The Who and *Summer Holiday* by Cliff Richard. Overall the album was an exercise in proving that it was possible to take a classic song and make something new and worthwhile out of it, so long as the approach was different and not a slavish imitation of the original. In this way it succeeds admirably with most of the album being performed solely by Gordon. There were exceptions in the shape of another 'musician's musician', Neville Marten's fuzzed up and very effective electric guitar on *Substitute* and Hilary Ashe-Roy's delicate flute on the Bach piece *Minuet*. But apart from the aforementioned Rick Wakeman tracks, these are the extent of the collaborative efforts here. This is certainly not any sort of 'full band' album, or anything approaching it, despite the rock nature of some of the tracks covered, but in many ways it is all the better for it and it is still quite fondly regarded by a great many of Gordon's followers. There are pieces included by some of the expected suspects from Gordon's sphere of influence such as John Renbourn and Django Reinhardt. But two of the most successful interpretations are undoubtedly the nimble-fingered acoustic reworking of *Layla* (it never fails to surprise when that familiar riff comes in, picked on the acoustic guitar) and the joyful skip through *Summer Holiday*, one of the most 'feel-good' tunes ever committed to vinyl. The whole package was presented in a fitting cover featuring the young childhood Gordon in sepia-tinted nostalgic glory, seated in a toy car on the front cover and staring wide-eyed into the lens on the reverse. Most appropriate!

This was the last new release of what had been a fairly busy 2003, but towards the end of the year the first shoots of another full-blown collaboration would appear — and it would not be the last such partnership over the years that followed...

28

Drifter

Away from the music, another significant 2003 event for the Giltraps was another house move, this time into the home they still occupy in Sutton Coldfield, just north of Birmingham. They had wanted to move for some time, if finances had only allowed it, because not only was the Solihull house not the biggest dwelling imaginable, but also Hilary wanted to return to the Sutton Coldfield area because her children had grown up there. One day out of the blue, Gordon took a phone call from his publisher, Simon Platz.

"He never rang me as a rule. He was just too busy. He was very much a big-time music publisher; his father was the late David Platz, who at one time owned the largest music publishing company in the world, with the likes of the Who, the Rolling Stones, Ralph McTell and T Rex under his belt. I'd been with the company since *Visionary* in 1975, when it was Essex Music. Simon took over the reins after David died and on this occasion he phoned and said 'I thought I'd just let you know that *Nightscreen* has come up trumps for us'. Now, I should explain that *Nightscreen* was a public service broadcasting thing that went on through the night, whereby ITV would show information about upcoming programmes, news, that sort of thing and they had music playing behind it. Unbeknownst to me they had picked up on *Troubadour*, which I'd made available as a library album and they'd been playing it solidly for months. Simon told me it had earned 'a substantial amount of money', which was giving me visions of about ten grand and I was quite excited. So I asked him how much we were looking at and he said 'I've done the figures and it's about a hundred thousand pounds'. Obviously, I nearly fell off my chair, and I asked him what my share was, to which he replied 'that is your share. It's 100,000 each'. There was a slight drawback, in that it pushed me to the 40% tax bracket, but I still made 60 grand, which was life-changing. So, that was what put us in a position to move. Otherwise we'd quite probably still be in Solihull now. Amazing really, that being taken up by that one thing made a lot more money than the album ever did in sales".

Before the music-making began in earnest again, 2003 saw one more bizarre event when Gordon was asked to play at the annual ball for the Grand Order Of Water Rats. This was quite an honour and he was given a piece of advice by his friend and fellow 'Rat', revered skiffle musician Chas McDevitt, who had seen him play a show at Windsor Arts Centre. Gordon had been including in his show a spoof on Deep Purple's heavy rock classic *Smoke On The Water*, which he would play on the wildly overdriven baby guitar, complete with some two-handed 'tapping', together in a medley with *God Save The Queen*, as Brian May had done memorably on the roof of Buckingham Palace[†], all rolled up as a humorous interlude. McDevitt saw this and said to Gordon after the show 'Oh, you've got to play that at the ball', which seemed a reasonable thing to do. When the evening arrived however, there was an unexpected change in plan: "During the show I thought it was time to do this spoof section, so I started to go into the melody of *God Save The Queen* and to my horror the whole room rose to their feet and stood up for the national anthem! My mind raced through this and I thought, 'I can't grind into *Smoke On The Water* now with them all standing there', so I had to just finish playing *God Save The Queen* straight, like a fool, before they all sat down again. Nobody twigged that it was supposed to be a bit of fun for a joke, and God knows what would have happened if I'd just ploughed into the big *Smoke On The Water* riff in the middle of it. I'd probably have been thrown out!"

A more serious musical endeavour began right at the end of the year, with Gordon teaming up with respected classical guitarist Raymond Burley to record tracks for a collaborative album called *Double Vision*, which would appear early the following year. He had first met Burley at a seminar in 1981 for RGT (the Registry Of Guitar Tutors) of which Gordon is a patron; the organisation was set up to provide consistency and quality in terms of guitar tuition and examinations. Raymond was there with his then-fiancée Siân — they are now married — and they got chatting. Gordon had been aware of Raymond's reputation and he agreed to send him some music, including the *Troubadour* album, to see what he thought. Raymond absolutely loved what he heard, which Gordon thought was wonderful given that he did not use classical technique nor have classical training. He was overjoyed that Raymond accepted the music for what it was and loved it accordingly and their friendship grew into this collaboration.

[†] May's performance was part of The Party at the Palace, a British music concert and celebration in commemoration of the Golden Jubilee of Queen Elizabeth II hosted at Buckingham Palace Garden on 3rd June 2002.

The tracks were recorded 'live' with no audience in the Holy Trinity church in Weston, Hertfordshire. The nature of the building gave the recording some excellent natural 'reverb'. In truth, the album is not entirely essential. The mix of the steel and nylon strings is interesting on the face of it and there are notable moments, such as the slightly disorientating moment when a new and unfamiliar lead melody comes in during *Heartsong*, when the listener is conditioned to hearing it in the familiar way. Moments such as this abound and in the end it sounds a little 'shoe-horned' together, though certainly skilfully performed as one would expect. It may not be an entirely successful experiment, but it will certainly have its rewards for those who seek a slightly different spin on the familiar material. When the album appeared it was packaged in a stylish cover by glass sculptor Debbie Timperley who created the duo's hands in glass for an eye-catching image. When the album was re-released a few years later on another label, it was not only oddly re-titled *Double Visions*, with an 's' tacked on but also in a cheap looking and far inferior cover design featuring dull photos of the two men, which is a shame. It did feature the original design on the inner, however. The pair would go on to work together further in the years to come, as we shall see.

Following the release of that album came an absolutely unique recording in the Giltrap discography. Titled *Live At Ambergate*, this was no regular live album; in fact it was a recording of Gordon playing, without accompaniment or audience, in Shining Cliff Woods, Ambergate, Derbyshire. The recording was made by Dallas Simpson, an enthusiastic exponent of what is known as binaural recording. What this meant in effect was that he wore in-ear microphones, so that what was recorded was exactly what he was hearing, in 'true' surround sound. If he walked around Gordon, you would hear him move around your head, especially if you listened via headphones. In fact, to emphasise this effect and the unique atmosphere of the performance, the album is book ended by tracks *Arrival* and *Departure*, which are simply Simpson approaching and leaving the location, with the natural sound of the trees, birds and insects filling the listener's head. Gordon runs through nine tracks from his recent catalogue and more of this ambient sound is included between each piece. While it may not be classed as the most definitive Giltrap recording, it is certainly the most unusual, and it has a charm and originality which sets it apart from its peers even to this day.

******

As interesting as these releases were however, it was clear that the time was ready for another studio recording of original material. This duly arrived later in 2004 as *Drifter*. There is an interesting story behind the recording of the album, concerning a violin used on some of the tracks. Gordon had bought this particular instrument from a car boot sale for £20 — not being any sort of expert on violins he bought it as much for the case as anything. However, it turned out to be far more than your average boot sale instrument, as he discovered when he asked two friends Cath and Geoff Olner (Geoff being violinist with the Sheffield Philharmonic orchestra at the time) to do a little investigative work. What they came back with astonished him. It turned out that the violin in question was by Giuseppe Pedrazzini, an early twentieth century Italian maker of exceptional repute, and that it was worth an astonishing £30,000. Not bad for a twenty pound investment!

Gordon had invited the noted violinist John Bradbury to do some sessions for the record. When Bradbury arrived at the house Gordon asked him if he would use the Pedrazzini violin if it was playable. After a brief play of it, Bradbury commented that it was an incredible instrument and possibly the finest violin he had ever played. It was eventually used on three tracks on the album. One amusing aside is that, before knowing the nature of the instrument, Gordon had a go at cleaning it up, using Duraglit polish, which turned out to be a disaster as it removed half of the varnish. Eventually he had to pay £100 to fix his cleaning attempt, five times the initial outlay! This financial penalty was soon negated, however, when the violin was eventually sold, through a dealer, for £23,000 (reportedly it would be worth nearer £60,000 today). Gordon had loaned it out to a couple of trusted people in the interim, and indeed John Bradbury himself had offered that same price of £23,000 for it after first playing it. At that time Gordon was not ready to part with it, but as he says now "I wish I'd sold it to John now. I'd have known where it was going to and that would have been nice". He actually had a feature in the Sun newspaper about the instrument and his incredible find, which ironically gave him his greatest number of national column inches for decades!

The *Drifter* album kicks off with *Mrs Singer's Waltz*, a track with a story behind it as Gordon explains: "This was one of the tracks with John playing the boot sale violin on it, beautiful playing. The piece was actually written at a soundcheck before a gig at a village hall and based around the middle section of my arrangement of *Here Comes The Sun*. The title came from a plaque on the wall of the venue, expressing thanks to 'Mrs Singer' for donating the funds enabling it to be built. Mrs Singer was from the famous Singer Sewing Machines family and as soon as I tied those things together, it had to be *Mrs Singer's Waltz*".

The following *Maddie Goes West* was named after the notable banjo player Madeline Martyn, who actually played on the track. Gordon insists that her playing does not do justice to her phenomenal ability, as she was not in the best of health at that time. She was about to embark for America as the first part of a round the world trip at the time, hence the title. *Lakeland Memories* was actually another commissioned piece for Clive Williamson, to celebrate a life together in the Lake District and evokes that area in quite charmingly 'English' fashion. The title track is notable for being performed on yet another car boot sale guitar, illustrating what a successful run of boot sale rummaging Gordon was having. Hilary is credited on this for some very effective 'wordless vocal' backing accompaniment.

The dedication of the next track *James' Jig* is quite a contrast, being named for Jim Marshall, originator of the famous amplifiers, a fellow Water Rat and described often as 'the Father of Loud'. But aside from his amplifier fame, the Giltraps own something else from his hand, in the shape of a bird table that he made! Apparently he used to make them as a way of relaxing after a hard day, which just goes to show that it really does take all sorts. The piece was actually written to commemorate Jim's 80th birthday.

A couple of interestingly named pieces follow, beginning with *Ravensbourn*, which takes its title from the river in south-east London where Gordon grew up, known locally as 'the Quaggie'. "It's a lovely word, isn't it, Ravensbourn?" says Gordon now. "It sounds rather more picturesque than the reality — though to be fair, it's a long river, so it probably does wind through some scenic areas before it adopts it's 'Quaggie' nickname by our old house". *Three Legged Horse* follows, taking its odd title not from a horse that Gordon had put a bet on or anything so specific, but simply because the tune has what he describes as a slightly 'wonky' feel to it. *Long Road Home* was written for an information film called *Healing Hands*, about the work of the Lincolnshire Hospice.

Deco Echo has a slightly longer story behind its intriguing title: "Now that's a funny thing. I got a call from a chap who worked for a music publishing company who said 'we're putting together an album of French music, some guitar music, some accordion music. I wonder whether you could write a piece in the style of Django Reinhardt?' I foolishly said yes and I came up with this piece. In the end it actually got used for television, in a programme taking a look behind the scenes on the *Poirot* series starring David Suchet. I was quite surprised, though very pleased, that they chose to use that instead of a genuine piece of

French gypsy jazz. It was just a pastiche of that style really, but I think I just about got away with it."

Three more relatively slight pieces follow this, with *Circle Of Friends* being titled after a circular wooden box owned by Gordon with the inscription 'Faith, hope, charity, caring, sharing, love, trust, peace' and around the edge, 'Circle of friends'. Loving the sentiment of this, he adopted it for the piece. The following *Triple Echo* is unrelated to *Deco Echo*, despite the titular similarity, while *On Reflection* was composed beginning in the key of B Flat and ending in D and seeing where it led in between the two.

After this comes another commissioned piece, this time written for Geoff and Cath Olner, who had done that valuable detective work on the boot sale violin. It was written to celebrate their wedding and was entitled *Those Who Bring Sunshine* — a title coined by the Olners themselves. As a notable aside, the piece features John Bradbury appropriately playing that said violin. A version of the traditional *Greensleeves* (supposedly composed by Henry VIII) follows, described by Gordon with candid honesty, as 'all right but not great', before *On Tiptoe* comes in, featuring more of the 'harping' technique he had earlier used on *Troubadour*. The album draws to a close with firstly, a rediscovered demo from some years earlier titled *A Hint Of Blue* and finally another commissioned piece called *John's Deckchair*. This was written as a surprise birthday present to John Adams from his wife Pauline and the unusual title in fact relates to the couple's holidays in Greece and John's favourite deckchair!

The album was housed in a striking sleeve, with a photograph showing Gordon in silhouette mode against the backdrop of an impressive sunset, looking for all the world like the 'drifter' of the title, wondering where his feet or his muse will lead him to next. The photograph started life as a humble holiday snap taken by Hilary, but it came out so well that it ended up gracing the album cover. There would be a few relatively low-profile years to come before further collaborations would once again see the Gordon Giltrap name boosted in terms of profile and set onto another different and unexpected, path...

29
Circle Of Friends

The following couple of years were a relatively fallow period in terms of new music. Very little of significance was released until 2009, but there were certainly interesting developments away from the world of new composition. 2006 brought one release of significance — a concert at the Symphony Hall, Birmingham, which was released as a DVD/CD pack and is still a performance Gordon regards fondly. Certainly the filming is extremely professionally done, highlighting the impressive surroundings of this handsome venue.

2007 brought with it an album of Gordon re-recording some of his favourite romantic pieces from his repertoire, called *Secret Valentine*. A more interesting release than that rather uninspiring description makes it sound. It came about from a project named Cool Acoustics undertaken by Loughborough University, whereby they were looking at the feasibility of using plastic for musical instruments. During the course of this research they had discovered a particular plastic material that seemed to be very well suited to the task and they approached Rob Armstrong to manufacture a guitar using it. He did so, producing two instruments with the back and sides made of wood but the entire top of the guitar from plastic polymer. Gordon tried the guitar and to his surprise found that the sound was excellent, so he undertook to record the *Secret Valentine* album entirely using this hybrid plastic instrument. Indeed the sound on the album is such that the listener would never guess this fact unless told about it in advance. It isn't a major release — a fact emphasised by the slightly 'Hallmark cards' design of the cover with its red heart design, but the story behind its origin makes it stand out as more than a 'filler' project.

Another live album, entitled *As It Happens* followed in the same year, but although it joins a hefty number of similar live releases sprouting up in the Giltrap catalogue, it is nevertheless one which Gordon recalls as being more notable than most. In contrast to some of the archival live recordings, some of which he was previously unaware of, this particular show was planned in advance to be an album. As such he had family and friends in the front row and he recalls the release very fondly.

The major project in 2008 became known as Three Parts Guitar, a trio formed with Raymond Burley and Gordon's old friend John Etheridge. This came about after the *Double Vision* album with Ray, and some live work together. As a commercial venture, however, it was doomed to failure because the pure classical guitar crowd who followed Burley were dismissive of Gordon, whereas Gordon's own audience were largely completely unfamiliar with Burley, as his reputation was mostly among his own 'scene'. So a lot of the reaction tended to be either a disdainful look or a shrug of the shoulders. Frustrated by this, both men were keen to keep the working relationship going. To this end Gordon suggested forming a trio with three guitarists all of differing styles, to attempt to bring in an inquisitive audience, so he gave John Etheridge a call. A friend from the days of Soft Machine and Second Vision, Gordon had first come across John in 1973 when he supported Darryl Way's Wolf, led by the former Curved Air violinist. John was the precociously talented jazzy guitarist in the band while the drummer was none other than a young Ian Mosley. It was through Mosley some years later that Gordon and John were introduced again. When the trio was mooted Etheridge was very keen and after christening themselves Three Parts Guitar, they began playing shows wherein each man would play his own set followed by a collaborative finale playing some of Gordon's repertoire. His was the 'common denominator' as he did not have the experience in the classical or jazz worlds — nor the musical sight-reading ability to feel comfortable taking on their works. The Giltrap material also had more commercial appeal. The shows were very successful, not least the one performed at the Symphony Hall in Birmingham in September 2008 to a capacity crowd, celebrating Gordon and Ray both turning 60. It was also Rick Wakeman's 60th birthday that same year and he appeared as special guest.

John Etheridge however, could not guarantee that the project would always be his number one priority, as he was also collaborating with classical guitar virtuoso John Williams. Feeling that the arrangement may be in some jeopardy, Gordon approached young guitarist Clive Carroll with a view to him stepping in if needed. Clive had come highly recommended by none other than John Renbourn. Having witnessed him play at a guitar festival in the North East of England, Gordon was astonished at his ability. A graduate of Trinity College Of Music, where he had attained Masters degrees in both composition and performance, Carroll is rated by Gordon as "without doubt one of the finest acoustic guitarists in Europe". Meanwhile however, when he went to John

Etheridge with the news that Clive would be happy to step in to allow John to fulfil his other commitments, John responded that there would be no need, as he really wanted to continue with the project. "He even said 'if you'll still have me', would you believe. So obviously I said that was marvellous, and the best option was to make it a quartet". This then turned into Four Parts Guitar, which continued for the following few years and to which we shall return.

Before that the following year the next recorded collaboration to be undertaken was with Rick Wakeman for an album entitled *From Brush And Stone*. After talking for some time about getting together the pair found that the time was at last right in terms of scheduling and other matters, so they began planning what format the release should take. Gordon had it in his mind to have another crack at his *Brotherhood Suite*, which he had still not managed to capture in a satisfactory fashion. He told Rick about this and its inspiration by the pre-Raphaelite artistic movement. Rick had a fascinating book about sculpture and decided that he would pen some short pieces inspired by the works therein. It was thus that the 'brush and stone' concept came about and certainly formed an intriguing and original basis for the album. It was agreed that the record would be split into two halves, with Gordon adding accompaniment to Rick's compositions and vice versa.

While expertly done, it comes across as a little less than it might have been — not by any fault of the material, or either of the two musicians, but rather by the demands on Rick's time which were, as they always are for this most hard-working and driven of musicians, considerable. So while Gordon had the luxury of months of work putting together some brilliant contrapuntal melodies and guitar arrangements for Rick's seven piano compositions, Wakeman himself simply had nothing like that amount of time available to him and provided his contributions to the Giltrap pieces in a matter of days. Thus, while the two men work together brilliantly on the Wakeman compositions (if not literally together, as they sent each other their recordings without having to physically be together), the Giltrap pieces, while benefiting from some skilfully lush keyboard textures, do not possess the same complexity of arrangement. Nevertheless, it was the most successful realisation of the *Brotherhood Suite* up to that point, with five pieces making up the suite and two others, *By Angle Tarn* and *Maddie Goes West*, making up the remainder of his seven contributions. Gordon describes his work on the Wakeman pieces as 'one of the most challenging, yet also most enjoyable, creative tasks I have ever undertaken'. Hilary once again acted as 'executive producer', listening to the parts Gordon had added, and also suggesting some parts that needed to be added to more than others. The album is a laid-back and mellow affair, but despite its slight shortcomings it certainly displays the compositional talents of two exceptional musicians. The cover design was also striking, featuring a bold monochrome line drawing of two clenched fists, one holding two paintbrushes and the other a sculptor's chisel, with a single splash of colour in the shape of the red paint on one of the brushes standing out in stark relief. The album would mark Gordon's only teamwork with Rick, but certainly not the end of his collaborative endeavours with the Wakeman family...

******

Around the same time as *Brush And Stone* was being worked on, Gordon appeared with Rick again, this time in a live setting. Rick was embarking on his *Grumpy Old Picture Show* tour, which featured an appearance from Gordon each night in a very cleverly put together segment. In fact, the pair were interviewed backstage at one of the shows in Wavendon for what became the bonus DVD with the *Brush And Stone* special edition CD. Even though the working partnership did not ultimately lead to anything more permanent or high profile, Gordon still insists that he looks back on the whole period with nothing but fond memories — and asserts that working with Rick gives an acute realisation as to what a genius the man actually is.

With this partnership running its course, it was back to more solo material. 2010 brought the release of the *Shining Morn* album. When it came to the making of this, Gordon had a definite aim in mind: it had to be "as good as *Troubadour*". While it doesn't quite manage that lofty ambition, it is nevertheless an enormously creditable album, but is slightly too long at 24 tracks. Most of the material is new and original, but there are a few revisits to past glories, with the intention of improving them.

The title of the album and of the track which bookends it in two differing versions, actually comes from something that Hilary's mother used to say to her as a child. She would open up the curtains in the morning and greet the day with the words 'Hail, shining morn!' Gordon found this to be such a joyful, optimistic and uplifting thing to say that he was inspired to use it as the title. The piece *Shining Morn* itself is present in two incarnations; opening the album is Gordon's solo guitar version, while closing proceedings is another version featuring Rick Wakeman alongside him, contributing some superb piano work. Both versions are excellent and have their own unique charms, but at its heart the piece is a joyous and infectious guitar composition, skipping along in such a way as to convey perfectly those long-ago words of greeting to the new day. It is an inspired way to open and close the record and gives the album a big plus point immediately.

Elsewhere are other delights among the new compositions. *Joy Ride* for example is another excellent composition taken to a whole new level by the flute playing of Hilary Ashe-Roy. Astonishingly done all in one take, his contribution to the piece gives it a feeling something akin to Focus and the masterful flute work of Thijs van Leer. The piece would surely be strong even on its own, stripped back to the guitar, but with the flute it becomes another huge highlight on the record. Ashe-Roy also shines particularly impressively on the haunting, introspective *Prayer For Phillippa*, written in memory of the daughter of Gordon's friends Dave and Paula Ellison. Two other very notable inclusions among the original pieces on the album are *Five Dollar Guitar* and *Forever Gold*. The former is a very uncharacteristic bluesy shuffle — written while watching an Eric Clapton documentary as it happens — which showcases a rarely seen side to Gordon's playing, while the latter was written to celebrate Cliff Richard's fifty years in show business (hence the *Gold* of the title). It works extremely effectively in its aim as Gordon puts it, to capture the 'swagger' of the early Cliff with the Shadows. Even though it is instrumentally far removed from the music it references, somehow the naïve, innocent enthusiasm of films such as *Summer Holiday* or *The Young Ones* are captured perfectly and you can almost hear Cliff turning up with the Shadows and exclaiming 'hey, let's do the show right here!' A very clever trick to pull off.

Several tracks on the album are old pieces revisited, for various reasons. One of the most notable is *Night* from the *Visionary* album. Shorn of its accompaniment from its original recording it is here expanded by the addition of an extra section of new music and is, if not necessarily an improvement over the classic original, certainly a very viable alternative version, which may be more to the taste of those who prefer a purer and less ornate Giltrap sound. *Ive's Horizon* dates back to the very first Giltrap album, the self-titled release from 1968. This particular iteration is performed on Gordon's fan-fretted Fylde 12-string, a magnificent instrument that gives the piece a far more impressive sonic quality compared to the original version. By contrast, *By Angle Tarn* is a piece included on the very recent *From Brush And Stone* album.

Another old piece given a strong coat of fresh sonic paint through the use of a new instrument is *The Passing Of A Queen*, which originally saw the light of day on the 1973 *Giltrap* album. The full-bodied baritone guitar employed here gives the piece a gravitas and ominous feel that evokes the mediaeval origins of its subject matter particularly strongly.

Finally, we have a new studio recording of the live tour-de-force *Dodo's Dream*. This is a difficult one to assess since, while it is sonically excellent, it is recorded using overdubbing, whereas the continuing appeal and huge popularity of the piece in live performance is the fact of it being performed entirely in 'real time', using delay and echo techniques. Removing this does lose some of this crucial magic, though it is undoubtedly a far more accurate reading of the piece in terms of how it has been performed latterly on stage compared to the original *Peacock Party* blueprint. A couple of final points of interest to note on the record are the rare appearance of Gordon playing bass guitar on the track *Ring Of Kerry* (a track recorded some time earlier but only now completed to his satisfaction by the addition of the accordion playing of Karen Tweed) and also the title of the piece *Roseberry Topping*, which once again, in familiar Giltrap fashion, refers to a geographical landmark — this time in North Yorkshire — and not, as it may appear, a dessert option!

When the album appeared on Floating World Records it did so in another less than impressive package design with the image of Gordon, complete with guitar over his shoulder, superimposed somewhat sloppily against a garishly rendered yellow sunrise. It did not do justice to the contents and somehow failed to convey the impression of a 'major' work. Happily this would be far from the case when the next major release appeared...

30
Ravens & Lullabies

2012 turned out to be a quiet year with the only new release being an odd kind of hybrid album entitled *Echoes Of Heaven*. The idea of the record was a collaboration with two Christian musicians Carol Lee Sampson and Martin Green (the latter also a clergyman), whereby they added words to a collection of his pieces which Martin felt had what he described as "a hymn-like quality". These pieces were then re-titled and sung by Carol. It sounds as if it could end up as rather a by-the-numbers effort, which does neither side any particular favours, but in actual fact it works quite well. Of course, the overtly Christian lyrics could be a distraction for anyone not of that persuasion who may find them evangelical, but the quality of the music shines through and it has to be said that Sampson has an excellent voice. The lyrics are quite well matched to the music in the main and it was recorded very quickly, using the original backing tracks and just adding the vocals. The album was re-released in January 2018 under the new title *Peace Will Fall*, which is actually the name of the closing track, a new composition previously unreleased and titled *All The Days Of May* in its instrumental incarnation. The only thing which Gordon insisted upon for this re-issue was that the version of *Heartsong* be removed, as he never felt it worked comfortably in its new guise and instead they added a version of *The Lord's Seat*, which already had an appropriate title!

During 2012 Gordon was beginning to feel a little restless. He had in his mind been putting out very similar albums ever since *Elegy* and he felt strongly that he had to mix things up a bit and produce something quite different. This was something that he ended up doing in a more dramatic fashion than anyone could have forecast when he teamed up with Oliver Wakeman for the decidedly progressive rock approach on the album *Ravens And Lullabies*, which appeared in 2013. Oliver is the son of Rick and had quite recently left Yes, where he had filled his father's shoes with some aplomb before being replaced by the returning Geoff Downes. As Gordon recalls: "I remember thinking that I had to get off that treadmill of making the same sort of albums over and over — I didn't want to do another Gordon Giltrap acoustic record. It would be good I'm sure, with lots of pretty guitar and everything, but I felt I needed to do something different and I thought the time was right to return to my 'prog rock roots' if you like. I didn't know what form it would take — I thought it would be all instrumental at that point — but I got the idea of approaching Oliver through something I'd read in the Classic Rock Society magazine, whereby someone had put forward a connection between my work and his and that it would be nice to hear us together. I'd met Oliver some time earlier at one of his dad's Christmas shows and we'd got on really well, so I gave him a ring and asked him if he'd like to play on this new album I was planning. He said he would, and that was that — except that within a few hours of putting the phone down I began thinking what a ridiculous request that was. I knew how good he was, he'd been good enough to fill his father's role in Yes, he'd produced some great material under his own name and it was obvious that he had inherited his father's genius. So I rang him back and said 'Oliver, this is a waste for you to just play on the album. Why don't we make an album together, as a partnership'. Thankfully he said he'd love to."

To start the ball rolling, Gordon went over to Oliver's home, met his family and they were getting on like the proverbial house on fire. What Gordon did not realise until later however, was the impact that leaving Yes had had on him, and to what extent it was driving him musically. "Being dismissed from Yes was a tremendous blow for Oliver, understandably. It wasn't through any fault of his playing, it was more that Trevor Horn, who was producing their album and Geoff Downes came as a sort of package. But Oliver really thought he had a future there and it was devastating for him and a big blow to his confidence, as it would be. But in a way, that drove him on, because he felt he had a lot to prove both to Yes and to the wider world — that he had great music in him, and that he was far from a spent force. And those inner demons manifested themselves in some great music".

One thing that Gordon admits he had no idea about is what a great songwriter Oliver was. He had thought of him just as a musician, but his compositional ability was brought home straight away when Gordon would bring ideas in and Oliver would say, "that will make the basis of a great song" — and he actually meant 'song' in its true sense, complete with lyrics and vocals. What he also was unaware of was how skilled a sound engineer Oliver was. Gordon had arranged for them to spend a day in his friend Paul White's studio — Paul didn't know much about Oliver either. He began suggesting one or two ideas, but it became obvious very quickly that Oliver didn't need the services of an engineer, as he was fully versed in recording techniques such as the ProTools software and he knew exactly what he wanted and how he wanted the album to sound. So at this point Gordon allowed him to take the reins: he arranged the Esoteric label being involved, he arranged the studio and he even arranged for vocalist Paul Manzi (also of Arena and other bands) to put down some vocals. "It just brought home to me again exactly how talented he is. It was quickly obvious that we didn't need Paul White or his studio and when he brought Paul Manzi in I thought he sounded great. So I just thought to myself, here's a guy who has talent to burn and is younger than my son. I was getting on in years and I just thought I'd try to tap into his energy a bit. Which is exactly what I did and I think it worked out in quite spectacular fashion in the end".

Listening to the album, the initial shock is of the ferocity and vitality of the electric guitar playing, causing the listener to check whether it is in fact that very same acoustic web-weaver Gordon Giltrap with fire in his fingers. After all, he had hardly played the electric guitar with any regularity for over thirty years. "What happened was that he asked me to come in and do some guitar parts and I said I hadn't got anything worked out yet, to which he replied 'that's all right, just come in and rock out"! I said 'Rock out? I'm an acoustic guitar player, Gordon Giltrap doesn't rock out!' But he assured me it would be fine. So I went in, picked up the electric guitar and started playing, working out some riffs, bending strings and generally going for it. He meanwhile recorded all this, went away and edited these bits together to produce these amazing sounding guitar solos! The way he made it work was astonishing, I couldn't believe it was me when I heard it".

Joining those who were taken aback by the sound was Del Newman, when Gordon sent him a copy of the finished album. He telephoned Gordon and was asked what he thought of it, "well, I think it's very good, but it's not *my* Gordon", which is a sentiment that one can understand him having to be fair. He went on to ask who the electric guitarist was. When Gordon assured Del it was himself, Newman was dumbfounded. He said that he had assumed it was, in his words, "some hot-shot session player", which is testament not only to Gordon's success in adapting back to the instrument, but especially to Oliver's creative genius.

Not that the recording was all plain sailing — indeed Gordon talks now about how hard a taskmaster Oliver could be and how hard he had him working. "It really took it out of me, the mental and physical pressure of it. But he couldn't help it, he was just such a driven person and if he hadn't been that way I don't think the album would have been as good as it was. But I was wondering once or twice if I'd get through it, because there were not only the physical demands but also the mental demands of having to come up with ideas and make them good enough. I put myself under undue pressure really, thinking that I had to be as good as anyone he'd worked with; I was thinking 'this guy has been in Yes, he's worked with Steve Howe and been in this iconic band, I have to match up to that', which wasn't the way to look at it of course, but that's how I was. But I got through it and I'm enormously proud of it, although it nearly drove me to the edge. I couldn't do it again though, I wouldn't be physically or mentally up to it, I'm sure".

This demanding, pressure-cooker working environment led to one or two inevitable clashes in the studio, as Gordon remembers only too well: "There was one time and I'm sure he won't mind me saying this, because it wasn't his fault really, when I actually cracked and lost it. The thing is, such was the pressure I felt I was under that I used to get up at 6am and rehearse at home before going into rehearsals with Oliver. I was actually rehearsing for rehearsals! I'd have all this stuff worked out in that way and I was prepared. Anyway, one time in particular I got there having spent hours working out a part to perfection, and when I played it he just went 'Okay, that's great, let's just change these chords' and I'd go 'but I've...' and he'd say 'oh, it'll be great, we'll just change this around...' — and I snapped. I remember I screwed up the sheet of music I'd worked out, hurled it across the room and shouted out a stream of expletives — which was most unsuitable language seeing as we were rehearsing in a church in a place called Bishop's Itchington at the time! Anyway, when I did that, he grabbed the ball of paper and was trying to smooth it out and apologising to me, saying it would be fine and that it was a privilege to work with me — and he obviously felt really bad. So in turn I felt sorry for him then, because I'd upset him and I thought that he must think he's working with a madman here; it was such a hair trigger we were on it was unbelievable."

Part of the problem was that this was unfamiliar territory for Gordon, who had always been his own boss in the studio, to all intents and purposes. Even back in the days of the Giltrap Band and the Triumvirate albums, he was the bandleader and what he said more or less went. There were other tense moments during the recording when Oliver asked Gordon to work out a part, to which he would reply "I'll do it Oliver, but only on condition that you promise not to edit it or change it! If I do this, you leave it alone" On this occasion, the entire struggle was worthwhile however, as the album proved to be a magnificent work. Some of the tracks were written by Gordon alone, some by Oliver, but several were actual musical co-writes while Oliver added the lyrics. The centrepiece of the album and in many ways its standout, is the ten-minute epic *Is This The Last Song I Write*, an Oliver composition. With its twists and turns, it is one of the finest and certainly most ambitious pieces of music Gordon has been involved with. It is helped by his own superb lead lines midway through the song. Clearly lyrically exorcising some personal demons after the Yes fallout, the song is moving on every level.

Elsewhere other highlights abound. Opener *Moneyfacturing*, a co-write "taken from one of my riffs", as Gordon says, is a driving heavy rocker peppered with stinging lead guitar breaks, a long, long way from his usual comfort zone. *Anyone Can Fly*, a favourite of Gordon's on the album, is a beautiful song written by Oliver for his as-yet unborn child. Originally a solo guitar piece from Gordon called *Mercurial*; the talent of Oliver was such that he was able to take this guitar instrumental, polish it and turn it into a tremendous song. The closing piece, *Ravens Will Fly Away*, another co-write, is the perfect way to finish the album with its soaring, uplifting feel. Elsewhere there are a couple of pieces whose titles bear some explanation: Oliver's *LJW* is titled after his wife's initials. Whereas Gordon's short *One For Billie* is actually named for Hilary, as Billie was her nickname as a child and is still used within her family.

Paul Manzi does a magnificent job on the vocals throughout, yet he does not sing on every song. The third track, *From The Turn Of A Card* is actually sung by Benoit David, with whom Oliver had worked with in Yes. He decided that it would be a good idea to draft him in for that one song, both because of his crystal-clear voice being very suited to it and also, cleverly, because it might help the album to be heard by curious Yes fans. Interestingly, Benoit actually did his vocal in Canada, recorded by his colleague in his 'other' band of the time, Mystery, in the shape of Michel St-Pere. The strong rock flavour of the album and its punchy production is aided by the involvement of two members of English progressive metal band Threshold, with that band's Johanne James occupying the drum stool and guitarist Karl Groom aiding Oliver's production in a mixing and mastering role.

Housed in a striking and enigmatically artistic package by Liliana Sanches and designed by Oliver, the visual impact of the record — including the beautifully illustrated lyrics in the CD booklet — matched its musical ambitions. There would have been little doubt in the minds of the casual browser exactly what type of music was contained herein. A two-disc deluxe edition included improved slipcase 'digipak' packaging and a second disc containing some excellent new live and studio recordings, including a new take on *Roots*, from the *Fear Of The Dark* album, which crackles with energy and creativity. There was, unfortunately, little money left after the recording to do as much serious PR for the album as the pair would have liked, but nevertheless the album sold more than respectively and one assumes, brought back the name of Gordon Giltrap into the minds of lapsed former fans. The next hurdle was to perform the album live and tour with it. This was to provide a whole new set of challenges...

31
Ravens Will Fly Away

When the time came to take the *Ravens* material out on the road for live shows, there were a couple of changes to the album personnel. Firstly, another Threshold connection was formed as their bassist Steve Anderson came in, replacing Liverpool-based session man Steve Amadeo. Secondly, and more significantly, the decision was taken to bring in another guitarist. Gordon had played all of the acoustic and electric guitars on the album, but live there would be a lot of quick changes between the two instruments if it was to work with one player and Gordon did not feel confident to do it. The reason was partly due to the logistics of changing instruments, but also, as he admits, he lacked the confidence to step too far away from his comfort zone of recent years. If he had elected to handle the electric lead guitar parts he felt that people would automatically expect him to be as he was 35 years prior, standing at the front and leading the band. With the advancing years and also the long period of time spent performing seated with the acoustic, the decision was taken, for the sake of the show to bring in Nick Kendall, who had come fresh from the *Rock Of Ages* musical in the West End.

This may have been a wise move in terms of the music, but it was an unsatisfactory one from Gordon's own point of view. Handling seated acoustic duties only, he was fine on the more delicate, less accompanied material, but when the whole band came in — which they did for a majority of the time — he largely disappeared. Reduced to playing fairly simple rhythm parts, the loud, 'full band' sections of the show would see him frantically strumming away in an effort to be heard and in the process not really doing justice to his talents. This is something with which Gordon concurs: "Yes, those shows really didn't do full justice to the album. But I simply didn't have the confidence to take on the lead guitar role, fronting the band playing the electric. So I chose to stick to the acoustic and I knew at the time that it wasn't showing me to the best of my ability. We also didn't really have long enough to rehearse as a band. The sound of the full band was loud when they all came in. I did get drowned out a little, but that wasn't surprising with Johanne James on the drums! He's a very powerful drummer to say the least and the band had to be loud to match him."

Still, imperfect as the live shows may have been, they still provided an opportunity to see Gordon playing with a full band again, something which long-time fans had all but given up on. His lead parts on the album had at least one admirer. With Nick Kendall learning them all, "He said they were really great parts", says Gordon today. "He'd learnt them all in order to play them accurately and I took this as a big compliment. He was a fine guitarist, very underrated."

The first opportunity for the band to showcase what they could do in the live arena was in the Autumn of 2013, when they appeared as headliners at the Summer's End progressive rock festival. Despite the sonic limitations, the performance was a triumph, with some tears of nostalgia shed by audience members of a certain age as Gordon strummed that familiar *Heartsong* intro to climax the show. With a full band behind him, driving home this iconic piece, many were transported back to those heady days of the Reading festival and other great gigs by the original 'band'. "The roof came off, didn't it?" he smiles. "I could feel it from the stage, a wonderful atmosphere and a wonderful ovation. I remember after the show, Hilary just came up to me and said 'Well done, love! Well done...'" This was intended to be a one-off appearance, but such was the reaction that more appearances were inevitably arranged. However, before that, Oliver and Gordon would work together in a different live capacity — as a duo.

The shows performed together unaccompanied were a very different beast to the full band shows. Low-key performances were the order of the day, with the pair playing material from their own repertoires and including a fair amount of storytelling and general interaction with the crowd — something that both men were born to do. Gordon had always possessed a personable style and ready wit from his old folk club days and Oliver had inherited some of his father's legendary raconteur delivery. With this mixture of musicianship and audience engagement in place, it was a winning combination that seldom failed to go down well with an audience. As a result, they were offered a series of shows leading up to the end of 2013 as support act to Barclay James Harvest.

Back in the 1970s, Barclay James Harvest, or BJH as their fans always referred to them, were something of a major concern. Admittedly one-step down from the 'big league' of Pink Floyd, Genesis and the like, they nevertheless produced a string of big-selling albums and performed to extremely healthy audiences. Their first break had come with the track

Mockingbird, from their second album *Once Again*, released in 1971. After this first 'anthem', as one might call it, they went on to release classic albums such as *Everyone Is Everybody Else* and *Time Honoured Ghosts*, and tracks such as *For No One* and *Child Of The Universe* became 1970s progressive rock touchstones. However, as the '80s wore on, all was not well in the BJH camp, and a schism developed between the band's two frontmen and chief songwriters, guitarist John Lees and bassist Les Holroyd. The band split into two camps in 1998, with two separate incarnations of the band emerging, one led by Lees and the other by Holroyd. Drummer Mel Pritchard joined Holroyd, while keyboard player Woolly Wolstenholme, who had left the original band in 1979, fell in with the Lees camp. Pritchard sadly succumbed to a heart attack in 2004, while Wolstenholme tragically took his own life in 2010.

The version of the band which Gordon and Oliver were invited to tour with were the John Lees variant, who had just released a new album entitled *North* (from the band's north of England origins) and which they were keen to promote with live work. The Giltrap / Wakeman duo were an excellent fit for the shows, as the symphonic / melodic style of the BJH material was very similar in tone to their own repertoire. As a lower key opening act, Giltrap / Wakeman were perfect. The tour began in November 2013 and the last gig together was not until early the following year, as a handful of gigs stretched to after Christmas.

In April 2014 a short tour of England with the *Ravens* band was arranged, including a notable show at the Robin 2 in Bilston on Gordon's Birthday. Paul Manzi came out with a birthday cake at one point during the show, complete with candles. Unfortunately as he bent down to allow Gordon to blow out the candles he got too near to them and his hair caught fire! Thankfully the flames were doused before any lasting damage was done. Sadly, following this landmark show, the project bowed out more with a whimper than a bang, as the last gig in Swindon was a slightly dispiriting and poorly attended affair. All in all, while the album was an unqualified triumph, the live shows will be looked back on as more of a mixed bag. Undaunted however, Gordon filled the next few months with some quite regular work for the Four Parts Guitar ensemble, which was proving very popular. One notable tale from around this time was when they had arranged a show — funnily enough, again at Swindon, at the Arts Centre — and John Etheridge still hadn't arrived ninety minutes or so before show time. Starting to get concerned, Clive Carroll suggested it might be wise to ring him to see if he was stuck in traffic. Gordon duly called and a cheery Etheridge on the other end, when asked how he was, replied that he was extremely content, sitting having a pot of tea outside his favourite cafe around the corner from his home. Slightly perplexed, Gordon replied, "Well, that's great John — but you do realise you're due onstage with us at Swindon Arts Centre tonight..."

His confused response that nobody had told him drew the answer from Gordon that, "if you look at your own website, John, it's down there in your gig list". A stream of expletives were followed by a panic-stricken Etheridge hanging up to rush back to jump in his car as quickly as he could! Clearly he would not be anywhere near the place by the start, so Gordon explained to the audience that "one of our number is delayed in traffic, but he'll be here for the second half". Sure enough, having apparently made a good fist of the land speed record along the way, he arrived during the interval and the audience were none the wiser that anything had been amiss. This was far from typical John Etheridge behaviour, but making such a superhuman effort to get there certainly showed the professionalism and dedication of the man.

Apart from this Four Parts Guitar work, 2014 was taken up heavily by a project initiated by Gordon's sound engineer friend Mark Sowden who had a vision of *Heartsong* reinvented as a Christmas song. Enlisting Paul White and his recording studio into the equation, Gordon was sufficiently intrigued by the idea to throw his full energy behind the project and he recorded a new backing track over which to overlay vocals. Several singers were approached, including Barbara Dickson who was forced to decline as it was out of her optimum range, but each time a vocal was attempted, the possibility of it succeeding artistically seemed to recede a little more. Both Gordon and Mark were frantically writing and rewriting lyrics but nothing seemed to work. After quite some time had been invested, Gordon reluctantly had to withdraw his involvement. He sees it now as being a job undertaken for the wrong reasons (namely making some money) and says that he began seeing more and more that a great piece of music was in danger of being cheapened and ultimately robbed of its magic. The words that he claims he had resounding in his head at the time were Peter Green's to him after his *Oh Well* single attempt, opining that, "you can't cover a classic". Along with the fact that it was beginning to affect his friendship with Paul White, it had to go and the project was abandoned.

Gordon has always liked to use his talents in the aid of a favourite charity and he had the idea during the latter half of 2014 to play some charity shows at St Giles Hospice in Sutton Coldfield — just a man and a guitar, no frills or publicity. Arriving for a prior appointment to discuss matters, instead of the main Hospice building, which he thought he was attending, it turned out to be the Day Centre that accommodates various groups on a non-residential basis. The lady in charge, Julie Nicholas, was sufficiently impressed by his talents to arrange a couple of lunchtime shows for the Multiple Sclerosis group, just as a 'local musician'. When he arrived for the first of these, he found it was packed and that there were even a couple of people with albums to sign and asking for their favourites to be played! The MS group and Gordon 'adopted' each other and he went on to play two full-scale fundraisers at a local church, raising around £2,500 for them. He even played a lunchtime show at the main hospice: a somewhat more sombre occasion with some terminally ill people. He was very touched indeed by one old gentleman who had been a wood turner and gave Gordon some beautifully crafted and painted Spalted Beech Mushrooms as a gift. All in all he found his involvement to be an extremely rewarding and in some ways, uplifting experience.

He could not have predicted however, the significance that having had this involvement with a hospice would have in his life in the following couple of years. In January 2015, he and Hilary took a trip to Center Parcs with their friends Geoff and Cath Olner, as they frequently had. One morning, Gordon awoke with a terrible feeling of heartburn and indigestion and over the following days and weeks began to experience further gastric issues. He doctor prescribed Lanzoprazole tablets to ease the symptoms, but also arranged for him to have further tests to hopefully rule out anything sinister. So would begin the darkest period of Gordon's life and one that would test his spirit and resolve to the fullest extent...

32
A Tapestry Of Tears

Although in early 2015 the doctor was quite confident that the gastric reflux symptoms he described would be easily resolved by the medication, he nevertheless referred Gordon to Good Hope Hospital in the Sutton Coldfield area to have an endoscopy. He told him that it wasn't the most pleasant of tests, but it would be worth it to have any complications ruled out.

After the endoscopy was complete the nurse told Gordon that everything looked clear, except that they could see what she described as "a little fatty lump" just at the top of the stomach. To take a closer look a scan was arranged at Heartlands Hospital in east central Birmingham. A short while after he returned to Heartlands to discuss the results of the scan. As it happened he could not make the original date, so rearranged the appointment. This did not seem like a problem, as the letter did not indicate that anything sinister was amiss. As he says now, "it never crossed my mind that it might be anything serious, because you're not looking for anything serious".

Thus it was in June 2015 that he was finally scheduled to go for the meeting. In March he had taken the role of Guest Presenter at the Classic Rock Society annual awards night, a duty he was performing for the second time. Looking back at photos from the event it is clear that he was unwell and his skin had a noticeable pallor. However, trouper that he has always been, he gave no indication on the night that he was feeling such discomfort and he delivered a thoroughly professional and engaging performance in every way. On the day of the appointment, accompanied by Hilary, he left her in the hospital cafe suggesting she get a cup of coffee, assuring her that he wouldn't be long. "So I was in this waiting room, still thinking it would be a routine consultation. I remember this doctor coming into the room, with a nurse accompanying him and he called me through. Funnily enough I still remember him carrying a folder with him. He ushered me into a room and asked if I knew why I was there, to which I replied in some puzzlement 'Well, yes.

I've been suffering from acid reflux and I believe you've found a little fatty lump'. His blunt reply to this was 'Oh no Mr Giltrap, I'm afraid it's far more serious than that. Let me show you your scan on the screen', whereupon he showed me the image. He pointed to the top of my stomach, where the fatty lump was supposed to be, and there was a large black shadow. 'That', he went on, 'is a tumour. It's called a GIST, which stands for Gastro Intestinal Stromal Tumour and you will require major surgery to remove it. The good news is that we can get rid of it and cure the problem; the bad news is that we will have to remove much of your stomach and also your spleen, you will be in hospital for ten days and there will be a three month recovery period'. Then he simply told me I had to fill out some forms and left — his bedside manner wasn't exactly comforting to say the least! To be honest, it was like being hit with a sledgehammer, completely out of the blue. After he left, I remember the MacMillan nurse asking me if I was okay and the only thing I could say was 'Well, no, because I've now got to go and tell my wife'. I went back down to find her sitting reading the paper. I adopted a cheery demeanour and asked 'Do you want another cup of tea love?' I was steeling myself to have to break this news to her, summoning the strength. So I sat down and told her exactly what they'd found and what I had to have done, but that they could cure it and that they had assured me I would be fine. I still remember the first thing she said to me: 'Well, at least you haven't come down to tell me you're going to be dead by Christmas'! Because that's what you have to cling to you see, that hope. Basically your world shrinks instantly to the size of a pinhead and the only thing that matters is that hope you can hold on to. That's what gets you through it."

The next step was another endoscopy, this time with a sample being taken from the tumour in order for a biopsy to be carried out. This was again at Heartlands Hospital, a difficult place to get to and from in the centre of Birmingham. Fortunately there was a boost as Gordon recalls 'I was talking to my friends Sue and Roger across the road, who had both recovered from cancer. They told me that it should be no problem to have my future treatment done at the Queen Elizabeth Hospital, or QE as it's known, which is much easier to get to by public transport and they were right. I was able to get my notes transferred over there".

The endoscopy was done at Heartlands before the transfer, in order to lose no more time, but that in itself was an interesting visit. When Gordon was called through the registrar who was checking his notes asked what he did for a living. When he said he was a musician this chap replied that he knew who he was and that as soon as he saw the name on his list he was looking for someone who looked like 'the'

Gordon Giltrap and that as soon as he saw him he that must be who he was. As it turned out, the registrar himself was a guitarist, had his own home studio and even used to work for Elton John's Rocket Records label! As Gordon says now "It's really funny, because that ended up being quite an enjoyable visit. I was chatting to that registrar and with having sedation they gave me coffee and a choice of sandwiches, so in the middle of all that darkness of the time I can look back and think, 'you know, that wasn't a bad day'!"

Following that procedure, the medical notes were transferred over to the QE. The next significant meeting was in August with an oncologist who told him they were going to put him on a course of a chemotherapy drug to specifically target the tumour and reduce it in size so that it could be operated on, an estimated six months or more down the line. By this time he was starting to suffer from some severe abdominal pain. A side effect of the drug was that it caused the tumour to bleed as it was attacking it. As a result he became anaemic and required two sets of blood transfusions. The first time had an immediate effect, as he recalls: "It was amazing. After that first transfusion I felt full of energy. In fact, I felt so good that I came home and started doing some recording. It was like filling your car up with juice, is the best way I can describe it". This boost didn't last too long, however, before he had to go for a second transfusion and this time he was so weak that even the short walk to the station was beyond him and he was taken by ambulance. He received two bags of blood, which saw him through until the following May when the surgery was to take place. A scan in December 2015 had showed a significant reduction in the size of the tumour, so it was decided at that point he would have a further three months on the medication before he was to be reassessed with a view to the surgery and so it was.

Before the surgery was due to take place on 5th May 2016 he had a meeting with his consultant surgeon, Professor David Gourevitch, who Gordon has no hesitation in describing as "the most remarkable man I have ever met in my entire life. An extraordinarily charismatic man and when you meet someone like that they can have a profound effect on you. At that first meeting he explained exactly what was going to happen; he said that he probably wouldn't carry out the surgery himself, but that he was overseeing the case. He actually did a drawing of my oesophagus and my stomach, showing precisely what the plan of action was. Hilary not only asked him if we could have the drawing but also asked him to sign it! He did so and we've still got it."

One of the things that gave him heart in the run-up to the surgery was the words of good friend Anne Sutcliffe, a former top anaesthetist.

One day she had been for a meal with Gordon and Hilary and she said when they came back, "I know that you'll come through this. I can tell by looking at you that you're in good health apart from this problem, and you'll be fine" — which was a massive boost coming from someone whose opinion they respected deeply. There was a further twist however when they found out that she had worked in surgery with David Gourevitch's father, Arnold, who himself was something of a legendary surgeon in Birmingham medical circles — notwithstanding the fact that his nickname was 'Slasher' Gourevitch!

Gordon's surgery was put back twenty-four hours owing to an emergency situation on that day — the last thing you want to happen when you are already facing a monumental and terrifying event such as that. The operating surgeon, Mr Samuel Ford, informed Gordon of this, knowing what a blow it would be given that he was mentally built up to get it over with. On Friday 6th May the surgery finally took place, but it was to be significantly more of a job than was originally anticipated. On opening him up, they discovered that the tumour was in fact more widespread than they had believed, and it was a significant challenge to remove it all. They did manage it but it took almost double the original estimate of three hours to do so. In the process they had to remove not only the spleen and a large part of the stomach but also some of the pancreas as the tumour had got its claws in there as well. After the surgery was completed, Gordon was transported to the Intensive Care Unit, with his appearance destined to be something of a shock to his loved ones. He was not only hooked up to several tubes and drains but initially he was also incubated for breathing purposes. He had come through the surgery, but a battle still lay ahead...

******

At this point we must backtrack a little to record the entry of a very significant person in this whole period into Gordon's life, some five years earlier. Carrie Martin is a singer and guitarist from Hull who, having given up music and the guitar entirely for some two decades when raising her family had ended up playing a support set at one of Gordon's shows, only a week after she picked up the instrument again, owing to the non-appearance of the scheduled support act. Gordon was very impressed with her talent and her kindness and openness as a person. He went on to act as her 'mentor' over the following few years. By the time of the surgery Carrie had become one of Gordon and Hilary's closest friends. She stayed with Hilary for the days at the time of and immediately following the surgery. This was of incalculable help to Hilary, which has Gordon even today expressing his feelings about it with undisguised emotion. "I can never thank Carrie enough for that", he says. "To come and stay like that, accompanying Hilary on all of the hospital visits was extraordinary. One thing Hilary hadn't done was to read up about the after-effects of the surgery and what to expect, but Carrie had. She was able to reassure Hilary when she became understandably very scared to see me the way I was and for someone who isn't even family to do that and help to support Hilary so much, is something I can never completely repay".

Carrie remembers the period as so: "Originally I was just going down for a couple of days, because Gordon was worried about Hilary while he was going to be having the operation, so the intention was to be there to see him into the hospital and to stay the next night. When it turned out to be a lot more serious, I ended up being there for about five days, until his family were able to stay. If we'd had any idea of the severity of how it turned out they would have all been there with us, but nobody expected it at all. I'd read up a bit about it, more than Hilary had, but neither of us dreamt it would be as bad as it was. When he came out of surgery we were both shocked and worried, but I remember not saying anything about it because I didn't know what he could hear and I didn't want to sound so worried. It was a strange situation for me really, because even though I knew him well, I didn't know him so well at that time for him to expect me at the bedside when he woke up!" Expecting it or not, as is sometimes the case with events such as this, good things were forged in the crucible of this traumatic time and Gordon, Hilary and Carrie all fully admit that their friendship might never have grown as strong as it subsequently did, were it not for her presence and support. While it is far from being something any of them would ever like to relive, there is an element of the proverbial 'silver lining' about the time in that way.

After the first couple of days in the hospital, when things were very much still in the balance recovery-wise, Gordon began to pick up strength once he had fully recovered lucid consciousness. The nursing staff at the Queen Elizabeth Hospital are singled out by him for his fullest praise — in particular one of his one-to-one nurses in the Intensive Care Unit, who he describes as "a lovely, kind Irish lady who looked like a pre-Raphaelite painting" and he has nothing but admiration for all of the staff with whom he had dealings. After the operation he saw Professor Gourevitch again, who reassured him that they had managed to get all of the tumour removed, despite its greater reach and size, though he did sound a slight note of caution.

"What he said to me was that although they had 'got it out and in the bucket' as he put it, there might be 'one or two pieces floating around', which could have broken away. He did say that if such was the case they would be able to deal with it, but in actual fact I didn't give that eventuality much thought. Despite any assurances, I simply didn't want to admit to myself that there could be any possibility of a recurrence or the need for further surgery, because that's the way your mind works at the time. You don't want to believe that could be a possibility, so you don't". He was also to find out from the surgeon, Mr Ford, that they had actually played Gordon's music in theatre during the surgery! There is a school of thought that believes that this can aid the patient, as they can still respond mentally to sound while under the anaesthetic. Who will ever know whether this was indeed the case?

Less than two weeks after the operation, Gordon had made such good progress that he was able to come home. He was still very weak, however and he began a gradual process of building up his strength by slowly increasing the distance he could walk; a mere few steps in the first instance developed into 25 yards up and down the road and then further excursions until he began feeling relatively strong. He was also having to gradually adjust to being able to eat solid food, which is a massive obstacle after any gastric surgery. As he regained his physical strength however, the demons which plagued him were of the mental variety, as his mind began traversing some dark places. Thankfully, and largely through his own selflessness a couple of years earlier, help was at hand for this.

When he had done his fundraising for St Giles Hospice he had no clue that within such a short time he would be ill in this way himself. He also had no clue that this charitable act would pay itself back to him. So grateful were the staff at the Hospice and the day centre that, when they knew of his situation, they immediately organised two sessions of counselling at a time when he needed it the most. This saved the crucial time which would have been taken up with waiting for a GP referral and which might have seen his mental outlook become yet more bleak. Enormously grateful for the gesture, he attended the sessions, which were of so much help that after the second one the counsellor declared that he would have the internal strength to combat these demons and regain his inner balance and so it proved. What they also did however, was to arrange for him to see a Reiki healer named Kim Quance, with a view to trying some alternative healing — a direction in which he had long shown an interest.

Reiki is a Japanese relaxation technique, which is also claimed to promote healing through the concept of the 'life force energy' that flows through everyone. Kim Quance, in addition to the regular Reiki work also administered a process called Energy Field Healing, which she felt strongly that Gordon could benefit from. In actual fact, he did so in exceptional fashion, as he enthuses about it now. "She did four of these sessions with me free of charge and I have seldom felt such comfort and help from anything. They were two-hour sessions. The first hour was simply talking and opening up completely. This was like counselling again and I absolutely embraced it. I laid my emotions bare and there were many tears shed during these sessions but every time I left I felt so uplifted it was incredible. It was meeting Kim and having this treatment that led me to even greater interest in this path of alternative healing and it is something in which I have absolute faith. In fact, going back to my younger days of course, I always had that element of seeking a truth, or a higher message in my spirituality and this was, to me, another path towards that ultimate goal. It was quite astonishing and helped me beyond measure."

Everything was going extremely smoothly in the recovery and rehabilitation process and it seemed as if everything was on track. Regular check-ups were still required however and at one of those he was given the news that he was hoping never to hear. A scan had revealed the presence of unknown deposits in the liver. While these were possibly something benign, there was no way to tell non-invasively whether this was the case or whether small rogue sections of the original tumour had travelled to the liver and set up home there. There was only one thing for it: only months after the worst experience of his life, Gordon was told that he would have to undergo further surgery, to remove part of his liver. The journey was not yet over...

33
A Promise Fulfilled

The warnings had been there. The possibility had been flagged up. But understandably, after enduring the gruelling tumour removal operation and its painful recovery process, the idea of going under the knife again was not one that had been allowed to even flit across the mind of Gordon Giltrap in 2016. Now that it had reared its head as a reality he was being forced to look it squarely in the eye and face up to it, probably the hardest things he had ever done. The reassuring words about it being 'relatively minor' in comparison, and 'purely to be absolutely safe' were fighting unsuccessfully for prominence in his worldview, as the thought of the beast needing to be slain one more time was almost too much for him to bear.

Still, bear it he did, as we all tend to find inner strength from somewhere in these situations. The surgery was scheduled for November 2016. Before it happened there was to be another significant event in the shape of the wedding of one of Gordon's students, Andrew Davis. The night before the ceremony Gordon and Hilary were booked into a nearby pub. They were sitting outside when a couple got out of a car and Gordon invited them to sit with them, as space was at a premium. The lady in question initially declined as she was going to have a cigarette, but having been assured that it was perfectly fine to do so, they got chatting. The conversation turned to Gordon's upcoming second surgery and the complications that had arisen from the first. After they had talked about it, she unexpectedly mentioned that she was, in actual fact a psychic and that he was going to be fine. Many people would scoff at this but to Gordon it was another brick in this wall of support that had been assembling itself ever since he received the payback help from the hospice staff.

Come the wedding day, they found themselves sitting with an elderly couple. Upon introducing themselves, the man informed them that he was a retired GP from Stoke On Trent. Gordon couldn't resist asking him whether he had much contact with the surgeons in the

Midlands area and he replied that he had known a few of them. Upon mentioning David Gourevitch as his consultant surgeon, Gordon was then astonished when this chap told him that by an amazing coincidence his father and David Gourevitch's father (the aforementioned Arnold Gourevitch) had in fact been prisoners of war together! As Gordon reflects on this web of synchronicity: "It just seemed to me that there was this coming together of people and events which conspired to give me support and strength. There had been this retired GP's story, the psychic lady, our good friend Anne Sutcliffe having worked with David's father and of course the path to the Reiki healing. In addition to all of that, when I saw my own GP I happened to ask him if he had encountered Anne and he announced that not only had he worked with her closely, but that she had in fact taught him an enormous amount. I felt very blessed at the time, if I'm honest."

The procedure was much simpler than the initial surgery, requiring only a short stay in hospital, but understandably enough in the build-up to the operation Gordon's mind had begun to make elaborate 'cat's cradles' of his thoughts and fears, filling him with trepidation almost, if not entirely, equal to the first surgery. In practice these fears were groundless as the offending portion of the liver was removed and upon investigation, found to be housing nothing more sinister than benign deposits unrelated to the tumour. The somewhat grim irony of this situation was that the removal of the liver section revealed the surgery to be ultimately unnecessary, but in order for that to be discovered it had to first be performed. A 'Catch-22' situation indeed!

One thing that Gordon did in the lead-up to the operation was to visit a clairvoyant / spiritualist down in Dorset, who came on strong recommendation. She did a tarot reading and assured him that she had dealt the cards twice and both times they had indicated that although he had an ordeal to go through he would be fine. Regardless of the veracity of such readings, it was certainly a valuable and reassuring thing to hear when he needed all the supportive words he could get. What was less comfortable however, was the spiritualism side of the meeting, as she claimed to have his parents with her in the room. As Gordon remembers it: "That was something I found very scary and unsettling, to be honest. She said my parents were there and she described my mother so perfectly that it unnerved me to quite an extent. It was frighteningly real to be frank. She said my mother had a message to tell me to 'do what he's told and do what the doctors tell him', which is exactly what she would have said had she been there. She also claimed my father was in the background and asking if I could forgive him as he had given me a hard time as a child. I said that of course I did, I'd forgiven him years ago; what right did I have to judge him anyway? But I really wasn't comfortable with that. She did me a cassette, but I had to get rid of it, I really didn't want to keep it around".

After the surgery Gordon was visited the following day by Hilary and her daughter Ruth, who were astounded to see him already sitting in a chair, talking and animated. Compared to the ghastly tube-ridden apparition which had shocked Hilary after the main surgery, this was a pleasant surprise indeed. Another visitor to the ward at that same time was the original surgeon Samuel Ford, who declared himself to be similarly impressed by Gordon's rapid recovery. While chatting to him he was able to relay the tale about the man whose father had shared the same POW camp with David Gourevitch's father, a story which left Mr Ford astonished by the coincidence of it. The final irony, if one wishes to call it that, of this second surgical procedure was that, despite the fact that it was much shorter in duration, less serious and quicker to recover from than the first, it actually required a bigger incision because the earlier incision had to be cut open again and then continued to the side where the liver resided. A total of 52 clips were required to close it up after completion!

Further follow-up scans are still required on a three or four monthly basis to ensure that nothing sinister returns, but thus far these have all proved negative and Gordon sees them as, while stressful and worrying each time, ultimately a small price to pay for being alive and well.

******

During this whole period, Gordon had been working on his first new album since the Oliver Wakeman collaboration and the dawn of 2017 saw the time draw near to release it. Once again however, this was not to be a solo endeavour as the album, entitled *The Last Of England*, emerged as a joint venture with keyboard player and producer Paul Ward, who Gordon had met years before in the unlikely surroundings of a Car Boot sale in a Lincolnshire field! Wanting someone to work with on the album rather than returning to the unaccompanied acoustic work, he took the suggestion of mutual friend Mike Stranks and phoned Paul, asking whether he would like to work on the album as a joint project. "I was quite honest with him", says Gordon about the phone call now." I told him I'd love to work with him but I couldn't afford to pay him! So we did it as a jointly credited venture, which I think was a fantastic decision in the way it turned out".

Some of the music had been newly composed before and after the first surgical procedure, but other pieces had been around for longer. It just accumulated to the point where it became obvious that there was enough for an album. One of the main aims was to finally record a definitive version of the long-gestating *Brotherhood Suite* and using the template of the *From Brush And Stone* version as the springboard, this was undoubtedly achieved. All of the guitar tracks for the album were sent over to Paul Ward and he set to arranging them and adding keyboard parts. Gordon was overjoyed at the quality of the job Paul did on the pieces commenting, "I knew that Paul would be the man for the job, he could use string samples and whatever else was required, but he exceeded my expectations. I can still remember him sending me the music back and listening to it on my iPad and weeping. It was that perfect!"

However, despite immediate success, the creative process was not without its pitfalls as one might expect with the work being carried out at such an uncertain and stressful time. One such occasion was when Gordon, to his later regret, accepted to write a commission piece. "I shouldn't have done it", he says now. "I was in a dark place after the first surgery and I know full well looking back that I was in no state of mind to do justice to something like that. The person in question had commissioned the piece for her husband and while the piece that I produced was a nice composition, it didn't gel with her expectations and demands for what it should have been. Add to that the fact that when she gave me the title she had chosen, the working title had already been registered with PRS and it becomes clear that I had made a pretty sizeable error of judgement. In the end I refunded the money and accepted my mistake". The piece in question did make it onto the album under the title *Plas Oriel* and although it is a pleasant piece, it understandably retains some difficult, personal memories for Gordon.

Nevertheless, such diversions were very much the exception. The album was released in January 2018 on the Angel Air label, complete with a beautiful pre-Raphaelite painting by Ford Maddox Brown, itself entitled *The Last Of England*, adorning its classy and effective packaging. The highlight of the album is inarguably the *Brotherhood Suite*, finally emerging from its long development as a perfectly formed and well-rounded suite of compositions. This to Gordon represented the culmination of decades' worth of work adding to, editing and honing the suite and gave him enormous pride and satisfaction when it was released to almost unanimous approval from fans and critics alike. This is not to say that the album stood and fell on the suite — quite the contrary, as it only took up the first half of the album. Other pieces such as *Ania's Dream* and perhaps most of all, the enchanting *The Anna Fantasia*, would be singled out in several reviews of the album as among his best work for some two decades.

Gordon is unequivocally delighted with how the album turned out, especially at such a time when he and others besides had begun to wonder whether he would ever produce another album of original material at all. "I think it's one of the best albums I've ever put out", he says now. "*Troubadour* is probably the high point for me, but this one is up there. Paul has to be singled out for massive praise, as the success of the album has so much to do with his contribution. After I did *Shining Morn*, I made a decision that I didn't want to do another similar solo album again, which is part of the reason for the collaboration with Oliver. I had to shake things up after a run of albums in a similar vein. This one continued that progression, being another collaborative work and yet completely different to what I'd produced with Oliver".

The album release was greeted with overwhelmingly positive reviews — in fact, one of the most supportive receptions afforded to a Giltrap album for many years — with some hailing it as a celebratory signal of redemption of a sort, after the events of the previous years. More shows began being added to the calendar as Gordon returned cautiously to the live arena again in a serious way. Not in terms of full tours or anything of that magnitude — he had already decided to tone down that level of work — but certainly in the way of successful one-off shows.

Towards the end of 2017 *The Last Of England* was treated to a high-quality vinyl release, complete with deluxe gatefold sleeve packaging, new sleeve notes from both himself and Ward and even a poster bundled in. The release came courtesy of a man named Pete Bonner, record dealer and owner of the small Psychotron Records label. A Giltrap admirer of old, he was only too happy to see the album realise its true destiny as a handsome, tactile offering. Some of the music had to make way for the reduced capacity of a vinyl disc — including, perhaps surprisingly, *The Anna Fantasia* — but that was hardly the key point of the release. *The Brotherhood Suite* stood untouched, making up the entirety of the first side and some of the second, rejoicing in its position at long last, as the cornerstone and main focus of a major release.

In a way, this represented something of a closing of a circle in Gordon's career as he delighted in the feeling of holding this treasured vinyl release in his hands long after he thought his records would not see that particular medium again. In very much the same way as the young, hopeful Gordon Giltrap had held his very first release, five decades previously. Older he may have been, wiser he most certainly was, but the sheer joy which that young man took in music for its own sake remained exactly as it had done, back to the day when he rescued his treasured guitar from its fate in the dustbin as a teenager. A perilous Journey in many ways but one that has been worth far more than the mere destination itself.

Afterword

Following the completion of this book, Gordon's son Jamie tragically passed away in unforeseen circumstances following a short illness. He had not been thought to be in any danger until his condition deteriorated and he passed away on the morning of 31st January 2018. He was just 46 years old.

Jamie had inherited his father's gift for music, working within the dance music genre under the name DJ Tango and Gordon's pride and joy in that fact never wavered, regardless of the difference in style and approach. Leaving behind a wife and young son, the tragedy of his passing cannot be overstated.

This book is respectfully dedicated to his memory.

Jamie Giltrap, 27th May 1971 — 31st January 2018.

Discography

This is a comprehensive list of the recorded output of Gordon Giltrap as a solo artist; as the Gordon Giltrap Band; with Accolade and the numerous joint projects he has been involved with over the years.

Albums

Gordon Giltrap
Transatlantic TRA 175, 1968

Portrait
Transatlantic TRA 202, 1969

Accolade (by the group Accolade)
Columbia SCX 6405, 1970

Accolade 2 (by the group Accolade)
Regal Zonophone SLRZ 1024, 1971
Gordon did not appear on this album but it includes his composition 'William Taplin'.

A Testament Of Time
MCA MKPS 2020, 1971

Giltrap
Philips 6308 175, 1973

Visionary
Electric TRIX 2, 1976

Perilous Journey
Electric TRIX 4, 1977

The Early Days
Allegro ALC 4052, 1978 (cassette only)

Fear Of The Dark
Electric TRIX 7, 1978

Performance
K-Tel NE 1081, 1980 (compilation)

The Peacock Party
PVK GIL 1, 1981

Live
Cube ICS 1001, 1981

The Platinum Collection
Cube PLAT 1005, 1981 (compilation)

Airwaves
PVK GIL 2, 1982

Elegy
Modern Music MODEM 1001, 1987

A Midnight Clear
Modern Music MODEM 1006, 1987
A collection of Christmas Carols.

One To One (with Ric Sanders)
Nico Polo NP002, 1989

Guitarist
Music Maker Records CMML 88006-6, 1990 (compilation)

The Peacock Party
BBC Enterprises CDPT 507, 1990 (CD release)

Elegy / Perilous Journey
BBC Prestige CDPM 850, 1991 (reissue 2 LPs on 1 CD)

Visionary / Fear Of The Dark
BBC Prestige CDPM 851, 1991 (reissue 2 LPs on 1 CD)

The Best of Gordon Giltrap
Prestige CDSGP005, 1991 (compilation)

A Matter Of Time (with Martin Taylor)
Prestige CDSGP007, 1991

The Eye Of The Wind (With the Birmingham Schools Concert Orch)
Accolade EYE T1, 1992 (cassette only)

The Solo Album
Prestige CDSGP021, 1992 (compilation)

On A Summer's Night
Music Maker Records CMMR 924, 1992 (Live at Warwick Folk Festival)

Gordon Giltrap / Portrait
Transatlantic Demon Records TDEMCD 15, 1993 (reissue 2 LPs on 1 CD)

Music For The Small Screen
Munchkin Records MRCD1, 1995

Live At The BBC
BBC Worldwide WHISCD009, 1995

The Brotherhood Suite (W/ Notts Education String Orchestra)
Munchkin Records, 1995 (cassette only)

Gordon Giltrap / Portrait
Transatlantic / Castle ESM CD 526, 1997 (reissue 2 LPs on 1 CD)

Troubadour
K-Tel ECD 3390, 1998

Visionary
Voiceprint / La Cooka Ratcha LCVP114CD, 1999 (reissue)

Perilous Journey
Voiceprint / La Cooka Ratcha LCVP113CD, 1999 (reissue)

Fear Of The Dark
Voiceprint / La Cooka Ratcha LCVP112CD, 1999 (reissue)

One To One (with Ric Sanders)
Terra Nova TERR CD017, 1999 (reissue)

Live At Oxford
Voiceprint / La Cooka Ratcha LCVP115CD, 2000

Part of the Picture
Snapper Music SMD CD 297 2, 2000 (compilation)

A Midnight Clear
Voiceprint / La Cooka Ratcha LCVP106CD, 2000 (reissue)

Music For The Small Screen
Voiceprint / La Cooka Ratcha LCVP110CD, 2000 (reissue)

Airwaves
Voiceprint / La Cooka Ratcha LCVP108CD, 2000 (reissue)

The Solo Album
Voiceprint / La Cooka Ratcha LCVP111CD, 2000 (reissue)

Janschology
Voiceprint / La Cooka Ratcha LCVP124CD, 2000

Collection
Voiceprint / La Cooka Ratcha LCVP117CD 2 CD, 2001 (compilation - studio/live)

Elegy
Voiceprint / La Cooka Ratcha LCVP107CD, 2001 (reissue)

The Peacock Party
Voiceprint / La Cooka Ratcha LCVP105CD, 2001 (reissue)

Troubadour
Voiceprint / La Cooka Ratcha LCVP147CD 2001 (reissue, w/ acoustic bonus disc)

On A Summer's Night
Voiceprint / La Cooka Ratcha LCVP109CD, 2001 (reissue)

Giltrap and Taylor
P3 Music P3M003, 2002 (reissue of A Matter Of Time)

Under This Blue Sky
Voiceprint / La Cooka Ratcha LCVP150CD, 2002

Gordon Giltrap Band Live 1981
Voiceprint / La Cooka Ratcha LCVP148CD, 2003

Fingers Of Fire
Arc recordings no cat. No. 2003 (live recording)

Remember This
Voiceprint / La Cooka Ratcha LCVP155CD, 2003

Double Vision (with Raymond Burley)
Voiceprint / La Cooka Ratcha LCVP158CD, 2004

Live At Ambergate
Voiceprint / La Cooka Ratcha LCVP156CD, 2004 (Binaural Recording)

The River Sessions
River Records RIVERCD036, 2004 (live 1979 recording)

Drifter
Voiceprint / La Cooka Ratcha LCVP159CD 2 CD, 2004 (live recording)

A Testament Of Time
Voiceprint / La Cooka Ratcha LCVP157CD, 2005 (reissue)

A Taste of Classical Giltrap (w/ Sheffield Philharmonic Orchestra)
Wates Group no cat. No. 2005

Captured From A Point In Time
Hypertension HYP 6251, 2006 (live recording)

Symphony Hall Birmingham
Voiceprint / La Cooka Ratcha LCVP160CD, 2006 (double-sided live CD and DVD)

Sixty Minutes with Gordon Giltrap
Voiceprint VP6003CD, 2007 (compilation)

Secret Valentine
Voiceprint / La Cooka Ratcha LCVP162CD, 2007

As It Happens...
Voiceprint VP458CD, 2007 (live concert in full)

From Brush and Stone (with Rick Wakeman)
Voiceprint VP445CD, 2009 (Early copies included a bonus DVD)

Double Vision
Floating World Records FLOATB6025, 2009 (reissue)

Troubadour (CD) / **Live at Ventnor Winter Gardens** (DVD)
Demon Edsel EDSX3007, 2010

Music For The Small Screen / The Solo Album
Demon Edsel EDSD2073, 2010 (reissue) *Also available digitally VEXEDSD2073*

The Peacock Party / Airwaves
Demon Edsel EDSD2074, 2010 (reissue) *Also available digitally VEXDIGI317*

Remember This / Janschology
Demon Edsel EDSS 1043, 2010 *Also available digitally VEXDIGI318*

Shining Morn
Floating World Records FREEM5023, 2011

4 Parts Guitar (with Raymond Burley, John Etheridge & Clive Carroll)
no cat. No. 2011

Echoes Of Heaven (with Carol Lee Sampson and Martin Green)
BigWeb Entertainment Limited BW 4207, 2012

Visionary
Esoteric Recordings / Cherry Red ECLEC2400, 2013 (reissue)

Perilous Journey
Esoteric Recordings / Cherry Red ECLEC2401, 2013 (reissue)

Fear Of The Dark
Esoteric Recordings / Cherry Red ECLEC2402, 2013 (reissue)

Live At Oxford
Esoteric Recordings / Cherry Red ECLEC2409, 2013 (reissue)

Ravens And Lullabies (with Oliver Wakeman, Paul Manzi, Benoit David, Steve Amadeo and Johanne James)
Esoteric Antenna / Cherry Red Records EANTCD21012, 2013 (2CD Signed ltd ed)

Ravens And Lullabies (with Oliver Wakeman, Paul Manzi, Benoit David, Steve Amadeo and Johanne James)
Esoteric Antenna / Cherry Red Records EANTCD1013, 2013

Time to Reflect: A Personal Anthology
4CD set Trapeze /Acrobat Music TRQCD1501, 2015

The Last of England (with Paul Ward)
Angel Air Records SJPCD485, 2017

The Last of England (with Paul Ward)
Psychotron Records PR1006, 2017 (Ltd edition of 500, orange vinyl)

Singles

No Way Of Knowing / I See A Road
Philips 6006 344, 1973

Lucifer's Cage / The Ecchoing Green
Electric WOT 11, 1977

Heartsong / The Deserter
Electric WOT 19, 1977

Oh Well / Reflections And Despair
Electric WOT 21, 1978

Weary Eyes / Nightrider
Electric WOT 27, 1978

Fear Of The Dark / Inner Dream
Electric WOT 29, 1978

Fear Of The Dark / Catwalk Blues / Inner Dream
Electric LWOT 29, 1978 (12")

Fear Of The Dark / Catwalk Blues / Inner Dream
Electric LWOP 29, 1978 (12" picture disc)

Fear Of The Dark (Edited Version) / Melancholy Lullaby
Electric INT 111.357, 1978 (Germany only)

Party Piece / Dodo's Dream
Pye Records WOT 38, 1979 (Ireland only)

O Jerusalem / Party Piece
Electric WOT 42, 1979

Theme From The Waltons / Birds Of A Feather
Cube Records BUG 89, 1980

Chi Mai / After The Storm (with Juan Martin)
PVK Records PV 105, 1981 *B-side, Juan Martin only.*

Magpie Rag / Gypsy Lane
PVK Records PV 101, 1981

Hocus Pocus / Dodo's Dream
PVK Records PV 111, 1981

Sunburst / Headwind
PVK Records PV 116, 1982

Heart Song / Weary Eyes
Old Gold OG 9235, 1982

Coppers Will Turn Into Silver / In The Bleak Midwinter
The Birmingham Mail, ZELSPS510, 1988

Heartsong / Magpie Rag
Music Maker Records SMMR903, 1990

Heartsong / Heartsong (1993 version)
Dodo's Dream (recorded al fresco) / Dodo's Dream (2018 version)
Angel Air Records, RAJP932, 2018 *Digital download only.*
The original version of Heartsong is remixed. The 1993 "All Star" version features Brian May, Steve Howe, Rick Wakeman etc.

Acknowledgements

I would firstly like to thank all of the people who kindly took time out to speak to me about their time spent with Gordon, all of whom were of enormous help: Bill Leader, Martin Turner, Eddy Spence, Shirlie Roden, Ric Sanders and Carrie Martin. Thanks to Janet (for endless encouragement and support), Stephen Lambe (for getting the ball rolling), Jerry Bloom at Wymer Publishing (for believing in the book) and all at the Classic Rock Society, particularly Miles Bartaby, without whom my writing career would not be where it is now.

Thanks to Hilary Giltrap for laughs, cream cakes and occasional cheese on toast! Finally and most importantly, the biggest thanks are due to Gordon for trusting in me to do his story justice and working tirelessly with me over this lengthy period. It's a debt I will always owe but hopefully telling this fascinating story will go some of the way!
Steve

Thank you to everyone who has been with me during various episodes of this 'Perilous Journey' of mine. You know who you are. A special heartfelt thank you to my lovely family: Hilary, Helen, Karen & Braden; Sadie, Gordon, Abbi, Kieran, Nathan, Lauren & Elijah; Rachael and Mylon; Ruth, Tom, Katie & Jimmy; Simon, Alex, Charlotte and Jack; Chris & Norman and a big thank you to Steve Pilkington and all at Wymer Publishing.

This book is dedicated to the memory of my dear son Jamie Giltrap, 1971-2018.
Gordon